The Euro and Economic Stability

The Euro and Economic Stability

Focus on Central, Eastern and South-Eastern Europe

Edited by

Ewald Nowotny

Governor, Oesterreichische Nationalbank, Austria

Peter Mooslechner

Director, Economic Analysis and Research Department, Oesterreichische Nationalbank, Austria

Doris Ritzberger-Grünwald

Head of the Foreign Research Division, Oesterreichische Nationalbank, Austria

PUBLISHED IN ASSOCIATION WITH THE OESTERREICHISCHE NATIONALBANK

Edward Elgar
Cheltenham, UK • Northampton, MA, USA

Published by
Edward Elgar Publishing Limited
The Lypiatts
15 Lansdown Road
Cheltenham
Glos GL50 2JA
UK

Edward Elgar Publishing, Inc.
William Pratt House
9 Dewey Court
Northampton
Massachusetts 01060
USA

A catalogue record for this book
is available from the British Library

Library of Congress Control Number: 2010926010

Mixed Sources
Product group from well-managed
forests and other controlled sources
www.fsc.org Cert no. SA-COC-1565
© 1996 Forest Stewardship Council

FSC

ISBN 978 1 84980 436 3

Printed and bound by MPG Books Group, UK

Contents

Contributors

Joaquín Almunia, former Commissioner for Economic and Monetary Affairs, current Vice-President and Commissioner for Competition Policy, European Commission, Belgium

Agnès Bénassy-Quéré, Director, Centre d'Études Prospectives et d'Informations Internationales (CEPII), France

Erik Berglof, Chief Economist, European Bank for Reconstruction and Development, United Kingdom

Antoine Berthou, Economist, CEPII, France

Zsolt Darvas, Research Fellow, Brussels European and Global Economic Laboratory (BRUEGEL), Belgium, Research Fellow, Institute of Economics of the Hungarian Academy of Sciences, and Associate Professor, Corvinus University of Budapest, Hungary

Vladimir Dubrovskiy, Senior Economist, CASE Ukraine – Center for Social and Economic Research, Ukraine

Lionel Fontagné, Paris School of Economics (Université Paris 1) and CEPII, France

Paul De Grauwe, Professor, Katholieke Universiteit Leuven, Belgium

Jaromír Hurník, advisor to the Board, Česká národní banka (Czech National Bank), Czech Republic

Asel Isakova, Economic Analyst, European Bank for Reconstruction and Development, United Kingdom, and Center for Economic Research and Graduate Education – Economics Institute (CERGE-EI), Czech Republic

Radovan Jelašić, Governor, Narodna banka Srbije (National Bank of Serbia), Serbia (resigned on 23 March 2010)

Peter Mooslechner, Director of the Economic Analysis and Research Department, Oesterreichische Nationalbank, Austria

Ewald Nowotny, Governor, Oesterreichische Nationalbank, Austria

Franziska Ohnsorge, Senior Economist, European Bank for Reconstruction and Development, United Kingdom

Nataliya Orlova, Chief Economist, Alfa-Bank, Russia

Doris Ritzberger-Grünwald, Head of the Foreign Research Division, Oesterreichische Nationalbank, Austria

Märten Ross, Deputy Governor, Eesti Pank (Bank of Estonia), Estonia

Sławomir S. Skrzypek, President, Narodowy Bank Polski (National Bank of Poland), Poland (died on 10 April 2010)

Ivan Šramko, Governor, Národná banka Slovenska (National Bank of Slovenia), Slovenia (until 31 December 2009)

Herbert Stepic, Chief Executive Officer, Raiffeisen International Bank-Holding AG, Austria

Helmut Stix, Economist, Oesterreichische Nationalbank, Austria

György Surányi, Regional Head of CEE, Intesa Sanpaolo Group, Italy

Zdeněk Tůma, Governor, Česká národní banka (Czech National Bank), Czech Republic

Gertrude Tumpel-Gugerell, Member of the Executive Board, European Central Bank, Germany

David Vávra, advisor to the Board, Česká národní banka (Czech National Bank), Czech Republic

Preface

The end of the 2000s and the beginning of the 2010s was characterized by a severe economic crisis, starting in financial markets and spreading to the entire economy. In such unstable times questions like 'Which factors have added to instability?' and 'What are the stabilizing factors?' were raised by many an economist or policymaker. In answer to these questions the natural candidates include currencies or exchange rate regimes. Thus, the euro came under close scrutiny, not only with regard to the euro area as such, but also with regard to our neighbouring region, the Central, Eastern and South-Eastern European (CESEE) countries.

Among this group of countries, only Slovenia and Slovakia have managed to introduce the euro so far. The others are still on their way, debating the right timing, but also the most appropriate exchange rate regime up-front. These questions are inherent to the enlargement process of the European Union (EU), and are thus anything but new issues. But has the crisis changed the answers? Did we get new insights concerning the right speed and the necessary preconditions for euro adoption? It is not clear if euro adoption will speed up in the near future, or if countries may refrain at least for a while, as they have found the exchange rate instrument to be a valuable tool that helped them survive the crisis relatively well.

The answers may depend on the starting point, de facto on the initial exchange rate regime of the countries concerned. Fixed-peg and flexible exchange rates ask for different solutions. Among countries with pegged exchange rate regimes, the crisis reinforced the prevailing euro-adoption strategies. Euro adoption was perceived as a credible exit strategy propping up confidence (by residents and non-residents alike) in the pegs, and as offering a relief to liquidity constraints and eliminating exchange rate mismatches while not imposing additional challenges on economic policies. For countries with floating exchange rates, the crisis had highlighted the vulnerabilities coming from large fiscal deficits. However, euro adoption should not be seen as a quick fix to economic vulnerabilities, but rather as part of a broader long-term policy strategy. Membership in the euro area was enhancing resilience, but it had not eliminated the need to work out underlying imbalances.

Another aspect is the degree of euroization. In the CESEE region this is an important issue, and it brings a completely new element into the stability debate. Has the euro been a safe haven for households' assets in CESEE countries before and during the economic and financial crisis, and will it be a safe haven in the near future? The answer to all three questions, provided by the Oesterreichische Nationalbank's (OeNB) Euro Survey, is 'yes', in particular for South-Eastern European (SEE) countries. Although the SEE economies stabilized and prospered in the 2000s, the extent of euroization of households' total financial assets still ranges from 31 per cent to 88 per cent in SEE. In particular, foreign currency cash holdings are an important component in households' portfolios. However, this phenomenon is not a completely new one. One can draw several comparisons with dollarization, which we find in Latin America as well as in Central Asia. But euroization involves several special issues, given that introducing the euro as legal tender is definitely an aim for all CESEE countries, at least in the very long term. And in this respect, the introduction process must follow a certain path defined by the institutional framework of the Eurosystem.

Without any doubt the euro area has weathered the crisis storm quite well. Although failing to prevent the build-up of internal and external imbalances, the common currency had indeed cushioned the effects of global shocks in the euro area. Overall the euro was an important stabilizing element in this battle. But one has to acknowledge that the euro area is not completely homogeneous, or not as homogeneous as economic textbooks would imply. Still, after several years of unification the euro area has transformed itself into a solid conglomerate that is characterized by a certain degree of economic divergence. This is due to country-specific factors, such as different industrial and trade structures, more or less openness and different labour force qualifications. Also prices have converged only moderately within the euro area so far, which could be attributed to certain 'reform fatigue' among member states. Euro area member states shared a high degree of product market regulation with little improvement happening over the last decade. After all, some euro area members still find themselves in a catching-up process. For our focus on CESEE, the last point is the most interesting one. Analysing the euro area in this respect increases our knowledge of catching-up processes in general, but also helps us to better understand and support the ongoing convergence processes in CESEE countries. Learning from each other has always been an issue, but like with other sciences, we can learn even more when the whole system is under stress.

The banking sector played a central part in the catching-up process of CESEE. For more than a decade, financial deepening and financial intermediation were positive elements, supporting growth and driving the economy. Domestic and foreign investments, based on high credit growth, were important factors; the foreign exchange component, which was (and still is) quite high in some of the CESEE countries, was risky, but under control.

In the crisis, Western banks found themselves in the middle of the storm, and irrespective of whether they had been instrumental in triggering and spreading the crisis or were its victims, they had to face enormous challenges in their home markets, and even bigger challenges in CESEE. The CESEE-related challenges were judged differently by the markets from one day to the other: prosperous countries which a bright EU or euro area perspective suddenly turned into risky emerging markets.

The mainly foreign banks weathered the storm quite well. In fact the banking system had been remarkably resilient, although some currencies had witnessed a sizeable depreciation during the crisis. Especially for economies with a floating exchange rate regime, an additional risk of foreign exchange fluctuation had been created by the high volumes of foreign currency loans granted in some Eastern European countries. The main strategy of the banks was not to pull out of the region and therefore not to destabilize markets and expectations further. In parallel, the financial support of several international and European institutions helped to stabilize the situation. These two elements and the supportive behaviour of many others – national economic policies to international investors – have prevented the worst. Still, banks would therefore have to adapt their business model accordingly. At least some of the most risky elements, such as foreign currency-denominated credits came under heavy debate, and regulators are looking for a new, more coordinated approach to react in an appropriate and timely manner, and to prevent circumvention right from the beginning.

Before the crisis, the argument that the introduction of the euro will sooner or later solve the problem was a common one. While this 'wait and see' approach may still seem attractive, it is no longer feasible. On the one hand, the crisis has shown that foreign currency credits add an additional risk to an already non-performing loans portfolio; on the other hand, some countries have postponed euro introduction even further. Therefore the crisis intensified the need for action.

This book, which is based on a Conference on European Economic Integration (CEEI) that the Oesterreichische Nationalbank (OeNB) held on the theme 'The Euro's Contribution to Economic Stability in CESEE' in Vienna on 16 and 17 November 2009, addresses the specific range of issues mentioned above. In addition, it contains a more broad-based academic contribution from Paul De Grauwe. He points out the discrepancy between the causes of the current crisis on the one hand and mainstream macroeconomic modelling on the other: whereas the crisis had come about as a result of inefficiencies in the financial market and economic agents' poor understanding of risk, standard macroeconomic models which have become popular in recent years were based on the unrealistic assumption that agents are capable of using and processing all available complex information. Hence, these rational expectations top-down models, as Professor De Grauwe refers to them, need to be replaced by what he dubs bottom-up systems, in which individuals understand only small bits of total information and apply simple decision rules.

Although these ideas are only a first step, they are quite important, as they prove that economic theory tries to find new paths and explanations for what is going on in our economies. This reassures us that theory and reality will come closer in the future, for the sake of preventing another global financial and economic crisis.

Ewald Nowotny
Peter Mooslechner
Doris Ritzberger-Grünwald

The academic view up front: towards a new macroeconomics

Paul De Grauwe

INTRODUCTION

One of the surprising developments in macroeconomics is the systematic incorporation of the paradigm of the utility maximizing forward-looking and fully informed agent into macroeconomic models. The most successful implementations of these developments are to be found in the Dynamic Stochastic General Equilibrium (DSGE) models that are increasingly used in central banks for policy analysis (see Smets and Wouters, 2003, 2007).

These developments are surprising. While macroeconomic theory enthusiastically embraced the view that agents fully understand the structure of the underlying models in which they operate, other sciences like psychology and neurology increasingly uncovered the cognitive limitations of individuals (see for example Kahneman, 2002; Camerer et al., 2005; Kahneman and Thaler, 2006; Della Vigna, 2007). We learn from these sciences that agents only understand small bits and pieces of the world in which they live, and instead of maximizing continuously taking all available information into account, agents use simple rules (heuristics) in guiding their behaviour and their forecasts about the future. The recent financial crisis seems to support the view that agents have limited understanding of the big picture. If they had understood the full complexity of the financial system they would have understood the lethal riskiness of the assets they massively took in their portfolios.

In order to understand the nature of different macroeconomic models it is useful to make a distinction between top-down and bottom-up systems. In its most general definition a top-down system is one in which agents fully understand the system. These agents are capable of representing the whole system in a blueprint that they can store in their mind. Depending on their position in the system they can use this blueprint to take over the command, or they can use it to optimize their own private welfare. These are systems in which there is a one-to-one mapping of the information embedded in the system and the information contained in the brain of one (or more) individuals. An example of such a top-down system is a building that can be represented by a blueprint and is fully understood by the architect.

Bottom-up systems are very different in nature. These are systems in which no individual understands the whole picture. Each individual understands only a very small part of the whole. These systems function as a result of the application of simple rules by the individuals populating the system. Most living systems follow this bottom-up logic. The market system is also a bottom-up system. The best description made of this bottom-up system is still the one made by Hayek (1945). Hayek argued that no individual exists who is capable of understanding the full complexity of a market system. Instead individuals only understand small bits of the total information. The main function of markets consists in aggregating this diverse information. If there were individuals capable of understanding the whole picture, we would not need markets. This was in fact Hayek's criticism of the 'socialist' economists who took the view that the central planner understood the whole picture, and would therefore be able to compute the whole set of optimal prices, making the market system superfluous. For further insightful analysis see Leijonhufvud (1993).

My contention is that the rational expectations models are the intellectual heirs of these central planning models. Not in the sense that individuals in these rational expectations models aim at planning the whole, but in the sense that, as the central planner, they understand the whole picture. These individuals use this superior information to obtain the 'optimum optimorum' for their own private welfare. In this sense they are top-down models.

In this chapter I will contrast the rational expectations top-down model with a bottom-up macroeconomic model. This will be a model in which agents have cognitive limitations and do not understand the whole picture (the underlying model). Instead they only understand small bits and pieces of the whole model and use simple rules to guide their behaviour. I will introduce rationality in the model through a selection mechanism in which agents evaluate the performance of the rule they are following and decide to switch or to stick to the rule depending on how well the rule performs relative to other rules.[1]

A BEHAVIOURAL MACROECONOMIC MODEL

In this section the broad outlines of the behavioural model are described (for more technical detail see De Grauwe (2009). The model consists of an aggregate demand equation, an aggregate supply equation and a Taylor rule.

Aggregate demand is determined by the:
- real interest rate
- expected future output (the forward-looking term)
- lagged output (the backward-looking term) reflecting inertia in output.

Aggregate supply (New Keynesian Philips curve) determines inflation as a function of:
- expected future inflation (forward-looking term)
- lagged inflation (backward-looking term) expressing price and wage rigidities
- output gap.

The *Taylor rule* describes how the central bank sets the interest rate:
- to keep inflation close to target (c_1)
- to stabilize output (c_2)
- to smooth interest rates.

Agents are assumed to use simple rules (heuristics) to forecast the future output and inflation. The way I proceed is as follows. I start with a very simple forecasting heuristics and apply it to the forecasting rules of future output. I assume two types of forecasting rules. A first rule can be called a 'fundamentalist' one. Agents estimate the steady-state value of the output gap (which is normalized at 0) and use this to forecast the future output gap. A second forecasting rule is an 'extrapolative' one. This is a rule that does not presuppose that agents know the steady-state output gap. They are agnostic about it. Instead, they extrapolate the previous observed output gap into the future.

This kind of simple heuristic has often been used in the behavioural finance literature where agents are assumed to use fundamentalist and chartist rules (see Brock and Hommes, 1997; Branch and Evans, 2006; De Grauwe and Grimaldi, 2006). It is probably the simplest possible assumption one can make about how agents, which experience cognitive limitations, use rules that embody limited knowledge to guide their behaviour. In this sense they are bottom-up rules. They only require agents to use information they understand, and do not require them to understand the whole picture.

As indicated earlier, agents are rational in the sense that they continuously evaluate their forecast performance. I apply notions of discrete choice theory (see Anderson et al., 1992; Brock and Hommes, 1997) in specifying the procedure agents follow in this evaluation process. After an evaluation of the forecasting rule they use, agents decide to switch to the alternative forecasting rule if the latter performs better than the one being used.

It should be stressed that although individuals use simple rules in forecasting the future, this does not mean that they fail to learn. In fact the fitness criterion used should be interpreted as a learning mechanism based on 'trial and error'. When observing that the rule they use performs less well than the alternative rule, agents are willing to switch to the more performing rule. Put differently, agents avoid making systematic mistakes by constantly being willing to learn from past mistakes and to change their behaviour. This also ensures that the market forecasts are unbiased.

A similar selection mechanism governs the use of forecasting rules of inflation. I assume two possible rules. The first one uses the announced inflation target to forecast the rate of inflation; the second one uses an extrapolative rule. This mechanism can be interpreted as a procedure of agents to find out how credible the central bank's inflation targeting is. If this is very credible, using the announced inflation target will produce good forecasts and as a result, the probability that agents will rely on the inflation target will be high. If on the other hand, the inflation target does not produce good forecasts (compared to a simple extrapolation rule) the probability that agents will use it will be small.

ANIMAL SPIRITS

I now present the simulations of the behavioural model in the time domain and I interpret them (for more information on how these simulations were designed, see De Grauwe, 2009). The upper panel of Figure X.1 shows the time pattern of output produced by the behavioural model. A strong cyclical movement in the output gap can be observed. The lower panel of Figure X.1 shows a variable called 'animal spirits'.[2] It represents the evolution of the fractions of the agents who extrapolate a positive output gap. Thus when the curve reaches +1 all agents are extrapolating a positive output gap; when the curve reaches 0 no agents are extrapolating a positive output gap. In fact in that case they all extrapolate a negative output gap. Thus the curve shows the degree of optimism and pessimism of agents who make forecasts of the output gap.

Combining the information of the two panels in Figure X.1 it can be seen that the model generates endogenous waves of optimism and pessimism. During some periods optimists (that is, agents who extrapolate positive output gaps) dominate and this translates into above-average output growth. These optimistic periods are followed by pessimistic ones when pessimists (that is, agents who extrapolate negative output gaps) dominate and the growth rate of output is below average. These waves of optimism

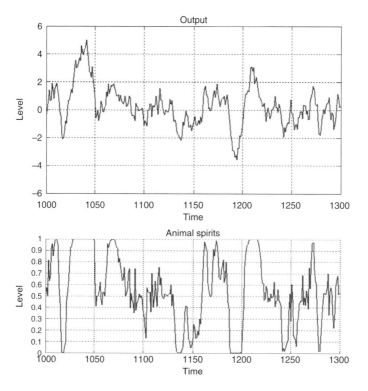

Figure X.1   Output gap in behavioural model

and pessimism are essentially unpredictable. Other realizations of the shocks produce different cycles with the same general characteristics.

These waves of optimism and pessimism can be understood to be searching (learning) mechanisms of agents who do not fully understand the underlying model but are continuously searching for the truth. An essential characteristic of this searching mechanism is that it leads to systematic correlation in beliefs (for example optimistic extrapolations or pessimistic extrapolations). This systematic correlation is at the core of the booms and busts created in the model. Note, however, that when computed over a significantly large period of time the average error in the forecasting goes to zero. In this sense, the forecast bias tends to disappear asymptotically.

Having presented the main features of the behavioural (bottom-up) model I now proceed to show how this model leads to a view of macroeconomic dynamics that contrasts greatly with the view obtained from the rational expectations (top-down) macroeconomic models. I concentrate on two areas. The first one has to do with the business cycle theories implicit in the behavioural and the rational expectations models. The second one focuses on the implications for monetary policies.

TWO DIFFERENT BUSINESS CYCLE THEORIES

The behavioural and rational expectations macroeconomic models lead to very different views on the nature of business cycle. Business cycle movements in the rational expectations (DSGE) models arise as a result of exogenous shocks (in productivity and preferences) and lags in the transmission of these shocks to output and inflation. Thus inertia in output and inflation are the result of the lagged transmission of exogenous shocks. One could call the inertia (and the business cycles) introduced in the DSGE model exogenously created phenomena.[3]

In contrast, the behavioural model presented here is capable of generating inertia (and business cycles) without imposing lags in the transmission process. This could be called endogenous inertia.

This difference between the two models is quite fundamental. In the rational expectations model and in the absence of lags in the transmission, agents immediately find the optimal levels of output and inflation after some unanticipated shock. This results from their top-down position, that is, they can instantaneously compute the effects this shock has on all the variables of the model making it possible to compute the optimal plan today and in the future. In order to produce the required inertia (and the business cycle movements), lags in the transmission preventing instantaneous adjustment to the optimal plan, are necessary.

The contrast with the behavioural model is great. Agents in this model do not fully understand how the shock will be transmitted. They have no top-down position. As a result they follow a procedure (heuristics together with a selection mechanism) that functions as a 'trial and error' learning mechanism aimed at revealing the information about shocks and the transmission process. This is a slow bottom-up process that uses backward evaluation processes. It generates an endogenous inertia (and business cycle) into the model.

The different natures of the business cycles in the DSGE models and the behavioural model also have policy implications. In the DSGE models now favoured by central banks, business cycle movements in output and prices originate from price and wage stickiness. In order to reduce this kind of volatility more flexibility in prices and wages is required. That is why many central banks call for more flexibility. In a more flexible world, central banks will not be called upon so often to stabilize output, and thereby set price stability at risk.

In the behavioural model, business cycle movements in output arise from informational inertia. Thus, even if prices and wages become more flexible, this will not necessarily reduce the business cycle movements in output. As a result, society's desire to stabilize output will not be reduced. And central banks that inevitably respond to these desires will face the need to stabilize output at the risk of reducing price stability.

THE ROLE OF OUTPUT STABILIZATION

Modern macroeconomics in general, and DSGE models in particular, have provided the intellectual foundation of inflation targeting. Until the eruption of the financial crisis in 2007, inflation targeting strategies had become the undisputed policy framework modern central banks should adopt. And most did. Inflation targeting, of course, does not imply that there is no role for output stabilization. DSGE modellers who have put a new Keynesian flavour in their models, have always stressed that wage and price rigidities provide a rationale for output stabilization by central banks (see Clarida et al., 1999; Gali, 2008). This idea has found its reflection in 'flexible' inflation targeting (Svensson, 1997; Woodford, 2003). Because of the existence of rigidities, a central bank should not attempt to keep inflation close to its target all the time. When sufficiently large shocks occur that lead to departures of inflation from its target, the central bank should follow a strategy of gradual return of inflation to its target.

Output stabilization in the DSGE world, however, is very much circumscribed. The need to stabilize arises because of the existence of rigidities in prices that makes it necessary to spread out price movements over longer periods. The limited scope for output stabilization is based on a model characterized by a stable equilibrium. There is no consideration of the possibility that the equilibrium may be unstable or that fluctuations in output have a different origin than price rigidities. Should the scope for output stabilization be enlarged? In order to shed some light on this issue we derive the trade-off between output and inflation variability in the context of the behavioural model, and we formulate some policy conclusions.

The trade-offs are constructed as follows. The model was simulated 10 000 times and the average output and inflation variabilities were computed for different values of the Taylor rule parameters.

The trade-offs are shown in Figure X.2 for different values of the inflation parameter c_1. Take the trade-off A–B. This is the one obtained for $c_1 = 1$. Start from point A on the trade-off. In point A, the Taylor output parameter $c_2 = 0$ (strict inflation targeting). As output stabilization increases we first move downwards. Thus increased output stabilization by the central bank reduces output and inflation variability. The relation

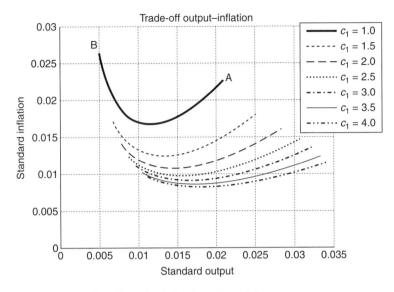

Figure X.2   Trade-offs in the behavioural model

is non-linear, however. At some point, with too high an output stabilization parameter, the trade-off curve starts increasing, becoming a 'normal'
trade-off, that is, a lower output variability is obtained at the cost of
increased inflation variability.

How can we interpret these results? Let us start from the case of strict
inflation targeting, that is, the authorities set $c_2 = 0$. There is no attempt
at stabilizing output at all. The ensuing output variability intensifies the
waves of optimism and pessimism (animal spirits) which in turn feed back
on output volatility. These larges waves lead to higher inflation variability.
Thus, some output stabilization is good; it reduces both output and inflation variability by preventing too large swings in animal spirits. With no
output stabilization at all ($c_2 = 0$) the forces of animal spirits are so high
that the high output variability also increases inflation volatility through
the effect of the output gap on inflation (supply equation). Too much output
stabilization, however, reduces the stabilization bonus provided by a credible inflation target. When the central bank attaches too much importance
to output stabilization it creates more scope for better forecasting performance of the inflation extrapolators, leading to more inflation variability.

Figure X.2 also tells us something important about inflation targeting.
We note that increasing the inflation parameter in the Taylor rule (c_1) has
the effect of shifting the trade-offs downwards, that is, the central bank can
improve the trade-offs by reacting more strongly to changes in inflation.[4]

The central bank achieves this improvement in the trade-off because by reacting more intensely to changes in inflation it reduces the probability that inflation extrapolators will tend to dominate the market, and as a result it reduces the probability that inflation targeting looses credibility. Such a loss of credibility destabilizes both inflation and output. Thus maintaining credibility of inflation targeting is an important source of macroeconomic stability in our behavioural model.

One can conclude that the behavioural model provides a different perspective about the need to stabilize output. This is a model that creates endogenous movements of the business cycle that are correlated with waves of optimism and pessimism. They are also unrelated to the existence of wage and price rigidities. These waves of optimism and pessimism both influence the output gap and in turn are also influenced by the output gap.

CONCLUSION

Macroeconomic models based on rational expectations assume extraordinary cognitive capabilities of individual agents. The latter are assumed to be capable of understanding the whole picture. Recent developments in other disciplines including psychology and brain science document that individual agents struggle with limited cognitive abilities, restricting their capacity to understand the world. As a result, individual agents use small bits of information and simple rules to guide their behaviour.

I have used these new insights to show how a macroeconomic model in which the cognitive limitations of agents take centre stage functions. Once one moves into a world of cognitive limitations one faces the problem that agents use simple and biased rules to forecast output and inflation. In order to provide discipline in the use of these rules, a learning mechanism was introduced that allows for the selection of those rules that are more profitable than others.

The ensuing behavioural model produces a number of results that distinguishes it from the rational expectations models. First, the behavioural model creates correlations in beliefs which in turn generate waves of optimism and pessimism. The latter produce endogenous cycles which are akin to the Keynesian animal spirits.

A second result is that the inflation targeting regime turns out to be of great importance to stabilize the economy in a behavioural model. The reason is that credible inflation targeting also helps to reduce correlations in beliefs and the ensuing self-fulfilling waves of optimism and pessimism. However, and this is where the behavioural model departs from the rational expectations model, strict inflation targeting is not an optimal policy. Some output stabilization (given a credible inflation target) also helps in reducing the scope for waves of optimism and pessimism to emerge and to destabilize output *and* inflation.

Finally, the behavioural model provides for a very different theory of the business cycle as compared to the business cycle theory implicit in the rational expectations (DSGE) models. In the DSGE models, business cycle movements in output and prices arise because rational agents cannot adjust their optimal plans instantaneously after an exogenous disturbance. Price and wage stickiness prevent such instantaneous adjustment. As a result, these exogenous shocks produce inertia and business cycle movements.

In the behavioural model, business cycle movements in output arise from informational inertia. Thus, even if prices and wages become more flexible, this will not necessarily reduce the business cycle movements in output. As a result, society's desire to stabilize output will not be reduced. And central banks that inevitably respond to these desires will face the need to stabilize output.

NOTES

1. The modelling approach presented in this chapter is not the only possible one to model agents' behaviour under imperfect information. In fact, a large literature has emerged attempting to introduce imperfect information into macroeconomic models. These attempts have been based mainly on the statistical learning approach pioneered by Sargant (1993) and Evans and Honkapohja (2001). This literature leads to important new insights (see for example Orphanides and Williams (2004), Gaspar et al. (2006), Milani (2007)). See also the fascinating book of Gigerenzer and Todd (1999) on the use of simple heuristics as compared to statistical (regression) learning.
2. The *locus classicus* is Keynes (1936). See also Farmer (2006) and Akerlof and Shiller (2009).
3. In a way it can be said that the lags in the transmission mechanism introduce an exogenous, some may say an ad hoc, element into the logic of the DSGE model. To give an example, Calvo pricing in which firms are constrained to adjust prices instantaneously (Christiano et al., 2001) is routinely imposed in DSGE models. It is clear, however, that such a restriction comes from outside the logic of the model. In a world where everybody understands the model and each other's rationality, which is at the core of the DSGE models, agents would want to go immediately to the optimal plan using the optimal price. They would not want to accept such a restriction.
4. A similar result on the importance of strict inflation is also found in Gaspar et al. (2006) who use a macro model with statistical learning.

REFERENCES

Akerlof, G. and R. Shiller (2009), *Animal Spirits. How Human Psychology Drives the Economy and Why It Matters for Global Capitalism*, Princeton: Princeton University Press.

Anderson, S., A. de Palma and J.-F. Thisse (1992), *Discrete Choice Theory of Product Differentiation*, Cambridge, MA: MIT Press.

Branch, W. and G. Evans (2006), 'Intrinsic heterogeneity in expectation formation', *Journal of Economic Theory*, **127**, 264–95.

Brock, W. and C. Hommes (1997), 'A rational route to randomness', *Econometrica*, **65**, 1059–95.

Camerer, C., G. Loewenstein and D. Prelec (2005), 'Neuroeconomics: how neuroscience can inform economics', *Journal of Economic Literature*, **63** (1), 9–64.

Christiano, L., M. Eichenbaum and C. Evans (2001), 'Nominal rigidities and the dynamic effects of a shock to monetary policy', *NBER Working Paper*, no. 8403, July.

Clarida, R., J. Galí and M. Gertler (1999), 'The science of monetary policy, a new Keynesian perspective', *Journal of Economic Literature*, **37**, 1661–707.

De Grauwe, P. (2009), 'Bottom-up versus Top-down Macroeconomic Models', paper presented at the Annual Research Conference of DG-ECFIN of the European Commission, 15–16 October 2009, Brussels.

De Grauwe, P. and M. Grimaldi (2006), *The Exchange Rate in a Behavioural Finance Framework*, Oxford: Princeton University Press.

Della Vigna, S. (2007), 'Psychology and economics: evidence from the field', *NBER Working Paper*, no. 13420.

Evans, G.W. and S. Honkapohja (2001), *Learning and Expectations in Macroeconomics*, Princeton: Princeton University Press.

Farmer, Roger E.A. (2006), 'Animal Spirits', *Palgrave Dictionary of Economics*, London: Macmillan.

Galí, J. (2008), *Monetary Policy, Inflation and the Business Cycle*, Princeton: Princeton University Press.

Gaspar, V., F. Smets and D. Vestin (2006), 'Adaptive learning, persistence and optimal monetary policy', *ECB Working Paper Series* No. 644, European Central Bank.

Gigerenzer, G. and P.M. Todd (1999), *Simple Heuristics That Make Us Smart*, New York: Oxford University Press.

Hayek, F. (1945), 'The use of knowledge in society', *American Economic Review*, **XXXV** (4), 519–30.

Kahneman, D. (2002), 'Maps of Bounded Rationality: A Perspective on Intuitive Judgment and Choice', Nobel Prize Lecture, 8 December, Stockholm.

Kahneman, D. and R. Thaler (2006), 'Utility maximization and experienced utility', *Journal of Economic Perspectives*, **20**, 221–34.

Keynes, J.M. (1936), *The General Theory of Employment, Interest and Money*, London: Macmillan.

Leijonhufvud, A. (1993), 'Towards a not-too-rational macroeconomics', *Southern Economic Journal*, **1** (1), July.

Milani, F. (2007), 'Expectations, learning and macroeconomic persistence', *Journal of Monetary Economics*, **54**, 2065–82.

Orphanides, A. and J. Williams (2004), 'Robust Monetary Policy with Imperfect Information', *Discussion Paper*, Board of Governors of the Federal Reserve System, Washington DC.

Sargent, T. (1993), *Bounded Rationality in Macroeconomics*, Oxford: Oxford University Press.

Smets, F. and R. Wouters (2003), 'An estimated dynamic stochastic general equilibrium model', *Journal of the European Economic Association*, **1**, 1123–75.

Smets, F. and R. Wouters (2007), 'Shocks and frictions in US business cycles – a Bayesian DSGE approach', *ECB Working Paper Series* No. 722, European Central Bank, February.

Svensson, L. (1997), 'Inflation forecast targeting: implementing and monitoring inflation targets', *European Economic Review,* **41,** 111–46.

Woodford, M. (2003), *Interest and Prices: Foundations of a Theory of Monetary Policy*, Princeton: Princeton University Press.

PART I

The stability merits of the euro

1. The euro's role on the world stage

Joaquín Almunia

The title of this book – *The Euro and Economic Stability: Focus on Central, Eastern and South-Eastern Europe* – could not be more pertinent. During the crisis, the euro effectively shielded members of the European monetary union (EMU) from the turbulences that proved so costly in times of stress in the past. But at the same time, we must recognize that the single currency is not a solution to all economic woes. The opportunity to learn from the lessons of this crisis and prepare a strategy that will strengthen Europe's response to any future adverse economic shocks is of utmost importance for all of us, and in particular for the European Union (EU) new member states (NMS), as many of them still face the challenge of adopting the single currency.

1.1   THE GLOBAL ECONOMIC CRISIS

But before referring to the Central and Eastern European (CEE) region, let me first turn to the impact of the crisis and the measures we have already taken to counter its devastating effects.

Financial markets were at the epicentre of the crisis. The EU and the euro area were not spared, with some large financial institutions on the verge of default. The risk of a collapse of the entire European financial system was no longer abstract – it had become a real danger.

The European reaction did not linger. The European Commission and the European Council quickly developed principles and objectives for a coordinated approach. For its part, the European Central Bank (ECB) was the first major central bank to address market tensions via enhanced liquidity provision to the banking system. Member states allocated sizeable public means to banking rescue packages. Since October 2008, the European Commission approved a total of over EUR 3.5 trillion (almost one-third of the GDP) of State aid measures to financial institutions. So far, EUR 1.5 trillion has been effectively used under the four main headings of debt guarantees, recapitalization, liquidity support, and treatment of impaired assets.

Credit restraint and sagging confidence hit business investment and household demand, notably for consumer durables and housing. The cross-border transmission was extremely rapid with the spectre of a new Great Depression looming large. Projections for economic growth were revised downward at a record pace.

The contraction now seems to have bottomed out. Still, GDP is projected to fall by about 4 per cent in the EU and the euro area in 2009. The cumulative output loss amounts to some 5 per cent of GDP since the recession started in the second quarter of 2008. In order to give you a sense of magnitude, this is about three times more than the average loss in the previous three recessions. Having said this, the situation would undoubtedly have been much more serious, had central banks, governments and supranational authorities, in Europe and elsewhere, not responded forcefully.

The EU's response to the downturn has been swift and decisive. The overall fiscal stimulus, including the effects of automatic stabilizers, amounts to about 5 percentage points of GDP in the EU in 2009 and 2010.

There are reasons to be optimistic about the near-term outlook. Financial conditions have improved over summer 2009, with several financial indicators returning to pre-crisis levels. Business and consumer confidence indicators have also improved in recent months. World trade has stabilized, and there are indications that the destocking cycle is bottoming out. The relative resilience of consumption has proved to be a stabilizing factor during the recession, as disinflation and relief measures included in fiscal stimulus packages have supported household incomes.

According to the European Commission's (2009a) latest forecasts, which were published at the beginning of November 2009, the EU and the euro area economies are emerging from recession in the second half of 2009. In the EU and the euro area, annual growth rates are expected to be 0.7 per cent in 2010 and gathering pace, at around 1.5 per cent in 2011.

However, I should stress that uncertainty about the strength and sustainability of the recovery remains. Banks are in the process of strengthening their solvency ratios, helped by the accommodative stance of monetary policy and rescue packages. But the stabilization in financial markets has yet to yield concrete outcomes for credit distribution to the economy. Moreover, deteriorating employment prospects are a huge source of concern which we need to address.

1.2   THE ROLE OF THE EURO

Now ten years after the inception of the euro, the crisis has put the single currency to a major test. But far from withering, the euro has weathered the storm well.

First, and most importantly, the euro prevented exchange rate and interest rate turbulences among the euro area member states. We know from experience how damaging such intra-European currency turmoil can be for the functioning of the single market.

Second, the euro area's stability-oriented macroeconomic framework has reduced the level and fluctuation of inflation and interest rates and kept expectations well anchored. It has also played a valuable role as an anchor of sound macroeconomic policies for member states actively pursuing the adoption of the euro, or whose currencies are linked to the euro.

Third, since the start of the financial turmoil, the ECB has skilfully managed liquidity and aggressively lowered interest to record low levels. This has helped to ease conditions in the interbank market and to anchor inflation expectations throughout this period of uncertainty.

Finally, but not of least importance, the governance structure of EMU – again, far from being perfect – facilitated the coordination of policy action across the euro area and the EU as a whole.

Imagine for a moment, how the crisis could have unfolded without the euro. The coordination problems would have multiplied. There would have been 16 European central banks that would have had to struggle for a coordinated liquidity provision while trying to keep exchange rates and inflation expectations in check, or engage in negotiations about currency swaps.

Why then, after ten years of successful EMU, did the crisis hit the euro area so hard? The single currency in itself is no panacea. The crisis has highlighted the unfinished business in the euro area. As argued by the European Commission (2008) in their report on 'EMU@10', unfinished business relates in particular to: (i) the accumulation of intra-euro area imbalances; (ii) the lack of a pan-European cross-border financial supervision and crisis management framework; and (iii) euro area governance. Let me address these three challenges in somewhat more detail.

Because of important macroeconomic imbalances accumulated over time, some euro area countries have been hit particularly hard. One group of countries have been running very large and persistent current account deficits and have registered a sharp deterioration in their net foreign asset positions. These external deficits reflect the strength of private domestic demand compounded by losses in price competitiveness due to an inappropriate response of wages to productivity growth. At the same time private sector debt has increased rapidly and external funding has tended to be channelled excessively into housing and consumption, contributing to the emergence of housing bubbles.

How to correct these imbalances? Taking measures to downsize and adjust oversized sectors, in particular housing, is part of the answer. It is also necessary to reduce high private sector debt and adjust unsustainable intra-euro area current account imbalances. Countries with entrenched current account deficits should restore competitiveness.

Conversely, other euro area member states have been running large current account surpluses. These member states have benefited from a strong export performance prior to the crisis, sometimes underpinned by robust gains in price competitiveness. However, to various degrees, their large current account surpluses also reflect comparatively weak domestic demand. They became particularly vulnerable to sudden reversals in global trade. As the global economy seems to be rebalancing, this group of countries also face formidable adjustment needs in terms of strengthening domestic demand.

The crisis put the spotlight on unfinished business also in terms of integrated financial supervision. I would not claim that better arrangements in this domain would have prevented the crisis. But the fact that progress in financial integration in the euro area was not matched by a parallel strengthening of supervisory arrangements certainly hampered the euro area's capacity to respond to the crisis. Our supervisory framework remains fragmented along national lines despite the creation of a European single market. Existing supervisory arrangements failed to promote a common supervisory culture.

The comprehensive packages of legislative measures proposed by the European Commission, building on the de Larosière report (2009), aims to significantly strengthen the supervision of the financial sector in Europe. This package represents the rapid and robust response to the shortcomings in European financial supervision and should help prevent future financial crises.

Finally, the crisis showed that the established mechanism of policy coordination within the euro area was not working sufficiently well. Indeed, if coordination had started earlier and had been more comprehensive, the aggregate impact of the euro area economic policy response could have been stronger. Coordination matters for the EU as a whole, but it is particularly important for euro area member states. More than ever, the euro area should exert leadership in these testing times.

1.3   THE NEED FOR COORDINATED EXIT STRATEGIES

On 13 November 2009, Eurostat (2009) published the flash estimate for the third quarter of 2009, posting 0.4 per cent GDP growth in the euro area and 0.2 per cent growth in the EU-27. This is in line with the European Commission's (2009a) autumn forecast and confirms positive momentum for 2010 and 2011. While 2010 will post a modest recovery still policy-induced, 2011 should see self-sustained growth. Therefore, it is imperative to continue implementing the agreed stimulus measures in 2010 and start withdrawing them in 2011 as these unprecedented stimulus measures in combination with automatic stabilizers and the sharp reversal of revenues have led to a significant deterioration of public finances.

The fiscal costs of the crisis and of projected demographic development compound each other and make fiscal sustainability an acute challenge. The European Commission (2009b) in its 2009 report on fiscal sustain-ability highlights the risks if no ambitious efforts to implement structural reforms and to consolidate government accounts are taken. If no fiscal consolidation measures are taken beyond the automatic withdrawal of the stimulus measures, the report projects that by 2015 the average debt ratio would be at around 100 per cent of GDP both in the EU and the euro area. The debt ratio would continue to increase to around 120 per cent of GDP in 2020.

In the light of these fiscal sustainability challenges the time is ripe to start articulating a comprehensive exit strategy from the crisis.

Do not get me wrong! It is still too early to start the exit strategy now. But in order to manage market expectations wisely in this uncertain environment, we need to prepare the exit strategy now and to commu-nicate clearly on it. By doing so credibly, monetary conditions could remain accommodative, which would avoid pushing up borrowing costs and making the fiscal consolidation longer and more painful than it would otherwise be. The Economic and Financial Affairs Council (ECOFIN) agreed in October 2009 that, beyond the withdrawal of the stimulus measures, substantial fiscal consolidation was required in order to halt and eventually reverse the increase in debt and restore sound fiscal positions. Provided that the European Commission forecasts continue to indicate that the recovery is strengthening and becomes self-sustaining, fiscal consolidation in all EU member states should start in 2011 at the latest. The timing and pace of the consolidation needs to take account of country-specific situations, which also implies that a number of countries need to reduce government deficits and debt accu-mulation before then.

I want to stress the importance of coordinated exit strategies across countries in the framework of a consistent implementation of the Stability and Growth Pact.[1] In line with this, the European Commission decided in October 2009 to initiate the excessive deficit procedure (EDP)[2] for nine EU member states on the basis of projected budget deficits above 3 per cent in 2009, and to adapt the EDPs launched in May 2009 for another four countries.

The timing, intensity and sequencing of policy withdrawal requires our attention. To be successful in this process, close coordination among all actors will be needed to ensure optimal cross-country differentiation but also cross-policy consistency.

In the euro area, coordination requirements are particularly strong, given growth spillovers between countries and the single monetary policy. But at the same time, the need for coordination extends beyond the EU scope. The global nature of the crisis calls for coordination of policies at a global level. At the St. Andrews meeting on 6 and 7 November 2009, G-20 Finance Ministers and Central Bank Governors committed to the further development of strategies for managing the withdrawal from the extraordinary macroeconomic and financial support measures. The participants of the meeting agreed to cooperate and coordinate, accordingly.

1.4 CENTRAL AND EASTERN EUROPE (CEE) AND SOUTH-EASTERN EUROPE (SEE) COUNTRIES AND THE CRISIS

The NMS from Central and Eastern Europe (CEE) were badly hit by the crisis, following a sharp decline of global demand and retrenchment of capital inflows.

Many of them fell into sharp recessions and their fiscal positions deteriorated markedly. However, the recession and financial strains were and remain stronger in those countries which already at the onset of the crisis had been suffering from major imbalances or policy weaknesses.

In the Baltic States, for example, several years of rapid catching up had been accompanied by accumulated imbalances. These imbalances, reinforced by the global financial crisis and the fading away of external demand, ultimately led to a sharp reversal of the cycle. Estimated GDP falls for 2009 in the Baltics are in double-digit figures.

High external and fiscal imbalances also increased exposure to the global economic downturn in some NMS with floating currencies, notably Hungary and Romania. By contrast, other CEE countries have been more resilient to the global crisis.

The EU rapidly showed its solidarity with its members in difficulty. In October 2008, Hungary asked for international financial support by the EU and International Monetary Fund (IMF) to counter pressures on its balance-of-payments (BoP) and financial markets. This led to the activation of the EU medium-term assistance facility.[3] Since then, two more programmes, in Latvia and Romania, have been launched, bringing the total commitments under the facility to EUR 14.6 billion. In view of the increasing needs, the ceiling of available EU assistance has been raised in two steps from EUR 12 billion to EUR 50 billion. This assistance is provided in the context of broader international support packages, implying an unprecedented degree of cooperation with the IMF and the close involvement of other actors (multilateral development banks, bilaterals).

In conjunction with the accompanying policy programmes, the international assistance has contributed to stabilizing market expectations and underpinning confidence. The BoP assistance has given the three countries breathing room to implement reforms necessary to restore access to private external financing and, ultimately, to honour their external debt obligations. Assistance also contributed to prevent a larger recession in the three countries. By providing significant financing to the budget, the programmes have allowed greater operation of automatic stabilizers than would have been possible otherwise. This has helped limit the social effects of the crisis. Importantly, the assistance is providing an opportunity to adopt long-due structural reforms in the countries concerned.

The EU BoP assistance to non-euro area member states is embedded in the broader policy framework set by the Treaty. Its elements include regular economic surveillance (particularly on fiscal and structural policies), support through structural funds, the single market framework and the euro adoption process. This broader institutional dimension is a crucial difference between EU member states and other emerging economies affected by the crisis.

The private sector has been involved in the crisis resolution efforts as well. Parent banks have so far provided the necessary funding to their affiliates in the new EU member states, and a significant deterioration of conditions in the substantially foreign-owned banking sectors in these countries has been avoided. In the context of the European banking coordination initiative – the so-called Vienna initiative[4] – parent banks have committed to maintain exposure to these countries and recapitalize their affiliates, if necessary.

More recently, the financial market situation in the NMS has improved. However, we should not have illusions on the pace of recovery. Even assuming continued forceful policy actions, the recovery is expected to be gradual. Some economies in the region are constrained in the use of fiscal stimulus. The scope for CEE countries to benefit from an export-led recovery is limited. Potential growth in the region is also unlikely to return to pre-crisis trends in the short term.

Policy challenges for the CEE countries remain significant. What is of key importance in the short term is to maintain resilience in view of persistent macro-financial vulnerabilities. Banking sectors continue to face important risks given the ongoing deterioration of asset quality. From a medium-term perspective, it is important to address further accumulated imbalances and re-establish a robust and sustainable growth and convergence path. This will require continued efforts particularly in the fiscal and structural fields.

The NMS, in their efforts to accelerate the catching-up process, have acquired over the years an important capacity to adjust. I am confident that in the face of the current challenge this capacity to adjust will prove invaluable.

Before concluding, let me briefly address the situation in candidate and potential candidate countries, where the crisis has so far been felt to different extents.

Some of those countries, particularly the most integrated in international trade and capital flows, felt the impact of the crisis more quickly and more severely and will post negative growth this year. Let me note that the banking sector in pre-accession countries has weathered the crisis remarkably well, thanks to its high degree of capitalization and liquidity, and – in the case of Turkey – due to a strong round of previous reforms. Only one ailing bank needed to be rescued, in Montenegro.

However, and in spite of fiscal adjustment measures taken in these countries, my main concern over the short and medium term relates to the continued deterioration of the fiscal situation.

The EU stands ready to help candidate and potential candidate countries in difficulty. EU macro-financial assistance can be provided, in conjunction with IMF programmes, to support them through the worst of the crisis. Earlier in 2009 Serbia and Bosnia and Herzegovina agreed programmes with the IMF. This in turn played an important role in enabling EU-based parent banks to maintain their financial exposure to these two countries. The EU will also contribute to these efforts. The European Commission recently proposed two macro-financial assistance loans in favour of Serbia and Bosnia and Herzegovina, of EUR 200 and 100 million respectively. These loans remain to be approved by the Council and the Parliament at the time of writing. Serbia also benefits in this context from exceptional EC budget support assistance expected to be released in 2009 and in 2010.

1.5   EURO ATTRACTIVENESS

Let me conclude on the EU members that are not yet integrated in the euro area.

The fall-out of the crisis – including the reappraisal of risk, tighter financing and liquidity conditions, and exchange rate volatility – has brought euro area membership to the forefront. The exit strategy will serve these countries in their preparation for euro adoption.

Among countries with pegged exchange rate regimes, the crisis has reinforced the prevailing euro adoption strategies. Euro area membership is perceived as a credible exit strategy propping up confidence (of residents and non-residents alike) in the pegs. Euro adoption is seen as offering a relief to liquidity constraints and eliminating exchange rate mismatches while not imposing additional challenges to economic policies.

For countries with floating exchange rates, the crisis has highlighted the vulnerabilities coming from large fiscal deficits against the background of tighter global conditions.

Euro adoption should not be seen as a quick fix to economic vulnerabilities. It should rather be part of a broader long-term policy strategy. As the crisis has amply demonstrated, membership in the euro area enhances resilience, but it does not eliminate the need to work out underlying imbalances that have been built up over the last years. Also, new entrants need to prepare thoroughly to cope with life under an irrevocably fixed exchange rate in order to successfully perform within the euro area.

The challenges of euro preparation should not be underestimated. For the recent new euro area entrants, preparation has involved the need to improve the state of public finances, in some cases changes to the exchange rate regime, and structural reforms to strengthen domestic adjustment capacity. In this respect, the crisis might serve to galvanize public and political support for the measures that are necessary to proceed with convergence and move closer to the goal of euro adoption.

Euro adoption remains a key anchor for medium-term policies and expectations for NMS. However, an accelerated euro area enlargement that would require a waiver or a loosening of the entry criteria specified by the Treaty is not an option. Without sustainable convergence, euro adoption may turn out to be a suboptimal strategy for the country concerned. And by heightening economic divergences and adjustment problems, it would also make the management of EMU more difficult.

Compliance with the convergence criteria in a sustainable manner is in the interest of both the prospective and existing members of the euro area. It signals the commitment and the ability to ensure a stable macroeconomic environment after irrevocably giving up the national exchange rate and monetary policy. It thus contributes in the best way to the smooth functioning and the stability of the euro area.

NOTES

1. The Stability and Growth Pact (SGP) is a rule-based framework for the coordination of national fiscal policies in the economic and monetary union (EMU). It was established to safeguard sound public finances, an important requirement for EMU to function properly. The Pact consists of a preventive and a dissuasive arm.
2. The SGP is the cornerstone of budgetary discipline. This Regulation is part of the pact, and its aim is to clarify and speed up the EDP so that it acts as a genuine deterrent. It supplements the 1993 Regulation laying down the procedure to be followed in connection with excessive deficits. Following discussions on the way the SGP is applied, the Regulation was amended in 2005.
3. Council Regulation (EC) No 332/2002 of 18 February 2002 establishing a facility providing medium-term financial assistance for member states' balances of payments.
4. The Vienna Initiative was created in early 2009 to coordinate the responses of major public and private shareholders to the financial crisis in Central and Eastern Europe. It brings together the home and host country authorities of the major EU-based bank groups, the bank groups themselves, the European Bank for Reconstruction and Development (EBRD), the International Monetary Fund (IMF), the World Bank, the European Investment Bank and the European Commission.

REFERENCES

De Larosière, Jacques et al. (2009), 'The High-level Group on Financial Supervision in the EU – Report', de Larosière Group, 25 February, Brussels, available at: http://ec.europa.eu/internal_market/finances/docs/de_larosiere_report_en.pdf.

European Commission (2008), 'Report on EMU@10: successes and challenges after 10 years of Economic and Monetary Union', European Economy, available at: http://ec.europa.eu/economy_finance/publications/publication12682_en.pdf.

European Commission (2009a), 'Forecasts', November, available at: http://ec.europa.eu/economy_finance/publications/publication16055_en.pdf.

European Commission (2009b), 'Sustainability report 2009', European Economy, **9**, available at: http://ec.europa.eu/economy_finance/publications/publication15998_en.pdf.

Eurostat (2009), 'Flash estimates', Eurostat news release, euroindicators, 13 November, available at: http://europa.eu/rapid/pressReleasesAction.do?reference=STAT/09/161&format=HTML&aged=0&language=EN&guiLanguage=fr.

2. The euro's contribution to economic stability in CESEE

Ewald Nowotny[1]

At the time of writing in Autumn 2009, the obvious points for starting a discussion of the euro's contribution to economic stability in Central, Eastern and South-Eastern European countries (CESEE) are the two anniversaries that we celebrated in 2009: the fall of the Iron Curtain and the introduction of the euro.

The fall of the Iron Curtain was, clearly, a milestone in the process of European integration. The breakup of what we knew as the 'eastern bloc' in 1989 ended the long-lasting division of Europe. This initiated a successful process of integration, which culminated in the 2004 and 2007 enlargement rounds of the European Union (EU). At least since then, cooperation and integration have been an integral part of our day-to-day European reality, a major element of our European identity.[2]

On 1 January 1999, 11 EU member states adopted the euro as their single currency. In the early stages of its existence, the euro was under heavy criticism. The well-known argument of proponents of the optimum currency area (OCA) paradigm associates the costs of joining a monetary union with the loss of domestic monetary policy. A currency union becomes costly if business cycles of individual countries are not synchronized highly enough. In the absence of country-specific monetary policies, an idiosyncratic shock cannot be absorbed through the real exchange rate but has to be digested via other channels, such as flexible wages, fiscal transfers or mobile factors of production.[3]

However this argument is very static. Joining a currency area leads to a boost in trade and hence to a convergence of business cycles. Moreover, in the current environment, the question of how costly idiosyncratic shocks can become are of minor importance. The crisis is a shock that has affected all economies. The first ten years of the euro have shown that the introduction of a single currency ensured price stability and spurred trade flows across the region. To put it in the words of Richard Baldwin (2006, p. 36) 'Most of the [trade] effect literature treats currency unions as magic wands. . . . The only question is: how big is the magic?'[4] Although there is no consensus about the magnitude of the trade effect triggered by the creation of the currency union, estimates point to a significant increase in trade and foreign direct investment within the euro area.[5] The rise in trade also went hand in hand with a surge in employment and a significantly lower price level than in the 1970s and 1980s. Therefore we can say that confidence in the euro is as large as the confidence markets used to have in its most stable predecessors.

Let me elaborate a little bit more on the current international role of the euro and its prospects for the medium term. In the first ten years of its existence, the euro has not only been a great success for its member states but has also continuously enhanced its international role. With the entry of Slovakia in January 2009, the euro area currently comprises 16 member states, with a total population of more than 330 million.[6] This compares with a US population of 304.5 million in 2008. Another important determinant is economic activity. While in 2008, the euro area's GDP at purchasing power was still below that of the USA, economic activity in the EU exceeded that of the USA. In other words, 2008 figures demonstrate that the potential euro area of the future outpaced the USA in terms of economic activity.

From a micro perspective, the use of the single currency outside the euro area is most prominent in its neighbouring countries, where strong cultural and political ties exist. As outlined in Chapter 10 of this book, which summarizes the latest findings of the Oesterreichische Nationalbank's regular 'Euro Survey'[7] the dissemination of euro cash holdings is strong in some (potential) EU candidate countries (the Former Yugoslav Republic of Macedonia, Serbia, Albania and Croatia). This highlights the perception of the euro as an anchor of stability and underscores its important role as an international means of payment and store of value. However, euroization can also be accompanied by certain risks, especially if financial markets are still to deepen. Foreign currency loans to households (predominantly denominated in euro) are substantial in some countries. Without euro area membership, balance sheet effects can seriously jeopardize households' ability to pay back their debt, which, ultimately, may feed through to the real economy.

At its tenth anniversary the euro was tested by a severe global financial and economic crisis. The world's worst recession since the 1930s posed a wide range of macroeconomic and political challenges for all affected economies, thus putting the single currency to the test. Rising spreads between German covered bonds and bonds of other euro area countries as well as diverging credit default swaps (CDS) on government bonds within the euro area are a major concern. Still, Nobel Prize Winner Milton Friedman's prophecy that 'when the global economy hits a real bump,

Europe's internal contradictions will tear (the euro) apart' proved wrong.[8] Quite on the contrary, it is the euro that functions as an anchor of stability and helps weathering the storms of the crisis. Still, there are some challenges ahead.

In its early stage, the crisis had been confined to advanced economies. Local and foreign banks in CESEE economies held only a negligible amount of so-called toxic assets. These innovative financial products and excessive risk taking put major banks under serious stress and prompted concerns about the adequacy of their business model. A post-crisis business model should therefore emphasize the importance of diversification of profit and funding sources, with the latter being most reliably provided by deposits. Also, for Austrian banks holding a major stake in the CESEE region, adaptations in their business models will be needed. This will concern the dynamics of granting loans and in particular, adequate recognition of the risks of foreign currency lending.

With the collapse of the investment bank Lehman Brothers, the crisis reached the CESEE economies during late 2008 and started to fully feed through to the real economy in early 2009. That said, the crisis turned from a financial market crisis into a broad economic crisis throughout the region. The global loss of confidence and the slump in demand for exports almost interrupted the convergence process of the catching-up economies. What followed were falling stock prices, increasing risk premia on bonds and – in some cases – a downward rally of currencies.

Since the crisis has severely hit the real economy of the region, the question arises how long it will take to bring the economies back to the growth track experienced in the last decade. Put differently, when will catching up to the euro area continue to take place at a fast rate? It is worth mentioning that there are several characteristics shared by most CESEE countries: their high growth rates have been accompanied by strong credit growth, remarkably high foreign capital inflows and widening current account deficits.

Whereas global imbalances have been one of the focal points of policymakers over the last years, imbalances have widened also within the euro area. Since the launch of the euro in 1999, the euro area has experienced significant divergence in the external economic positions of its member states. Two groups of economies emerged: surplus countries and deficit countries, with the two CESEE countries that have already introduced the euro falling into the second category. The determinants of the trend of divergence in competitiveness and current accounts are manifold. Changes in price competitiveness can reflect convergence in the price level of tradable goods, the Balassa–Samuelson effects and the response to cyclical differences between euro area countries.[9]

It is possible that the euro has amplified the divergence trend in current accounts since it grants better access to international capital markets for catching-up member states and hence allows running larger trade deficits. The imbalances might be attributed to domestic demand pressures, surging private and external debt and the inefficient use of foreign capital (for example, housing booms).

Adjusting imbalances remains a serious challenge particularly within Economic and Monetary Union (EMU).[10] Whereas the global crisis has dampened growth dynamics and lowered potential output of both advanced and catching-up economies, it has accelerated the adjustment of imbalances. To a large part, this adjustment is achieved through the trade channel, with demand for imported goods decreasing more strongly than demand for exports of the CESEE region. That said, it remains key to understand the determinants of these imbalances, while close monitoring remains essential in the near future.

A number of chapters in this book elaborate on the euro's role as a shelter, a term which came into vogue during late 2008 and mid-2009. Developments in these two years provide ample evidence that the euro has been an anchor of stability throughout the CESEE region. This is closely linked to the highly effective measures the European Central Bank (ECB) has taken to support the functioning of financial markets. The launch of international financing packages for some countries of the region (among them Hungary and Romania), increasing confidence and an improvement in the global risk appetite have contributed to a recent easing in financial market strains. We all hope that this is not only a 'recent easing' but that the economies will recover from the crisis quickly. However, 'coming back to normality' also bears the risk of missing chances. It is important to take the opportunity the crisis offers and bear in mind the lessons we have learned so far: enhanced regulation, coordination and transparency will ensure a sustainable long-term functioning of financial markets and help prevent such a global downturn in the future.

The surge in investor confidence we currently see in the markets can be partially attributed to the adapted monetary policy of the ECB. This helped ensure stability in the markets, not only within but also beyond the borders of the euro area. The ECB reacted promptly to the challenges brought about by the crisis, taking both traditional and unconventional measures. Along with other major central banks, the ECB gradually cut interest rates; they are now at historically low levels – the lowest since the ECB's establishment. Liquidity provided through unconventional measures aimed at ensuring that policy rate cuts are effectively passed on to the economy. These instruments also made it possible to provide stimuli to the economy when interest rates are already very low. In addition the

ECB signed swap agreements to provide European central banks outside the euro area with euro funding.[11]

The year 2009 will undoubtedly enter the textbooks as the year dominated by the biggest economic crisis seen in decades. Certainly it will also be remembered as a year in which strong and coordinated policy efforts were undertaken to shield the real economy, financial markets and banking sectors around the globe from the most adverse effects of the global downturn. As a case in point I would like to point out the Vienna Initiative, which was launched in early 2009 to avoid uncoordinated national crisis responses. A key element of the multi-institutional forum is the commitment of major banks to maintaining their exposure to the CESEE region. Containing financial outflows is important to regain financial stability. In times of crisis, this is a strong sign and complies with the long-term investment perspective of the – mostly Austrian – banks operating in the region. No doubt, a decade ago, a lack of coordination would have resulted in national interests prevailing, which would have made it nearly impossible to quickly and efficiently counter the crisis.

The measures taken are only one side of the coin when it comes to discussing the euro's role as a shelter. It is plain to see that EU membership alone has stabilized the region. It boosted access to international financial markets and enhanced the provisioning of indirect support to local banks. Membership in monetary union would have further increased access to liquidity during the crisis and provided shelter against speculative currency attacks. Moreover, the longer-term benefits of monetary union include lower transaction costs, increased competition and consequently lower profit margins, stronger financial market integration and a credible monetary policy target towards price stability.

Capital flows have enabled the financing of current accounts and have been an important ingredient of the CESEE growth model so far. However, whether in or outside the euro area, some CESEE countries will have to adjust their growth model in order to render their internal and external imbalances more sustainable. Higher returns attracted capital inflows from Western Europe but in light of the crisis, one was tempted to ask whether this source of financing would dry up.

This leads me to the question: is rapid euro adoption reasonable for CESEE countries? During the crisis a relatively short-lived debate evolved whether countries outside the euro area should be allowed to join monetary union immediately. This would have meant to abolish – or temporarily suspend – the convergence criteria laid down in the Maastricht Treaty. In this respect, the exchange rate mechanism (ERM) II is an important instrument to stabilize acceding countries' exchange rates and guarantees a smooth transition from a national to the single currency. It is important to note that the convergence criteria are key determinants of the sustainability of the fixed exchange rate implied by adopting the euro.

While entering the euro area is obligatory for almost all EU members, choosing the right moment is a demanding task. There are several factors that affect the decision. To start with, the mobility of capital and labour and the flexibility of domestic wages are essential factors for gauging the readiness of a country to join monetary union. Besides that, one should bear in mind the Maastricht criteria, in particular convergence in prices, a focus on long-term interest rates and fiscal stability.

Against the backdrop of the current crisis, the discussion is revolving around the fiscal stance of countries. The decline in growth rates has put serious pressures on the budget and fiscal positions in the region. It is therefore a challenge to manage the trade-off between providing support to those hit hardest by the crisis and correcting fiscal imbalances to ensure sustainability and to qualify for EMU.[12] Let me emphasize that the CESEE region is very heterogeneous and that achievements with respect to the particular factors mentioned before vary from country to country. Hence the timing of euro adoption remains a country-specific task and should be decided on a case-by-case basis.

Let me conclude and stress that European integration is closely linked to the creation of the EMU, which ultimately led to the birth of the single currency. Having successfully weathered the storms of the worst financial and economic crisis of post-war history, the euro has been and will continue to be an important anchor of European integration.

NOTES

1. Martin Feldkircher, of the Oesterreichische Nationalbank's (OeNB) staff, contributed to these remarks.
2. Nowotny, E. (2009), 'Editorial', *Focus on European Economic Integration* (FEEI) special issue: '1989–2009 twenty years of East-West integration: hopes and achievements', OeNB.
3. OeNB (2009), 'The euro – a stability anchor in turbulent times', speech by OeNB Governor Ewald Nowotny, Bologna, 10 September 2009.
4. Baldwin, R.E. (2006), 'The euro's trade effect', Working Paper Series 594, European Central Bank. The exact citation of Baldwin's statement: 'Most of the Rose effect literature treats currency unions as magic wands – one touch and intra-currency-union trade flows rise between 5 per cent and 1400 per cent. The only question is: how big is the magic?'
5. European Commission (2008), 'EMU@10: successes and challenges after 10 years of Economic and Monetary Union', *European Economy*, 2/2008.
6. European Central Bank (2009), 'Statistics pocket book', available at: http://www.ecb.int/pub/pdf/stapobo/spb200910en.pdf (accessed September 2009).
7. Dvorsky, S., T. Scheiber and H. Stix (2009), 'CESEE households amid the finan-

cial crisis: euro survey shows darkened economic sentiment and changes in savings behavior', Focus on European Economic Integration Q4/09, OeNB, 71–83.

8. Milton, F. (1999), available at: http://news.goldseek.com/MillenniumWave Advisors/1212336000.php (accessed September 2009).

9. European Commission (2009), 'Special report: competitiveness developments within the euro area', *Quarterly Report on the Euro Area*, **8**, (1).

10. Arghyrou, M.G. and G. Chortareas (2007), 'Real exchange rates and current account imbalances in the Euro-area', paper presented at Money Macro and Finance (MMF) Research Group Conference 2006, Money Macro and Finance Research Group, 38th annual conference, 13–15 September 2006, University of York.

11. OeNB (2009), 'The euro – a stability anchor in turbulent times', speech by OeNB Governor Ewald Nowotny, Bologna, 10 September 2009.

12. Backé, P. (2009), 'The monetary integration of Central and Eastern European EU member states: achievements and prospects', *Focus on European Economic Integration* (FEEI) special issue: '1989–2009 twenty years of East-West integration: hopes and achievements', OeNB, pp. 71–83.

PART II

A case for rapid euro adoption?

3. Serbia: on the de-euroization road to the euro

Radovan Jelašić

Although still outside the euro area, both private and legal entities in Serbia have already implemented the euro as a means of payment. An anecdote valid even today tells more than any study can: 'What does a Serb do if he has no more dinars? He changes 100 euro!' So every citizen of Serbia keeps only the bare minimum of Serbian dinars (RSD) in his pocket but always has at least EUR 100 with him in case of an emergency.

One of the key questions of the Serbian macroeconomic puzzle for the last four decades has been and still is: 'Can we allow the exchange rate to float and, if so, to which extent if we already have a high level of euroization?' Serbia, being the only country with a floating exchange rate in ex-Yugoslavia, faces an additional challenge, namely every time the floating gets more intensive, our currency regime is immediately proclaimed a failure compared to the 'stability' of the other ex-Yugoslav countries. Therefore, it was not a surprise that at the beginning of the economic crisis (with the fall of Lehman Brothers in September 2008) resulting in RSD depreciation of some 23 per cent, the discussions only intensified regarding the exchange rate mechanism. Unfortunately, however, those discussions did not go in the direction that the National Bank of Serbia (NBS) would have liked – how to lower the dependence of the economy on the EUR exchange rate development; rather it focused on how to cut the corners like Montenegro (unilateral euroization) or implement maybe another exchange rate regime, particularly a currency board such as Bosnia-Herzegovina or Bulgaria, in order to secure 'stability'. So while on one side the NBS was trying to exploit the effects of the crisis in order to ensure a faster de-euroization process with all of its benefits, on the other side there were not only unhedged borrowers (companies, private individuals, even the government) but also populist politicians, and even some economists that still believed in the common (false) wisdom that a weakening of the RSD/EUR exchange rate was the main driver of inflation, which was definitely not the case in Serbia either. How successful the NBS will be in using the effects of economic crisis in order to strengthen the role of the RSD still needs to be seen.

3.1   EXCHANGE RATE REGIME AND NBS POLICIES

Floating exchange rate regime has definitely determined not only NBS monetary and supervisory policy but all other activities as well. In order to secure a larger playground for the floating exchange rate regime, NBS prescribed not only a high capital adequacy ratio (12 per cent) in order to provide a sizable solvency buffer for banks, but also a high foreign exchange (FX) reserve requirements ratio (40 per cent for FX savings of citizens, and 45 per cent for foreign borrowing) in order to secure the necessary liquidity in times of crisis. In practice, the capital adequacy ratio was even higher (21.3 per cent at the end of 2009) as banks, although aware of the 150 per cent limit on consumer loans compared to capital set by the NBS in mid-2007 (200 per cent in 2006), decided to increase their capital even more in order to profit from the very attractive consumer lending boom. Moreover, a regulation of the NBS requiring more capital from unhedged borrowers, namely 125 per cent, and limiting private borrowing to 50 per cent of monthly disposable income – otherwise they needed to provision such loans to the full extent – contributed that the quality of the loan portfolio was relatively high and well provisioned. Although the high capital and reserve requirement ratios, as well as other restrictive supervisory measures, increased to some extent the cost of borrowing in the Serbian banking system, as the crisis hit Serbia as well, Serbia was able to manage the crisis locally, without requiring additional capital or liquidity from abroad. Moreover, additional stress tests carried out as a part of the 'Vienna agreement'[1] as of March 2009 and the Financial Sector Assessment Program (FSAP)[2] as of June 2009 proved that the Serbian banking sector does not require extraordinary recapitalization even if the negative macroeconomic assumptions materialize.

As far as monetary policy is concerned, by keeping a relatively high reference rate, also compared to other countries in the region, at the onset of the crisis (end of September 2008), some RSD 245 billion (EUR 3.2 billion) was invested in NBS repo papers. (Real interest rates in Serbia were, since the introduction of the NBS two-week repo rate as a reference rate in September 2006, relatively high in comparison with the region, see Figure 3.1.) This was especially important as the high RSD liquidity was also used in order to convert it for urgently needed FX funds from the

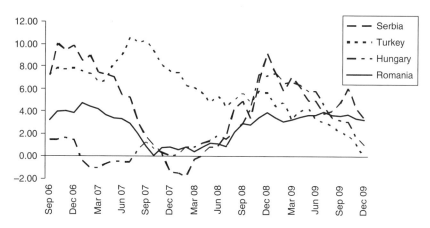

Note: Real reference rate = rate of the respective central bank – CPI

Source: Economic Analyses and Research Department, National Bank of Serbia.

Figure 3.1 Reference rate in Serbia and the region (in real terms)

NBS when households withdrew some EUR 1 billion savings within six weeks during October and November 2008.

Strict enforcement of the NBS' fit and proper policy resulted in a substantial improvement of the ownership structure of banks in Serbia. Namely, by the end of 2006, the stake of banks in the hands of strategic owners from the European Union (EU) reached 78 per cent, while the share of banks majority-owned by the state went down to only 15 per cent, and 7 per cent being owned by local private shareholders. Access of those banks that are majority EU-owned to additional capital and liquidity from international financial markets, their respective governments, the ECB and other international financial institutions was also essential in order to secure the stability of the banking sector and the confidence of the Serbian public.

Last but not least, one of the key reasons why the NBS was so active regarding consumer protection issues was to raise public awareness of risks involved in taking EUR- or CHF-denominated loans. Educational materials distributed by banks in more than 3 million flyers and brochures, public statements, and the establishment of a consumer hotline and so on, contributed to the fact that nobody could criticize the central bank that it did not warn the public in advance.

Compared to measures aimed at lowering the level of euroization, the main goal of the policies mentioned above was to minimize the impact of potential RSD depreciation on the stability of the entire financial sector.

Time did prove that those measures were very useful, as – despite a high level of euroization that made a strong depreciation during the crisis even more painful – Serbia's banking system retained its stability. Needless to say, the NBS did favour RSD over EUR with almost every regulation, but at this level of euroization, the NBS could not fight this battle alone. In addition to that, the economic boom that Serbia went through till the onset of the crisis made our efforts for de-euroization even harder due to a very simple reason: why should debtors take a RSD loan that carries a higher interest rate when the EUR loan not only comes with a lower interest rate, but the RSD is also appreciating, thus making the servicing of EUR loans in RSD cheaper!

3.2   CITIZENS PREFER TO SAVE IN EUROS

Citizens of Serbia are both saving and lending in EUR, which makes the life of banks compared to countries such as Poland or Hungary easier, as they can easily hedge their FX position. A practical proof of this constant back and forth changing between currencies is that in Serbia there are around 2 100 exchange bureaus in addition to some 2 600 bank branches where one can instantaneously change RSD into EUR and vice versa, paying a relatively small fee.

As far as private individuals' savings are concerned, 91.4 per cent are FX-denominated (thereof 95 per cent in EUR as of 30 September 2009, see Figure 3.2) and only 8.6 per cent are in RSD. This is actually a logical behaviour of households taking into consideration the hardships they went through during the last four decades. In addition to the turbulent political challenges, citizens also experienced economic deterioration:

- Average yearly inflation rate of 25.2 per cent in the period from 1960–2009 (excluding the hyperinflation in 1992, 1993 and 1994);
- Average depreciation of the Yugoslav, and then Serbian, dinar was 22 per cent in the period from March 1994–January 2010;
- Hyperinflation in the period of 1992–93 – at its height inflation was running at 64.6 per cent per day;
- Loss of some EUR 4.2 billion FX savings – repayment started in 2001 with the final payment due in 2016;
- Loss of entire RSD savings (life insurance premiums collected for 30 or 40 years were worth a box of cigarettes, sometimes only matches);
- Pyramid banks, and so on.

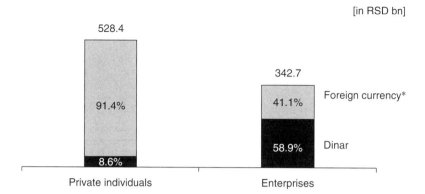

Note: * thereof in EUR 95% (for private individuals) and 93% (for enterprises)

Source: Economic Analyses and Research Department, National Bank of Serbia.

Figure 3.2 Structure of deposits (as of 30 September 2009)

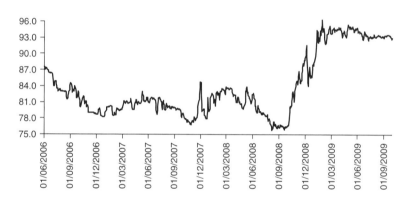

Source: Economic Analyses and Research Department, National Bank of Serbia.

Figure 3.3 Exchange rate EUR/RSD

Although since the beginning of the transition process in October 2000 the exchange rate was fairly stable, with some appreciation starting in June 2006 until September 2008 followed by depreciation from October 2008 until November 2009 (see Figure 3.3), there were no major changes regarding the currency structure of savings. Shifting to RSD from EUR did not take place despite the fact that the NBS was offering attractive RSD-denominated bonds directly to private individuals during the time period December 2005–June 2006 and paying interest rates of even 25 per

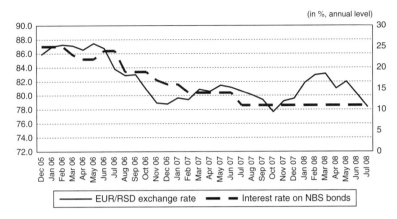

Source: Economic Analyses and Research Department, National Bank of Serbia.

Figure 3.4   Exchange rate EUR/RSD and interest rate on NBS bonds

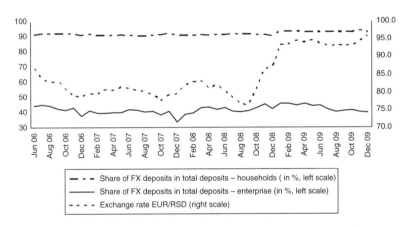

Source: Economic Analyses and Research Department, National Bank of Serbia.

Figure 3.5   FX deposits and exchange rate

cent p.a. If one adds to that an appreciation of RSD, the yield measured
in EUR was highly attractive (see Figure 3.4). Despite that, there was
not even a minor shift in the structure of deposits from EUR to RSD
(see Figure 3.5). Definitely, households have a much stronger ability to
remember than bankers (particularly investment bankers) and no gain,
regardless of how attractive it is, will make them forget the losses of the
last decades. Needless to say, once more we had proof that it is easier to

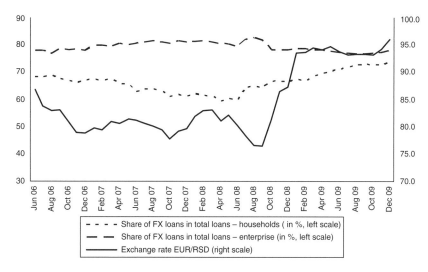

Source: Economic Analyses and Research Department, National Bank of Serbia.

Figure 3.6   FX loans and exchange rate

convince investors in London, Frankfurt or Vienna to trust the RSD than citizens of Serbia.

But what about taking loans, why is it more attractive to take them again in FX (see Figure 3.6)? (FX loans are also taken in RSD but they are indexed with the EUR (CHF)/RSD exchange rate development in order to minimize the FX risk of the banks.) There are several reasons behind that.

'A lower interest rate equals a cheaper credit' – households tend to forget, or prefer not to take notice that there must be a good economic reason why RSD loans are offered with higher interest rates than those in EUR or CHF. Although most of the banks, particularly the ones from Austria, had already faced strong criticism in the 1980s in their home country regarding CHF-denominated loans, it did not stop them from offering the very same product to households in Serbia. What regulations of the NBS were not able to achieve, the economic crisis did. Namely, almost all banks unilaterally ceased to offer CHF-denominated loans in early 2009.

A lower interest rate results in lower monthly payments, and that automatically increases the amount one could borrow from the bank. This reason is especially important due to the explosion of housing prices in the period from the beginning of 2005, and therefore a need for taking a larger mortgage loan year by year.

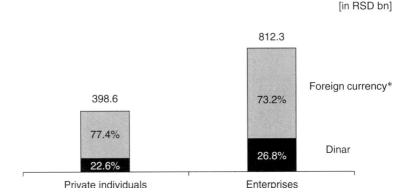

Note: * thereof in EUR 68.35% (for private individuals) and 79.81% (for enterprises)

Source: Economic Analyses and Research Department, National Bank of Serbia.

Figure 3.7   Structure of loans (as of 30 September 2009)

That no alternative product was offered in RSD was also an important reason for households to take FX-denominated loans. Even today, the only source of long-term RSD loans is the banks' capital and that is mainly invested in safe treasuries or NBS repos.

Hope that despite the potential upside, risk regarding the exchange rate will be limited and that salaries will increase more than the exchange rate movement (actually it was the fact from the beginning of the transition period all the way until the end of 2008).

Generally speaking the above mentioned situation proves a very interesting development, namely that people do think differently regarding exchange rate risk depending on which side of the bank's balance sheet they are. When depositing their money citizens prefer to keep it in EUR despite the fact that it brings a lower interest rate than in RSD. Obviously, 'safety first' is the key guideline. This principle was overriding despite the very high EUR-denominated income during the time of the appreciating RSD. On the other hand, when we are talking about taking out a bank loan, the majority is FX-denominated (EUR 68 per cent and CHF 32 per cent as of 30 September 2009, see Figure 3.7) but for completely different reasons. Well, strangely enough, there are many people who deposit and lend in FX at the same time.

In addition to legal entities it is worth mentioning an additional entity that is exposed to FX risk more than anything else, namely the state. Therefore, even exchange rate adjustment to the new macroeconomic environment is not warmly welcomed in Serbia as the majority of the country's liabilities are FX-denominated, while all regular budgetary income is denominated in RSD. As 87.2 per cent of public debt is FX-denominated (as of 31 December 2009), a weaker RSD means automatically a larger burden to financing the FX debt from the budget.

3.3   EXCHANGE RATE ADJUSTMENT

Serbia, during the time of crisis, adjusted mainly through the exchange rate to the new macroeconomic circumstances due to several reasons. Adjustment through fiscal policy is not only politically unpopular, but it takes a relatively long time to find the politically acceptable common denominator in the case of coalition governments (the larger the coalition the more time is needed to find a common ground for joint action). In addition, fiscal policy adjustments have also substantial limits, namely cutting a budget deficit by 1–2 per cent of the GDP is usually treated as very ambitious.

In Serbia, the level of fiscal deficit will be lowered from 4.5 per cent of GDP in 2009 to 1 per cent over a time period of 5 years (2015). Although it does seem to be an ambitious plan at first glance, the structure of this adjustment, that is, reduction of revenues by 1.1 per cent (from 38.3 per cent to 37.2 per cent of GDP), compared to the decrease of expenditures by 4.5 per cent (from 42.8 per cent to 38.3 per cent), does represent a major milestone in public finances.

Structural changes as a means of adjustment are time-consuming and have a time lag of 2 to 3 years. Needless to say, carrying out unpopular structural changes especially in times of economic hardship is not something that the political elite prefers.

Serbia agreed to speed up its structural reforms in several areas as a part of its IMF program, but one needs to be realistic regarding the extent and speed of such reform under current macroeconomic circumstances.

Compared to the two categories mentioned above, exchange rate movements mean an instantaneous adjustment. An additional benefit of this category for the political establishment is that the public usually perceives the exchange rate as being only and exclusively a central bank issue (responsibility). Needless to say, this instrument also has its economic limits, namely the stability of the banking sector, effects on price stability and so on.

Serbia adjusted mainly through exchange rate depreciation; as from September 2008 till January 2010 RSD depreciated by some 23 per cent compared to the EUR. Despite that sharp move, the negative effects of such adjustment were rather small, largely thanks to the previously built up strong buffers. The cumulative consumer price index (CPI) rate for the period of May–December 2009 was basically zero (in December 2009, year-on-year only 6.6 per cent), and non-performing loans (NPL) of the banking sector stabilized at a level of around 10 per cent, after a substantial increase during the first half of 2009.

Like every economic crisis, the current one also presents not only a threat but a chance as well.

Could the time after the crisis be used to lower the level of euroization? Based on the harsh experience of currency depreciation together with wage freezes in both 2009 and 2010, both legal and private entities should have changed their attitude toward FX-denominated loans. Of course, the distance between knowing that something is risky and doing something in order to mitigate that very same risk is large. Both the central bank and the government need to provide hedging instruments not only to banks but to borrowers as well in order to provide with them a tool for mitigating FX risk. Needless to say, as both the CPI and the NBS reference rate are decreasing, although still with a higher nominal rate, RSD loans should be more attractive. By neglecting these crisis' lessons regarding the FX-denominated loans, one will plant an even bigger crisis in the future.

Will central banks get more support in implementing countercyclical measures in the area of monetary and supervisory policy than before? Will it be supported by legislation as well? Promotion of countercyclical measures during the economic boom was neither popular nor easy in any of the areas that central banks are in charge of. Often it was central bankers who implemented such measures, prompting heavy criticism as hardliners and bureaucrats from both the public and government. Unfortunately, as time is passing, chances that such countercyclical measures would be strengthened by additional laws are diminishing very fast. In many aspects it is already business as usual, and several laws mitigating the effects of the next crisis have got stuck in the legislative process in Serbia.

Did governments learn how expensive the servicing of FX loans could be in the case of currency turbulences? In the case of Serbia, where at the beginning of the crisis almost the entire public debt was foreign currency-denominated, just a year later this figure changed substantially. Namely, during 2009 for the first time ever, the increase in public debt (total of EUR 1.4 billion without the debt write-off for Kosovo and excluding the IMF allocation of EUR 424.6 million!) was 72 per cent denominated in RSD while only 28 per cent in EUR. This change increased the stake of RSD-denominated debt to 12.8 per cent within just one year (the stake of RSD-denominated debt was only 2.5 per cent in 2008). Although nominal interest is higher on RSD-denominated debt than on the FX ones, in real terms it is actually cheaper.

Will some governments, but also central banks, use the crisis in order to speed up their reforms for a faster implementation of EUR as a legal tender and continue demanding a relaxation of the current preconditions for entering EMU? Lowering the threshold for entering the euro area would definitely result in more relaxed macroeconomic policies, not only within but particularly outside the euro area. For countries such as Serbia it would set a bad precedent as it would be even harder to take tough economic decisions in order to join both the EU and later on EMU.

All in all, being outside the euro area but having the euro as a parallel currency substantially limited Serbia's policy choices. For the NBS, the economic crisis did serve as a good proof that it pays off to be consistently restrictive in both monetary and prudential policy. The economic crisis also provides a great opportunity to speed up the de-euroization process. This may sound illogical for outsiders, but de-euroizing today will help Serbia to increase the number of policy choices available to a faster and easier EU and EMU membership tomorrow.

NOTES

1. One of the main actions taken by the NBS in the scope of anti-crisis measures, also referred to as financial sector support program (FSSP) – included bilateral agreement between NBS and representatives of the 12 largest foreign-owned banks. The program provided the following outcome: NBS agreed to provide special liquidity tranche for the banks as well as to put forward temporary measures of the relaxation of the current regulations. Banks agreed to retain the level of exposure to Serbia that included the direct channel via cross boarder borrowing and indirect channel via domestic banks existing portfolios at the level of 31 December 2008 considering that objectively crises spillover took place during the last quarter of 2008.
2. Financial Sector Assessment Program performed by the International Monetary Fund (IMF) and the World Bank (WB) – comprehensive analysis of the entire country's financial sector performed in coordination with domestic institutions such as NBS, Ministry of Finance, Statistical Bureau, Deposit insurance agency as well as private sector representatives, Association of Serbian Banks, individual banking sector representatives. The outcome is a detailed objective external report on the state of the financial sector with recommendations by the IMF and WB.

4. A case for rapid euro adoption?

Sławomir S. Skrzypek*

The chapter presents considerations about adopting the euro in light of the financial disturbance of 2008 and beyond. First, arguments for and against rapid euro adoption are considered, presenting the broader context of the balance of costs and benefits in the euro area countries so far, and pointing out challenges emerging from the crisis. The second issue raised here is the potential risk of euro overvaluation as a consequence of potential changes in the international monetary system.

PAST EXPERIENCE – NET BALANCE OF THE EURO ADOPTION

A case for rapid euro adoption can be considered from three different time perspectives: past (experiences of the euro area members), present (euro blessing – stabilizing role of the euro as a global currency and the actions taken by the European Central Bank (ECB) and future (growth potential, which is a key condition for closing the gap between the East and the West).

There is a broad economic consensus reflected in the literature that euro adoption can impact positively on the economy. However, the experiences of its member states show that many other growth factors can be very important for the smooth functioning of a monetary union – such as the labour force, research and development, rule of law, quality of governance, and so on. While the euro has been key in fostering economic growth, past experiences show that it is unable to create real convergence on its own.

Bearing this caveat in mind we should distinguish between costs and benefits on the one hand and threats and opportunities on the other hand. In other words, if you have some competitive advantage, the euro can definitely boost it. But if you do not have any edge, the euro cannot substitute

---

* Sławomir S. Skrzypek, President of the National Bank of Poland, died on 10 April 2010 in the air crash that killed the Polish President and a number of other senior Polish officials. The chapter presented here was the last version approved by the author before his tragic death.

for it. The experiences of the euro area countries prove that a positive balance is not at all certain at every point in time. The net effect depends on the strength and flexibility of economy, in particular the completion of necessary structural reforms which enhance the ability to operate in the highly competitive environment of the euro area. Fiscal policies and labour and product markets are the key elements which need to work better.

Euro adoption is seen as a historical chance, mainly for countries that are in the process of catching up with more developed member states. Subject to the right speed of this complex process, joining the euro area is a chance to gain access to a deep and broad financial market and to benefit from modern technology inflows and a more stable environment. These benefits, however, are accompanied by quite a wide range of threats: the loss of autonomous monetary policy and nominal exchange rate as well as the risk of a credit boom to name just a few. Of course, this risk of credit boom is currently smaller, but it can rise again once the euro area recovers from the present crisis. This means that in order to benefit from euro area participation, the economy has to be prepared to operate in a more competitive environment.

Since 1999, European Economic and Monetary Union (EMU) has had an impact on various aspects of its member state economies. The majority of EMU effects are in line with mainstream economic theory. The common currency promoted FDI flows, both inside and outside EMU, and enhanced integration via trade (especially intra-industry) and deeper financial market links.

As a consequence of introducing the common currency the standard theory predicts business cycle synchronization, higher GDP growth due to increased trade volume and investment flows and gradual equalization of major macroeconomic variables, with income convergence being the resulting process. The empirical evidence on these theoretical predictions is however mixed.

If we imagine that the crisis hits particular EMU member states asymmetrically concerning strength, onset and duration, we can clearly see that policy response coordination might turn out to be ineffective or virtually impossible. The recovery would also be long and uneven. But the euro is not just an umbrella for EMU member states. Providing a relatively stable environment, it becomes a stability exporter to its neighbours. For the non-euro European Union (EU) member states, the confirmed endogeneity of business cycle synchronization is a good message since improper monetary policy reactions are one of the most important fears connected with euro adoption.

Another issue is whether the euro promotes income convergence. According to statistical data, it does not necessarily so, even if two catching-up countries – Greece and Spain – experienced relatively high GDP growth rates throughout the first decade of EMU. The general lack of convergence is sometimes attributed to the broadly reduced motivation to reform in particular countries after the creation of EMU. Some countries may moreover have lost some growth momentum due to fiscal and monetary tightening before adopting the euro. Moreover, many studies show that all kinds of structural reforms are generally more costly in a monetary union than under a flexible nominal exchange rate regime. The apparent lesson is the necessity to undertake the required reforms in the areas of public finance, labour and product markets well ahead of adopting the euro.

Another worrying phenomenon is the emergence of current account imbalances and asset price bubbles. Of course the euro is not the only one to blame, but it did facilitate capital flows into real estate sectors in Southern Europe and to industrial sectors in Northern Europe, causing imbalances and weakening the euro area's resilience to the crisis. These new asymmetries are yet another aspect of divergence inside EMU. Current account imbalances are evident if we compare Southern European countries running deficits with Northern European states running surpluses. The gap was widening at a fast pace for most of the period since EMU creation, but it did not lead to any policy reaction.

The crisis revealed many imbalances that need to be corrected. One of them, which will stay long after the ongoing crisis fades away, is the quality of fiscal policy. The current rules, set by the Stability and Growth Pact, might need to be rewritten in order to guarantee strict rather than rough discipline. An example worth following might be the case of Germany, where a nominal deficit rule will be substituted by a rule based on the structural deficit.

In order to avoid serious problems inside EMU more and more arguments emerge in favour of increased policy coordination. If the existing divergences persist and if new asymmetries are allowed, the income convergence process might be reverted, and even nominal convergence is threatened, making common monetary policy more difficult.

LIVING WITH OR WITHOUT THE EURO IN TIMES OF CRISIS

The above dilemma highlights the main topics related to the euro, such as: is it better to be a member of the euro area during the crisis or not? The answer differs for different countries. Undoubtedly, in the first phase of the crisis the euro served as an umbrella. If Ireland or Spain had been outside the euro area, their currencies would probably have suffered heavily under the severe tensions in financial markets. As an international currency, the euro ensured stability not only in the euro area, but also in the EU and in Europe. For Europe as a whole, the euro was an important and credible nominal anchor.

Yet at later stages of the crisis, the common currency and common monetary policy did not allow for currency depreciation and for the use of national monetary policies because these tools had disappeared. Even if such depreciation had been justified by fundamentals, it could not materialize. Adjustment in the euro area has to be achieved through prices, wages and productivity channels, which is more complex than using the exchange rate channel. This also applies to countries which are not in the euro area but have pegged their currencies to the euro. However, if we have to choose between being a member of the euro area and being a member of the EU with the exchange rate pegged to the euro, the answer is simple – it is better to be the euro area member.

But the reality is more complex than the choice between floating and fixed exchange rates only. 'No single currency regime is right for all countries at all times', Jeffrey Frankel stated in 1999 (Frankel, 1999). A case in point is Poland, which benefited from the depreciation of its national currency because of its relatively low trade openness ratio compared to the Baltic states.

Moreover, Frankel introduced the concept of 'the impossible trinity', which means that in the case of full capital liberalization, in the long run, you have to trade-off pure float against exchange rate stability. If you fulfil some requirements (mainly connected with the optimum currency area), a monetary union can allow you to have pure float and a fixed exchange rate at the same time.

The resilience of an economy to the consequences of a crisis depends on the elasticity of its labour and product markets and on its international competitiveness. Countries that performed better in this regard deal with the crisis without severe problems. Despite the fact that the euro is a shield for the member countries, it is not the only factor which ensures smooth functioning in the globalized economy. Although the euro integrated financial markets, access to the funding during the crisis was dependant on long-term credibility.

In order to understand the euro's present role in the financial crisis, experiences of different European countries should be taken into consideration. We can distinguish three groups of countries:

- countries which have adopted the euro;
- countries which are in the EU, but not in the euro area (namely Denmark, Sweden, the UK and the countries that have joined the EU since 2004);

- countries which are in Europe, but are not EU members (such as Ukraine and Iceland).

The first group of euro area members seems to be in the most comfortable position. Undoubtedly, the euro is an international and credible currency and it has served as an umbrella for its member states. Thanks to a more cautious monetary and fiscal policy reaction as well as trustworthy institutions, the euro acted as a 'safe haven' currency, which was particularly visible in 2009. However, despite the euro's positive influence, some countries have experienced tensions: Ireland, Greece, Portugal and Spain lost their favourable ratings because of the increasing credit risk. The scale of financial-market disruptions and the lack of confidence led to flight-to-quality and flight-to-liquidity behaviours. Every sign of uncertainty caused disproportional risk aversion and perturbation in the financial markets of those countries which were more exposed to financial risks. The financial crisis showed that it is not enough to have international currency. The ability to maintain credibility can be also very important. If a country is credible, the euro can strengthen this credibility. Otherwise, having an international currency can be of little benefit.

The second group comprises EU member states which do not belong to the euro area. This is the most differentiated group. It contains developed countries (namely Denmark, Sweden and the UK (EU-3) as well as new member states of the European Union. The EU-3 countries suffered some perturbations because of weak economic performance, limitations resulting from a hard peg (Denmark), high risk exposure of financial systems and a rapid decrease in trade (Sweden and the UK). Moreover, according to Buiter (2009), they belong to a group of countries characterized by the 'inconsistent quartet', namely: a small country with a large internationally exposed banking sector, a non-global currency and limited fiscal capacity relative to the size of the financial sector. These factors increase their potentially damaging vulnerability, not only in the era of crisis.

The group of new EU member states is highly heterogeneous. The most severe consequences of the crisis appeared in Hungary and Latvia, which received international support from the International Monetary Fund (IMF) and the ECB. Their position, despite deep structural problems, is strengthened by their EU membership. In contrast, the countries that are neither in the euro area, nor in the EU are in the worst situation. This is the case of Ukraine and Iceland. They cannot count on the umbrella of EU institutions and the common currency in each and every case. In other words, unless you are Switzerland or Norway, remaining outside the EU may prove quite costly.

Thus, it is very important to belong to the EU and the euro area, but doing so does not fix every problem.

It is worth adding that although the ECB is the central bank for the euro area countries, during the financial market turmoil in 2008 and beyond it appeared to exercise the stabilizing role of a central bank also outside the euro area. The ECB provided liquidity not only to the banking system in the euro area, but also in other EU member states, such as Hungary and Poland. Agreements on financial swaps with Sweden and Denmark also aimed at preserving liquidity in the global financial market.

EURO ADOPTION – AS FAST AS POSSIBLE BUT IN LINE WITH FUNDAMENTALS

Keeping in mind the above circumstances, it is difficult to find arguments in favour of rapid euro adoption. Joining the monetary union is a long-term decision which requires large-scale preparation. Efforts should be concentrated on achieving sustainable compliance with the convergence criteria, enhancing the quality of factors influencing international competitiveness and introducing structural reforms to improve the flexibility of shock-absorbing mechanisms.

In spite of the fact that in the long run euro area membership can prove beneficial, there is a lot of uncertainty in the short run related to financial turbulence and its repercussions for the real economy. To some extent, current crisis changes the attitude towards the balance of cost and benefits. In pre-crisis times financial and trade integration was a source of many profits, but nowadays it may rather propagate the crisis. Moreover, the current economic situation undermines the ability to sustainably fulfil monetary and fiscal conditions. This means that it would be difficult to have a stable currency within the framework of the exchange rate mechanism (ERM II). The current crisis changes the political, economic and social landscape all over the world. It is a time for a global reassessment of the main rules prevailing over the last few years.

INTERNATIONAL CONTEXT

These changes will probably affect the role of the US dollar on the world economic stage. The depreciation of the world's leading currency has a deep economic and financial basis. First, the USA has accumulated giant private debt volumes because of the low saving level of American households. As a result, the American current account deficit is very high and the country has a negative investment position. Such a high level of debt for such a big country is a first (Rybiński, 2007). Moreover, the financial crisis has significantly pushed up public debt. In 2009, the US budget deficit exceeded USD 1 trillion for the first time. Given the US dollar's role as the most important international currency external creditors have become stuck in a dollar trap. Countries once eager to accumulate US debt cannot leave the dollar as a reserve currency abruptly now because a significant drop in the dollar's value would diminish the worth of the rest of their USD-denominated securities. To some extent, countries which heavily bought American assets cannot stop accumulating them to avoid the dollar's abrupt depreciation. Furthermore the largest US creditor – China – has its currency pegged to the USD. That is why the dollar's stabilization, as it were, depends on China's competitors in the global market. In the first decade of October 2009, Asian countries bought USD in order to avoid its weakening against domestic currencies, which could worsen their competitiveness against China. That is why in the short run an abrupt flight from dollar is rather unlikely. At the same time, by diminishing US demand for foreign products, the dollar depreciation will decrease US imports and thus improve the current account balance. Reduced exports to the USA should, in turn, influence the demand structure in Asian countries, where domestic demand should rise.

THE EURO'S ROLE ON THE WORLD STAGE

Considering the euro as an international currency we should take into account a number of factors.

First, the main feature which allowed the euro to fulfil the function of an international currency was the high integration of financial markets. Elimination of the exchange rate risk united a fragmented financial structure into a common, integrated, deep and diversified market comparable in some segments to the US markets. The integration of the euro area financial markets progressed quickly in those market segments that were important for monetary policy implementation (see Table 4.1). That was the main rationale for the private and the public sector alike to use the euro as a store of value. As a result, the euro speeded up the evolution of international debt securities and influenced the structure of foreign exchange reserves. Taking into account the use of the euro in issuing securities, two measures can be distinguished: narrow – referring to the euro-denominated debt outside the euro area; and broad – referring to all international securities denominated in euro. In the latter case, the euro surpassed the US dollar (see Figure 4.1).

Table 4.1   Functions of an international currency according to Cohen

Function/ Euro experience	Private sector	Euro experience	Public sector	Euro experience
Store of value	Investment currency*** Financial instruments denomination, portfolio allocation	Increase in issue of international debt securities from 30% to 48% – broad measure (mid-2007) Low capitalization of euro stock exchanges	Foreign exchange reserve currency*** Denomination of official foreign exchange reserves	Increase in global foreign exchange reserves denominated in euro from 18% in 1999 to 26.5% in 2008
Unit of account	Invoicing of foreign trade**	In 2007 goods turnover settlement in € depending on the country accounted for: • imports: from 35% to 73% • exports: from 40% to 70 %	Anchor or reference currency in exchange rate regimes**	45 currencies of European, African and Asian countries are linked to the euro
Medium of exchange	Vehicle currency*	Euro is the second behind the dollar vehicle currency. Its share in international financial markets turnover since the year 2000 is stable at the level of about 37%	Intervention currency in foreign exchange markets*	Importance of the euro in this function results to some extent from its unit of account function

Note: * moderate increase in euro's importance, ** significant increase in euro's importance, *** essential increase in euro's importance.

Source: NBP Report (2009), ECB (2009) and NBP's modifications.

Second, thanks to the economic and political importance of the euro area, the euro has become the second most important international currency in the world. The euro area is the world's largest exporter, whose GDP accounts for about 15 per cent of the world's GDP.

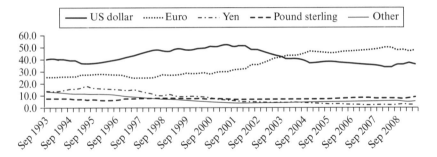

Source: National Bank of Poland's (NBP) calculations based on the data of BIS.

*Figure 4.1   Currency shares in outstanding debt securities (broad
        measure) – in percentages*

Third, the introduction of the euro also played the role of a catalyst
in the international monetary system. It led to a multiple international
system based on two important currencies. The benefits of such a situation
stem from the following reasons (Knight, 2008):

- provision of an alternative monetary anchor;
- more adequate composition of foreign exchange reserves;
- 'spare tyre' in case of disruptions in financial markets.

Fourth, the euro is commonly used as an invoicing currency in trade
outside the euro area. This way of reducing the exchange rate risk has to
some extent contributed to trade and investment creation in the euro area
and beyond.

Despite the above achievements, the euro is still a regional currency used
mainly in the euro area neighbourhood. However, it has a high potential
to become a global currency.

THE EURO: A SHELTER?

The euro appeared to be an efficient shelter against negative effects stemming from the crisis as it offers a well proven defence to all countries
having access to the ECB's credit lines. Obviously, the euro's shelter effect
seems to have been even greater for the actual members of the euro area.
There is a broad consensus that some of the countries affected by banking
tensions would have been definitely worse off had they opted to stay
outside the euro area.

That is why it is no exaggeration to say that the shelter effect offered by the euro can be easily compared to a medicine which is efficient in alleviating serious pain. But as in the case of medicine, there is a risk of serious abuse, such as excessive reliance on the effect of shelter offered by the euro. This risk is even higher in the case of the current euro area members, whose economic performance diverges markedly. Countries which were less eager to implement unpopular structural reforms are lagging behind those countries which were determined enough to pursue strategies aimed at making their domestic economies more flexible.

The risk of excessive reliance on the shelter effect seems to be smaller in the case of countries outside the euro area. If the ECB is dissatisfied with progress achieved in addressing structural rigidities in these countries, it can simply switch off the previously launched credit lines. That is why the risk of excessive reliance on the euro's shelter effects concerns current euro area members.

Given that, what incentives are used to encourage laggards to implement unpopular structural reforms? If membership in the euro area gives a country tight protection, incentives to implement reforms are far from being efficient. This is a serious problem causing dangerous divergence that may pave the way towards serious tensions within the euro area.

Being aware of threats stemming from excessive reliance on the euro's shelter effect it is essential to focus on structural reforms and make every effort aimed at launching indispensable reforms prior to joining the monetary union. Once these reforms are implemented no one will accuse new members of being tempted by the possibility to rely excessively on the euro's credibility.

THE EURO: A SAFE HAVEN?

One of the advantages of the Cold War period was the certainty with which the safe haven currency could be named. Prior to the end of the Cold War, this title belonged to the Swiss franc, possibly on account of Switzerland's neutrality. As late as in the 1980s, China settled a significant share of its foreign trade in Swiss francs. Pinpointing a currency unanimously recognized as a safe haven currency today is a more complex affair. The concept of a safe haven currency would imply a currency which is able to preserve its purchasing power and provide refuge in times of unprecedented turmoil. Following the launch of the euro in 1999, the new currency was widely expected to challenge the dollar's dominant position. Unlike in the case of the Swiss franc or the German mark, the dollar's ability to preserve purchasing power was relatively modest, above all because of the underlying structural weaknesses (incorporated twin deficits). The euro (which luckily lacks the structural weaknesses associated with the greenback) supported by the zealous approach of the ECB towards monetary stability should have emerged as a serious alternative to the US dollar.

Despite its potential, the euro seems to hold little appeal for investors in times of severe tensions. This became quite clear in autumn 2008, when at the height of the turmoil, the exchange rate of the euro against the greenback lost more than a quarter of its value in the span of two months. And even at the time of writing, the euro's fortune relies extensively on trends in equity markets.

The strength of the euro goes hand in hand with growing appetite for risk. Once the latter disappears, the former loses much of its appeal. During serious turmoil, investors like to flee to safe and stable bond markets. German bonds offer quite a few advantages, but they are not strong enough to challenge the US Treasuries, which offer much higher liquidity. Moreover, the ability to offer liquidity in times of crisis, which by definition squeezes liquidity, obviously matters a lot. When it comes to the euro, the lack of a common fiscal policy gives investors a serious reason to think twice before they even start to deliberate on going for a safe haven currency.

To summarize, it is ironic that the currency which was supposed to challenge the dominant position of the US dollar has been unable to attract investors in times of heightened tensions. Furthermore, with its strong reliance on exposure to risk, the euro is an unlikely candidate for being a safe haven currency on the FX markets.

IMPLICATIONS FOR THE POLISH ECONOMY

A potential depreciation of the dollar and simultaneous strengthening of the euro will have a significant impact on the Polish economy. Taking into account the structure of Polish foreign trade, the processes taking place in the euro area countries, especially in Germany, will influence the foreign demand for Polish exports (see Figures 4.2 and 4.3). It is very likely that the zloty strengthens as the euro appreciates, because Poland managed to steer a relatively smooth course through the crisis.

However, the zloty may weaken if global risk aversion rises again or given a deterioration of perspectives for Poland and other countries in the region on account of problems with fiscal consolidation. When participating in ERM II, a depreciation scenario is less probable given a low tolerance for current exchange rate deviations on the weak side of the parity;

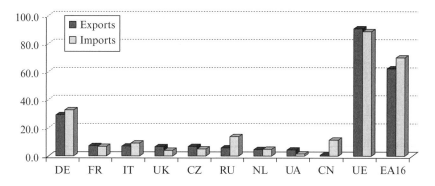

Source: NBP calculations based on the data of Central Statistical Office (2009).

Figure 4.2 *Polish foreign trade turnover with the most important trade partners in 2008 (in billion euro)*

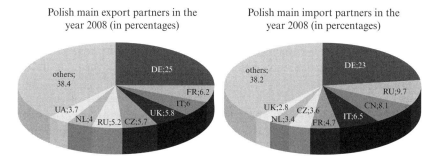

Source: NBP calculations based on the data of Central Statistical Office (2009).

Figure 4.3 *Geographic structure of Polish exports and imports in 2008*

yet the difficulty of meeting the nominal convergence criteria, turmoil in international financial markets or a currency crisis might trigger a depreciation nonetheless. A strong euro coupled with an even stronger zloty vis-à-vis the euro may deteriorate the competitiveness of Polish exports outside the euro area. This kind of problem may be eased by the floating exchange rate, which is unavailable in ERM II.

Having in mind the current euro achievements as an international currency, dollar depreciation would encourage euro appreciation. Such a development of the EUR/USD relation is likely to take place in a few years and may exacerbate the differences between European countries – creating difficulties for countries which peg their exchange rate to the euro (for example the Baltic countries) and for countries that wish to adopt the euro (like Poland). If the zloty's final anchoring to the euro occurs at a moment when the euro is overvalued, this may have a significant impact on the competitiveness of the accession country.

CONCLUSION

Joining the euro area is a historical chance for the new member states of the EU and at the same time fraught with challenges. Despite immediate benefits such as the elimination of transaction costs and exchange rate risk and despite the prospect of more stable macroeconomic conditions, what matters in the long run is the quality of the growth factors. The latter should be seen as a key condition for closing the gap between Eastern and Western Europe.

Our research shows clearly that the magnitude of benefits exhibits a clear tendency towards conditionality. In other words, a number of conditions must be met for a given country to overcome the challenges and take advantage of the opportunities stemming from euro area membership. It is a well-known fact that enhancing flexibility requires time. However, the so-called euro blessing is already being felt throughout the continent.

A rapid euro adoption may require urgent improvements of competitiveness and the ability to absorb shocks. In an uncertain environment such as the one caused by the financial turmoil of 2008 and beyond, it is difficult to fulfil the nominal and real convergence criteria in a sustainable manner. Ironically, choosing the slower but more certain path of economic reforms aiming at greater economic flexibility would thus appear to be the fastest way to join monetary union. Without consistent amelioration of the underlying economic foundations, too rapid euro adoption can be 'a short-term gain and a long-term pain'.

The analysis of potential changes in the international monetary system shows a risk for the euro to become overvalued, given the decreasing role of the US economy in the world and the depreciation of the US dollar, possibly as a consequence of the extraordinary monetary and fiscal policy measures undertaken in the more recent past. If the world were to turn away from the US dollar, the euro might become the only real alternative. One of the factors making this scenario more likely is the existence of deep and integrated euro financial markets and the trust enjoyed by EU institutions. However, given further deterioration of economic and fiscal conditions in the euro area member states, particularly in peripheral economies, the euro may also depreciate.

REFERENCES

Buiter, W. (2009), 'Can the UK government stop the UK banking system going down the snyrting without risking a sovereign debt crisis?', *The Financial Times*, 20 January.

Central Statistical Office (CSO) (2009), *Foreign Trade, January–December 2008*.

European Central Bank (ECB) (2009), *The International Role of the Euro*, July, Frankfurt am Main: European Central Bank.

Frankel, J.A. (1999), *No Single Currency Regime is Right for All Countries or at All Times*, Graham Lecture, Princeton University.

Knight, D. (2008), 'The euro as a catalyst for global financing market deepening', speech at the Brussels Economic Forum 2008 on 'Economic and Monetary Union in Europe: 10 Years On', Basel: Bank for International Settlements.

National Bank of Poland (NBP) (2009), *Report on full membership of the Republic of Poland in the third stage of the economic and monetary union*, Warsaw: National Bank of Poland.

Rybiński, K. (2007), *Globalizacja w trzech odsłonach*, Warszawa: Difin.

5. The Czech Republic on its way to the euro: a stabilization role of monetary policy revisited

Jaromír Hurník, Zdeněk Tůma and David Vávra[1]

5.1 INTRODUCTION

With the onset of European monetary integration eventual euro area membership was associated with several positive effects that were expected to have improved the long-term macroeconomic performance of member countries in terms of price stability and long-term output growth and were thus considered by European and national authorities alike to provide the economic rationale for the common currency project. However, ten years after the establishment of the euro area, the long-term effects on macroeconomic performance other than the delivery of price stability remain to be proved. It can be argued, of course, that this by itself is a huge success and such argumentation is right, except for two observations. First, apparently more was expected on the real side, or at least the real-side improvement was often used as an argument in the debate. Second and more importantly, if price stability is the only clear macroeconomic result of euro area membership, then what is left for a country that has achieved price stability on its own?

Providing an economically meaningful answer to this question requires reframing the debate about euro area membership as a debate about the choice of the exchange rate regime. Indeed, it is not surprising that the monetary policy framework is neutral in the long run in terms of real economy effects and that price stability can be achieved under various regimes. Then only the question of the relative size of nominal versus real shocks and implied macroeconomic volatilities under floating or fixed exchange rate regime remains relevant for economic analysis.

In this chapter we assess the relative importance of independent monetary policies, and of the exchange and interest rate channels in reducing macroeconomic volatility. The absence of exchange rate shocks under euro area membership will *ceteris paribus* reduce macroeconomic volatility (especially so for nominal variables). However, the fixed exchange rate also removes the stabilization role of the exchange rate. The absence of this stabilization channel will *ceteris paribus* increase macroeconomic volatility. The volatility increase after euro area membership may be even higher if most of the shocks affecting the economy are asymmetric, because the European Central Bank's (ECB) interest rate will not respond to them. Our main question is whether the removal of exchange rate-specific shocks under euro area membership will be enough to offset the effect of missing exchange and eventually interest rate stabilization channels in their effects on macroeconomic volatility.

In this respect our experiments show that inflation volatility is likely to increase following euro area accession, while euro area membership is unlikely to bring about a significant change in the volatility of consumption growth. This demonstrates that monetary policy based on a flexible exchange rate has provided a sound stabilization mechanism for the Czech economy and that the advantage of euro area membership can not be easily (if at all) assessed with economic analysis.

The chapter is organized as follows. Section 5.2 briefly discusses expected benefits and costs associated with monetary union membership in general and euro area membership in particular, while Section 5.3 reviews the empirical evidence regarding these benefits. Section 5.4 provides the body of our analysis discussing the applied methodology to volatilities measurement and achieved results. Finally, Section 5.5 concludes.

5.2   EXPECTED BENEFITS AND COSTS

In this section we summarize expected benefits and eventual costs associated with monetary union membership in general and euro area accession in particular. For this purpose one can rely on official European Commission (1990) documents, advanced textbooks of international economics such as Obstfeld and Rogoff (1996), or seminal research contributions to the field such as Frankel and Rose (2002). Although disagreeing about the order of transmission channels, all sources agree that the following channels should lead to higher long-term GDP or GDP per capita in the end.

First, euro area members should save transaction costs associated with currency conversion, local pricing behaviour and market imperfection in general. According to the European Commission's (1990) estimation, transaction costs associated with currency conversion alone accounted for 0.25 to 0.4 per cent of European community GDP at the time.

Second, euro area members may benefit from importing a more credible monetary policy and from a credible commitment to a low inflation
environment. In addition to inflation itself, this should reduce country
risk premiums and long-term real interest rates, which together with lower
inflation should lead to lower nominal interest rates, higher investment
and eventually higher output growth. The European Commission (1990)
had originally estimated the long-term output level to eventually increase
by 5–10 per cent thanks to a decline of risk premiums by 0.5 percentage
points.

Third, irrevocably fixing the nominal exchange rate insulates the
economy from speculative bubbles on the foreign exchange rate market
and any other exchange rate and monetary disturbances that could otherwise trigger temporary fluctuations in the nominal exchange rate, thanks
to price rigidities in the real exchange rate, and consequently in output and
inflation. In this respect the European Commission (1990) also stresses the
boost to firms' willingness to trade internationally, with eventual spillovers
to output, though smaller firms and countries with less developed financial
markets are seen as the main beneficiaries.

Given those arguments and original estimations, most new European
Union (EU) members from Central and Eastern Europe are more or less
explicit in their accession strategies about the benefits they expect. Thus,
the Bank of Slovenia (2003, p. 10) simply stated: 'Slovenia would certainly
benefit from joining the common currency area', while the National Bank
of Slovakia (2003, p. 5) was fairly precise: 'According to available estimates, the major benefit is annual one percentage point increase in economic growth as a cumulative effect of lower transaction costs, eliminated
exchange rate risk against the euro, and lower risk premium and interest
rates'.

On the cost side, the most prominent argument in the literature is 'no
monetary policy reaction to country-specific shocks'.[2] Given a country-
specific negative productivity shock, the only adjustment channel left to
the economy is, after all, the labour market with eventual fiscal policy
support. Shock asymmetries among euro area members have been discussed widely, starting with the seminal contribution of Bayoumi and
Eichengreen (1992) and Feldstein (1998) on eventual negative consequences for the stability of output and inflation.

Another cost argument is the fact that the nominal exchange rate may
serve also as a shock absorber, in case shocks are either real (productivity or preferences) or foreign nominal. This type of argument follows the
traditional debate of choice of the optimal exchange rate regime (Obstfeld
and Rogoff, 1996) though it has not been discussed extensively in the
context of the euro, assuming implicitly that losses from nominal exchange

rate volatility outnumber eventual gains from the 'shock absorber' role accompanied by stabilizing monetary policy.

5.3 EMPIRICAL EVIDENCE OF BENEFITS AND COSTS

With the euro area having been in existence for more than ten years, expectations of benefits and costs may now be confronted with facts. In this regard it is useful to split the debate in two parts: achievement of price stability with consequences for risk premiums and long-term interest rates; and impact on trade and output.

Regarding price stability, there is little doubt that the ECB has been able to maintain price stability within the euro area. Mongelli and Wyplosz (2008) point out that: 'Over the first five post-war decades, with a few exceptions, inflation in all euro area countries was never as low as it was during the first ten years of the euro', adding that inflation dispersion among the euro area countries has declined to a level similar to the one observed in the United States. The import of credible monetary policies and the application of the dynamically consistent policy rule of euro area membership certainly caused inflation expectations and country risk premiums to decline in countries that had not been seen as 'best performers' in respect of inflation before euro area membership. Consequently many euro area member countries enjoy lower long-term interest nowadays than they would otherwise.

There is dramatically less consensus when it comes to the debate about the euro's impact on trade and output. Concluding that membership in a currency union increases trade among members three-fold, Rose (2000) provoked an enormous stream of literature discussing an eventual bias in his estimation of the trade effect in general but also focusing on the euro area's trade effect in particular. Regarding the euro area, in a summary provided by Baldwin (2006) the trade effect varies across studies from around 6 to 25 per cent, and is likely to vary from country to country and industry to industry. More recently, in a meta-analysis of 61 studies (28 for the euro area) on the trade effect of currency unions, Havránek (2009), finds no trade effect for the euro area at all other than a publication bias.

The relatively low intensity of the euro's 'trade effect' has important consequences for the euro's eventual effect on income. Following the conclusion of Frankel and Rose (2002) that 'by raising overall trade, currency unions also increase income', the lower the trade effect is, the lower the effect on income is likely to be. This is of special importance as according to Frankel and Rose (2002, p. 438), the 'trade' channel is probably the only one in place: 'we test and find no support for the common argument that currency unions improve income through other channels, e.g, by enhancing the central bank's credibility or stabilizing the macroeconomy'.

Based on different methodology Giannone et al. (2008) also come to the conclusion that GDP growth has probably not been affected a lot by the euro area's creation, or at least ten years have not been enough to prove it.

Interestingly, all the above-mentioned estimations discuss the impact of euro area membership on trade and eventually on the long-term level of output growth, while there has been little discussion about the euro's effect on the volatility of output (or consumption) and inflation. Thus, we have little information about how the non-existence of exchange rate and monetary shocks and, conversely, the non-existence of the exchange rate as a shock absorber and the stabilization role of country-independent monetary policies affect the overall volatility of output and inflation in member countries.

Naturally, one reason for this is probably the difficulty of distinguishing this particular effect on volatility from the stabilizing effect stemming from the import of a better monetary policy that certainly played a role in many euro area member countries. Indeed, to properly identify the 'shock-volatility' effect one needs a country that pursued a credible monetary policy even before joining the euro area.

5.4   MACROECONOMIC VOLATILITY AND EURO AREA MEMBERSHIP

We now turn our attention to quantifying expected impacts of the euro adoption on macroeconomic volatility in the Czech Republic – by macroeconomic volatility we mean volatility in inflation and consumption growth measured by standard deviations. Previous sections suggested that the choice of the fixed exchange rate and euro area membership do not have a detectable impact on the long-term mean of economic variables other than inflation (and some other nominal variables) in some cases. We now therefore judge the normative implications of the regime choice against the effect on their variance.

We study the relative importance of the exchange and interest rate channels in reducing macroeconomic volatility. The absence of exchange rate shocks under euro area membership will *ceteris paribus* reduce macroeconomic volatility (especially so for nominal variables). However, the fixed exchange rate also removes the stabilization role of the exchange rate – systematic exchange rate movements following the changes in interest rates. The absence of this stabilization channel will *ceteris paribus* increase macroeconomic volatility. The volatility increase after euro area accession can be even higher if most of the shocks affecting the economy will be asymmetric (country-specific), because the ECB's interest rate will not react to them.

Our most important question is: is the removal of exchange rate-specific shocks under euro area membership enough to offset the effect of missing exchange (and eventually interest) rate stabilization channels in their effects on macroeconomic volatility?

5.4.1   Methodology

In quantifying macroeconomic volatility, we use the core macroeconomic projection model of the Czech National Bank (CNB). The model is a standard New-Keynesian DSGE model with a well-defined steady state and transition dynamics driven by a mix of nominal and real rigidities. The model features a list of idiosyncratic structural shocks whose variances were calibrated to fit the model's filtration on historical data. A brief model description including the methodology used for identifying shocks can be found in Hurník et al. (2008). For a full model description, including its parameterization and test of its forecasting properties, see Andrle et al. (2009).

To identify structural shocks we apply the same methodology and the same set of variables as Hurník et al. (2008), but we use a different time span, namely the period from 1998Q1 up to and including 2009Q3.

In a nutshell, a reduced form of the model serves as a starting point for the identification of structural shocks based on the method of Kalman filtration. The Kalman filter applies a reduced form of the model extended for measurement equations that map observed variables to the unobserved. Based on the state form of the model and using observed variables, the Kalman filter identifies all unobserved variables that are part of the model including structural shocks. For linear systems it represents an optimum estimate in terms of the least squares criterion (Hamilton, 1994). The application of the filter itself takes on the recursive algorithm form, wherein the conditional probability density of state variables is updated in line with observed variables. Table 5.1 provides an overview of the observed variables.

Due to the presence of trends within the model and resulting non-stationarity of certain variables, the unconditional variance does not have a finite value, which is why a diffuse Kalman filter is applied (De Jong, 1991).

The estimated realizations of structural shocks are subsequently used for the historical simulation of the model to quantify the overall volatility

Table 5.1   Observed variables for shock identification

CPI (*q-o-q*)	Real consumption (*q-o-q*)
Consumption deflator (*q-o-q*)	Real investment (*q-o-q*)
Investment deflator (*q-o-q*)	Real exports (*q-o-q*)
Import deflator (*q-o-q*)	Real imports (*q-o-q*)
3M nominal interest rates (level)	Foreign output (*q-o-q*)
Nominal wage	Foreign prices (CPI, *q-o-q*)
(average wage in business sector, *q-o-q*)	
Nominal exchange rate (*q-o-q*)	Foreign 3M interest rates (level)

of inflation and consumption growth as well as contributions of particular shocks to overall volatility.

The model's structural shocks give rise to the volatility of model variables. Because we study the long-term effects of a regime change we focus on their unconditional (that is, long-term) volatility. In the model, the unconditional variance of model variables roughly matches the observed historical variance of the corresponding macroeconomic data.

In simulating the impacts of euro area membership, we perform two experiments by changing the model specification and calibration of shock volatilities. These changes should reflect the following features of euro adoption: (i) fixed exchange rate (that is, non-existence of nominal exchange rate); (ii) the loss of the domestic reaction function; and (iii) import of the ECB's monetary policy that reacts to symmetric (euro area-wide) shocks and ignores country-specific ones.

In the first experiment we study volatility under the assumption that all structural shocks that do not disappear with the euro adoption are specific to the Czech economy, that is, they are asymmetric and the ECB does not react to them. In particular, we make the following changes to the model. First, we switch off the central bank reaction function and fix the exchange rate as the new nominal anchor, and second, we remove all identified exchange rate specific shocks affecting the behaviour of domestic interest rates, such as risk premiums.[3]

In the second experiment we study volatility under the assumption that all structural shocks are symmetric, meaning, common to the euro area and the ECB reacts to them. We make the same alterations to the model as in the first experiment, but in addition we make foreign interest rates move according to a Taylor rule similar to the original policy rule describing the behaviour of the CNB.[4]

In both experiments, we assume the volatilities of all structural shocks other than exchange rate-specific shocks to remain unchanged with or without the euro.

In summary, the model describing the behaviour under the euro has a fixed exchange rate, but the interest rate reaction to shocks is switched off in experiment 1 (asymmetric shocks) and switched on in experiment 2 (symmetric shocks). This allows us to study the relative importance of the exchange rate channel in reducing macroeconomic volatility.

5.4.2 Methodological Caveats

Our methodology is potentially prone to some criticism. First, though a general equilibrium in principle, the model can still be subject to Lucas critique. In particular, one could argue that parameterizations of certain behavioural processes (for example those governing the formation of expectations) will be affected by the regime change. Many other parameters may not be deep enough – rather, they may represent complex reduced form functions of 'true deep' parameters. To the extent that this is the case and the parameters would change by euro adoption, the model cannot be used to study the behaviour of the economy under the euro.

However, as the model embodies a robust consensus on how the economy functions and is built as a general equilibrium, we have little means of improving its immunity against the Lucas critique. Specifically, we have no priors on how to change the model specification or its calibration after transiting to the euro. Hence, our best qualified guess is to leave the model parameterization unchanged in the first approximation.

Second, the specification of shocks and estimation of their variances is very much driven by our specific historical experience and the model's historical fit. There is little doubt that going forward the absolute magnitudes as well as the relative importance of shocks and their volatilities will change, with or without the euro. For instance, the high importance of technology shocks in the transition period is likely to subside over time, as the economy converges towards the EU. To what extent this process can depend on euro adoption is an open matter, though, and we have no priors that a certain group of shocks would become more or less important following euro adoption (with the exception of exchange rate and monetary policy shocks).

However, even if euro adoption has no effect on the variability of shocks, a changing relative importance of shocks going forward would still affect our results. Euro adoption affects the model's reaction to different shocks differently. For instance, assuming adoption of the euro has little effect on how the model reacts to a technology shock, but it has a large effect on how it copes with a domestic demand shock. If technology shocks disappear in the future, euro adoption will have a large impact on macroeconomic volatility, and vice versa.

In order to address this weakness we divide the structural shocks into several groups and test the robustness of our results by alternatively assuming that one of these groups will eventually disappear by calibrating their variances to zero. We then rerun our experiments and compare the resulting macroeconomic variances again under these alternating assumptions.

Finally, our treatment of symmetric and asymmetric shocks and the European Monetary Union (EMU)-wide policy reaction is very primitive. Our model is not a two-country model and cannot capture the synchronization of economic cycles in Europe, feedback loops between the small open economy and the EU, and ECB reactions. Yet, it is difficult to say a priori which groups of shocks will be felt symmetrically and which ones will not, and so at minimum our approach provides a crude corridor for future volatilities under the euro.

In summary, despite these caveats we believe our approach is a step in the right direction in examining macroeconomic volatility under euro area membership. The model embodies a robust consensual view of how the CNB – the leading forecasting and analytical institution for the Czech economy – expects the Czech economy to behave. Further work will need to investigate if all parameters are deep enough to survive the regime change and refine our crude approach towards identification of shock volatilities and their classification to symmetric and asymmetric.

5.4.3   No Euro

As our benchmark we use model volatility corresponding to historical observations. We focus on the volatility of inflation and consumption growth. Inflation, because it is the target variable under the CNB's current monetary policy regime (and also the numeric objective of the ECB). Consumption growth volatility serves as a proxy for utility.

Figures 5.1a and 5.1b show the evolution of conditional volatility (measured by standard deviation) of inflation and consumption growth and its decomposition into relative contributions of main groups of structural shocks: monetary policy and exchange rate shocks; technology shocks; price-specific, demand-specific and foreign economy shocks. The figures describe how the conditional volatility and shock contributions gradually increase with the forecasting horizon until they converge to their unconditional values.

In terms of inflation, the most important sources of volatility are technology, price-specific, and external shocks. While the contribution of the exchange rate is important, it is by far not a dominant source of inflation volatility in the Czech economy. Besides, exchange rate volatility plays

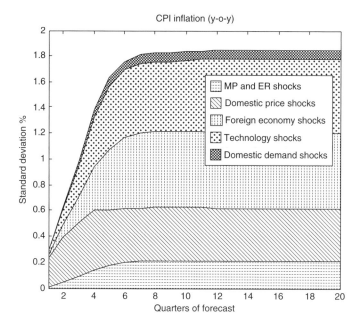

CPI inflation (y-o-y)

Legend:
- MP and ER shocks
- Domestic price shocks
- Foreign economy shocks
- Technology shocks
- Domestic demand shocks

(y-axis: Standard deviation %, from 0 to 2; x-axis: Quarters of forecast, from 2 to 20)

Source: Authors' computations.

Figure 5.1a   Standard deviation of inflation forecast error – no euro

almost no role in explaining the variance of consumption growth. Demand and technology shocks dominate.

For comparison and robustness, we re-compute the unconditional volatilities assuming higher variance of the exchange rate-specific shocks (see Figures 5.2a and 5.2b). This experiment is motivated by the fact that the years 1998 and 1999 saw a dramatic increase in short-term exchange rate volatility – far in excess of historical averages that have guided the calibration of model shocks. According to some measures, volatility increased three to five times, and although it has subsided since, it is still well above the historical averages. Should the higher volatility persist for a longer period, one can expect higher macroeconomic volatility overall. The attractiveness of euro adoption would be higher.

In examining how sensitive macroeconomic volatility is to higher exchange rate variance of the crisis period, we increase the variance of the exchange rate shock threefold. Figure 5.2a shows that this induces an increase in overall inflation volatility by about 20 per cent (compared to Figure 5.1a). Under this assumption the monetary and exchange rate shocks become the dominant source of inflation volatility. At the same

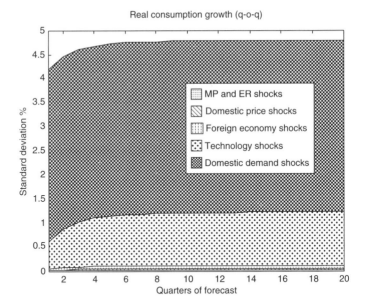

Source: Authors' computations.

Figure 5.1b   Standard deviation of consumption growth forecast error – no euro

time, the effect on consumption growth variance remains negligible (Figure 5.2b versus 5.1b). This suggests that monetary policy is effective in insulating the real economy from impacts of nominal exchange rate shocks – much more effective than in insulating inflation from such shocks.

5.4.4   Asymmetric Shocks

In this experiment, both the exchange rate and interest rate stabilization channels are switched off. Figure 5.3a shows that inflation volatility increases substantially despite the absence of exchange rate shocks. Technology and foreign economy shocks have now become the dominant source of volatility, and the overall standard deviation of inflation is up more than 2.5 times.

For consumption growth, the difference is less dramatic (Figure 5.3b). Standard deviation is also up, but only by about 10 per cent, which we do not consider a robust result given the uncertainties in the methodology and model specification.

By a way of example, Figures 5.4a and 5.4b explain why we can expect

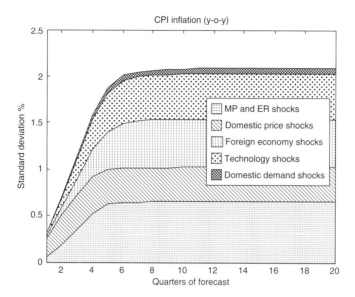

CPI inflation (y-o-y)

Legend:
- MP and ER shocks
- Domestic price shocks
- Foreign economy shocks
- Technology shocks
- Domestic demand shocks

Source: Authors' computations.

Figure 5.2a *Standard deviation of inflation forecast error – no euro (three times higher ex rate shock volatility than history average)*

higher inflation volatility under the euro when neither interest nor the exchange rates react to shocks. They show the responses of model variables to unitary unexpected one-period shocks that are important volatility sources – exchange rate shocks (Figure 5.4a) and technology shocks (Figure 5.4b). Figure 5.4b shows model reactions under 'no euro', 'euro with asymmetric shocks' and 'euro with symmetric shocks' assumptions.

Figure 5.4a displays how an exchange rate-specific shock causes volatility of inflation and the real economy necessitating a corrective policy rate reaction without the euro. This is the volatility that will be removed by adopting the euro. However, Figure 5.4b shows that volatility of inflation and consumption following a labour technology shock is much higher in the absence of the exchange and interest rate channel under the euro (dashed versus solid line). It is this additional volatility that explains the results of Figures 5.3a and 5.3b.

5.4.5 Symmetric Shocks

In this experiment, the exchange rate channel remains switched off, but domestic (that is, EMU-wide) interest rates react to all shocks using an

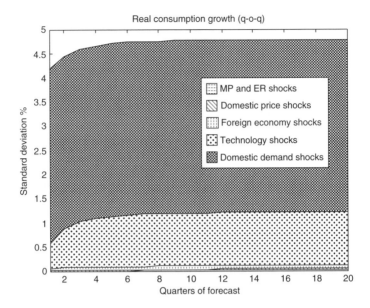

Source: Authors' computations.

Figure 5.2b   *Standard deviation of consumption growth forecast error – no euro (three times higher ex rate shock volatility than history average)*

ECB-like Taylor rule. Figures 5.5a and 5.5b show that inflation volatility is still higher than in the benchmark 'no euro' case (less than two-times), but much lower than in the case of asymmetric shocks (when both channels are switched off). The simulated ECB interest rate reaction helps in reducing overall inflation volatility caused by euro adoption, however the absence of the exchange rate channel still makes inflation more volatile than without the euro. At the same time, consumption growth is marginally less volatile now than in the benchmark 'no euro' case. But as before, we treat the results for consumption growth with caution, as the differences are very small.

Figure 5.4b provides the background. With the euro, inflation after a technology shock is less volatile, when the interest rate reacts (dashed lines). Even then, though, it is still more volatile than without the euro, when both the interest rate and the exchange rate channels are at work (solid line). Consumption growth, on the other hand, fluctuates less under the euro with just an interest rate reaction than without the euro, when both exchange and interest rates respond.

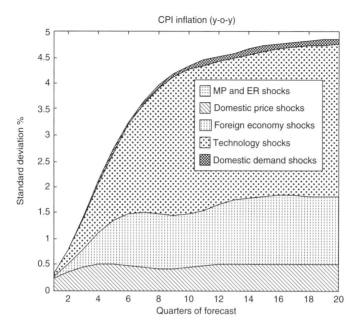

CPI inflation (y-o-y)

Source: Authors' computations.

*Figure 5.3a   Standard deviation of inflation forecast error – euro with
          asymmetric shocks (no interest rate reaction)*

5.4.6   Robustness with Respect to Changing Shock Variability

We now test how robust our results are with respect to changing relative
importance of shock groups in future. Table 5.2 shows absolute contributions of each shock group to an increase in standard deviation of inflation
and consumption growth from the baseline 'no euro' case, for both asymmetric and symmetric shocks.

In terms of inflation, the results are robust and we can expect an increase
in volatility after euro adoption irrespective of whether the shocks will
be symmetric or asymmetric or whether their relative importance will
change.[5] This is because each shock group adds positively to the overall
variance.

The largest addition to inflation volatility comes from technology
shocks in the asymmetric and from foreign shocks in the symmetric
case. However, even if the technology shocks completely disappear in
future, inflation will still be more volatile under the euro than without it.

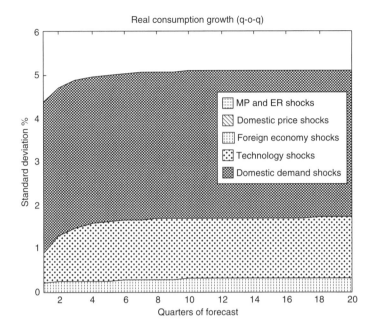

Source: Authors' computations.

*Figure 5.3b   Standard deviation of consumption growth forecast error –
euro with asymmetric shocks (no interest rate reaction)*

The same holds for other shock groups, most notably foreign economy
shocks.

The relative comparison of symmetric and asymmetric euro cases is less
robust to these changes. For instance, without technology, shocks inflation will be less volatile if shocks are asymmetric (and interest rates do not
move) than when they are symmetric.

The results for consumption growth are not as robust to changes in
the relative importance of individual shock groups as those for inflation. Although the absence of domestic demand shocks will not alter
the sequence, the absence of technology shocks will make consumption
growth least volatile in the 'asymmetric euro' case, followed by 'no euro'
and 'euro with symmetric shocks'.

Besides, if foreign economy shocks become the most dominant in
future, we could even expect to have the lowest consumption growth volatility without the euro. This is because the economy with the euro reacts to
foreign shocks with more volatility than without the euro – but in history
these shocks have not been the dominant source of volatility.

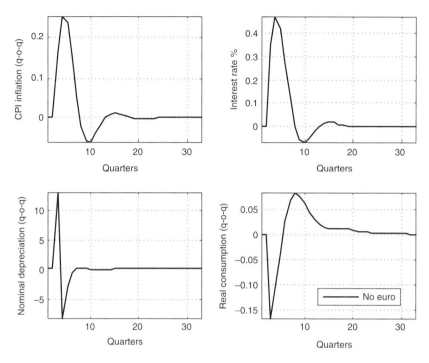

Source: Authors' computations.

Figure 5.4a   Impulse responses to unexpected one-period exchange rate shock – no euro

5.4.7   Some Empirical Evidence

The above evidence naturally raises a question whether the above-proposed increase in volatilities is observed in the data. That means to search for volatilities in inflation and consumption growth before and after currency union membership among the currency unions' members. For the comparison to be relevant, however, the analysis must concentrate on countries that had a credible monetary policy even before joining the currency union. Otherwise the analysis would be biased by the overall stabilization implied by the import of better monetary policy.

Unfortunately, we do not have enough observations to test our hypothesis. Only a few countries satisfy our criteria. Indeed, only Germany and Finland qualify as countries that entered the euro area with an independent and credible monetary policy. The rest was either more or less pegging

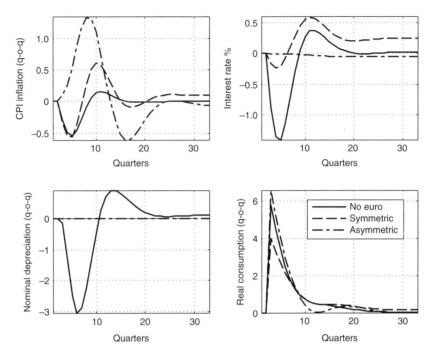

Source: Authors' computations.

*Figure 5.4b   Impulse responses to unexpected one-period labour
technology shock – no euro, euro with symmetric shocks, euro
with asymmetric shocks*

against the Deutsch Mark or its monetary policy would not have qualified as
a low inflation-oriented credible monetary policy. Unfortunately, even for
those two countries the analysis is only indicative, because of the short data
sample before euro area membership. It is not that the data are not available, but the data sample is shortened by the structural break that appears
at the beginning of the 1990s and is associated with the re-unification of
Germany and the break up of the Soviet Union. Using the data from 1994
thus gives us only five years of observation before euro area membership.

In providing indicative evidence in question, Table 5.3 shows standard
deviations of quarterly inflation and consumption growth for Germany
and Finland, and Table 5.4 for Sweden as the control country. We include
Sweden as a non-member country with a sound monetary policy to control
for a common factor that could influence the volatilities in question one
way or the other.

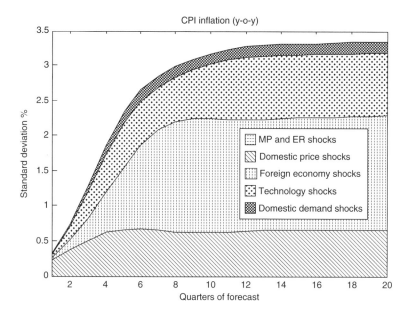

Source: Authors' computations.

Figure 5.5a   Standard deviation of inflation forecast error – euro with symmetric shocks (interest rate reaction)

It is evident that while in Germany (and Sweden) the volatility in inflation has remained the same, it has increased by roughly 40 per cent in Finland. Regarding consumption growth we see an increase of 20 per cent in Germany and of more than 60 per cent in Finland. Consumption volatility increases also in Sweden, but only by 10 per cent.

Given the size of the Finnish economy and its openness, results for Finland are probably more relevant for the Czech economy than those of Germany. With all the caveats, however, these examples do show that euro area membership can be associated with an increase in inflation and/or consumption growth volatilities and that our model-based projections should be treated seriously.

5.5   CONCLUSION

Ex ante, euro area membership was associated with several benefits and many believed that it would eventually improve the long-term macroeconomic performance of member countries in terms of price stability and

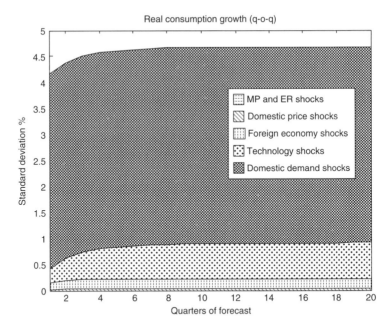

Figure 5.5b   *Standard deviation of consumption growth forecast error –
euro with symmetric shocks (interest rate reaction)*

Table 5.2   *Absolute contribution of shock groups to increase in standard
deviation of inflation and consumption growth after euro
adoption*

Variable	Scenario/ shock group	Tech- nology	Foreign	Domestic price	Domestic demand	Mone- tary and exchange rate	Total
Inflation	euro asymmetric	2.3642	0.7329	0.086	0.0393	−0.2089	3.0135
	euro symmetric	0.3314	1.0321	0.2512	0.0924	−0.2089	1.4982
Consumption growth	euro asymmetric	0.2865	0.2142	−0.0072	−0.1724	−0.0086	0.3125
	euro symmetric	−0.4169	0.1095	0.0044	0.2027	−0.0086	−0.1089

Source: Authors' computations.

Table 5.3   *Inflation and consumption growth volatilities in Germany and Finland*

Time	Germany (volatility, stand. dev.)			Finland (volatility, stand. dev.)		
	1994Q1–1998Q4	1999Q1–2008Q2	Diff. (%)	1994Q1–1998Q4	1999Q1–2008Q2	Diff. (%)
Inflation	1.53	1.44	−5.9	1.09	1.52	+39.4
Consumption growth	2.41	2.97	+23.1	1.10	1.81	+64.5
GDP growth	2.55	2.25	−11.8	2.39	2.52	+5.4

Source: IMF database and authors' calculations.

Table 5.4   *Inflation and consumption growth volatilities in Sweden*

Time	Sweden (volatility, stand. dev.)		
	1994Q1–1998Q4	1999Q1–2008Q2	Diff. (%)
Inflation	1.49	1.55	+4.0
Consumption growth	2.07	2.28	+10.1
GDP growth	2.11	2.07	−1.9

Source: Sweden Statistics and authors' calculations.

long-term output growth. Expected effects of those benefits were estimated a priori by both European and national authorities, but ten years after the euro area's establishment only the achievement of price stability is beyond any doubt. Of course, this is not little by itself, but more had apparently been expected on the real side. However, the magic that was expected to increase the long-term real economy performance has not arrived.

It is only natural then to reframe the debate of euro area membership as the traditional debate about the choice of exchange rate regime. Indeed, if the long-term real economy effects are negligible and price stability was in place before accession, only the question of macroeconomic volatilities remains valid for an economic discussion.

In this respect our experiments show that in case of a country with a sufficiently credible monetary policy, inflation volatility is likely to increase following euro area accession. For instance, in the Czech case the likely increase in inflation volatility is significant and unambiguous, irrespective of whether interest rates respond to shocks or not and whether certain shock groups will become more or less important in future. At the same time, in this case euro area membership is not likely to fundamentally change the volatility of consumption growth. The more asymmetric shocks are, the more we can expect consumption growth to be more volatile under the euro than without it. However, if the shocks are more symmetric, consumption growth can be less volatile than without the euro, and especially so if technology shocks dominate. Alas, the differences are relatively small and so the results are much less robust to possible alternative models or specifications than those for inflation. For instance, if technology shocks decline in importance in future, consumption growth is likely to be more volatile with the euro.

In a nutshell, the results demonstrate that monetary policy based on a flexible exchange rate and a credible inflation-targeting regime has provided a sound stabilization mechanism for the Czech economy and that the advantage of euro area membership can not be easily (if at all) assessed by economic analysis. Although euro adoption would remove an important source of volatility, the absence of the exchange rate reaction would bring about even more volatility – especially so for inflation and possibly also for consumption growth depending on the nature of shocks.

The relative size of the identified exchange rate shocks to the rest of the shocks is simply not high enough to rationalize the fixed exchange rate regime and abandonment of the flexible exchange rate and independent monetary policy. Naturally, one can never exclude the possibility that this is going to change in the future, and one should not forget that this is a country-specific conclusion.

NOTES

1. Zdeněk Tůma is the governor of the Czech National Bank (CNB), Jaromír Hurník and David Vávra are advisors to the Board of the Czech National Bank (CNB). The authors are thankful for comments from M. Hampl and T. Holub. Research assistance of Jaromír Toner is gratefully acknowledged. The chapter is based on the analysis first presented at the conference Prague Twenty 'On Euro', 12 November 2009. The views expressed herein are those of the authors and do not necessarily reflect the views of the CNB.
2. Other arguments that can be found in the relevant literature (see Obstfeld and Rogoff, 1996) are a split of seigniorage revenues among the currency union member countries and impossibility of inflation being used to lower the real level of the public debt. With respect to the euro area both can be certainly neglected.
3. We ignore the possibility that a small risk premium and its shocks will likely persist even after euro adoption.
4. The rule is somewhat modified to reflect the higher perceived sluggishness with which the ECB has been changing its policy rates relative to the CNB. Specifically, we increase the autoregressive coefficient from 0.75 of the CNB rule to 0.95. We calibrate the variance of the policy shock in this rule to that of the present CNB rule.
5. This assertion is made only with respect to a shock group as a whole – the variances of individual shocks making up the groups are not perturbed in the experiment. Hence, it is possible that the results would have changed with respect to some individual shocks.

REFERENCES

Andrle, Michal, Tibor Hlédik, Ondra Kameník and Jan Vlček (2009), 'Implementing the new structural model of the Czech National Bank', Working Paper No. 2, Czech National Bank.

Baldwin, Richard (2006), 'The euro's trade effects', Working Paper No. 594, European Central Bank.

Bank of Slovenia (2003), 'Programme for ERM II entry and adoption of the euro', Joint Programme of the Slovenian Government and the Bank of Slovenia, Ljubljana, November.

Bayoumi, Tamim and Barry J. Eichengreen (1992), 'Shocking aspects of European monetary unification', Working Paper No. 3949, National Bureau of Economic Research.

De Jong, P. (1991), 'The diffuse Kalman filter', *The Annals of Statistics*, **19** (2), 1073–83.

European Commission (1990), 'One market, one money: an evaluation of the potential benefits and costs of forming an Economic and Monetary Union', European Economy No. 44, October.

Feldstein, Martin (1998), 'The political economy of the European economic and monetary union: political sources of an economic liability', Working Paper No. 6150, National Bureau of Economic Research.

Frankel, Jeffrey and Andrew Rose (2002), 'An estimate of the effect of common currencies on trade and income', *The Quarterly Journal of Economics*, **117** (2), 437–66.

Giannone, Domenico, Michele Lenza and Lucrezia Reichlin (2008), 'Business cycles in the euro area', Working Paper No. 14529, National Bureau of Economic Research.

Hamilton, J.D. (1994), *Time Series Analysis*, Princeton: Princeton University Press.

Havránek, Tomáš (2009), 'Rose effect and the euro: is the magic gone?', MPRA Paper 18479, University Library of Munich, Germany.

Hurník, Jaromír, Ondra Kameník and Jan Vlček (2008), 'The history of inflation targeting in the Czech Republic through the lens of a dynamic general equilibrium model', *Czech Journal of Economics and Finance*, **58** (9–10), 454–69.

International Monetary Fund, 'International Financial Statistics', Washington, DC: IMF, http://www.imfstatistics.org.

Mongelli, Francesco P. and Charles Wyplosz (2008), 'The euro at ten: unfulfilled threats and unexpected challenges', Fifth ECB Central Banking Conference – 'The Euro at Ten: Lessons and Challenges', Frankfurt am Main, 13–14 November, http://www.ecb.int/events/conferences/html/cbc5.en.html.

National Bank of Slovakia (2003), 'Strategy of the Slovak Republic for the adoption of the euro', BIATEC, **XI** (8), 1–10.

Obstfeld, Maurice and Kenneth Rogoff (1996), *Foundation of International Macroeconomics*, Cambridge: MIT Press.

Rose, Andrew (2000), 'One money, one market? The effect of common currencies on international trade', *Economic Policy*, **XXX**, 7–45.

Sweden Statistics, http://www.scb.se/.

6. Preparing for euro adoption

Gertrude Tumpel-Gugerell[1]

For the European Central Bank (ECB), the topic of the optimal timing of euro adoption for the European Union (EU) countries in Central and Eastern Europe (CEE) that have not yet done so is very important. According to the Maastricht Treaty, all EU countries are called upon to adopt the euro at some stage. So it is not a question of if, but rather of when to join.

However, to ensure that the monetary union is working smoothly, it is essential – and the Maastricht Treaty has foreseen this – that the countries joining the euro area have achieved a sufficient degree of sustainable convergence. This is first of all in the interest of the country concerned. Moreover, sustainable convergence is a cornerstone of the European Monetary Union (EMU) on which the success story of the euro is built. Since its introduction back in 1999, the euro has become one of the major currencies of the world. The low inflation environment in the euro area can be largely attributed to the well anchored inflation expectations and the high credibility of the ECB's monetary policy strategy to ensure price stability over the medium term. During the global financial crisis, it became apparent that the euro has been an important shelter for the euro area countries to protect them against what otherwise may have resulted in an exchange rate and balance of payments crisis.

In the following this chapter discusses the economic situation in the CEE countries and their prospect of joining the euro.

THE CEE COUNTRIES HAVE BEEN STRONGLY HIT BY THE FINANCIAL CRISIS

Following the bankruptcy of Lehman Brothers, the CEE countries have been strongly hit by the global financial crisis, although at varying degrees across different countries. Due to the slump in global activity, heightened risk aversion by international investors and a de-leveraging by financial institutions, most CEE countries have seen a significant weakening of export demand and a substantial worsening of their external financing conditions. It seems that financing difficulties have been particularly severe in those countries that had accumulated large imbalances during pre-crisis times and whose debt structure was characterized by significant currency and maturity mismatches. In some countries balance sheet effects associated with large exchange rate depreciations posed a risk to financial stability.

The financial crisis reversed some of the impressive progress that the CEE countries had already made in terms of convergence. In the years preceding the crisis most CEE countries were growing rapidly. However, excessive credit growth, substantial wage increases and house price bubbles, contributed to the overheating of some of the economies. This in turn led to a widening of the positive output gap and a non-sustainable deterioration of the current account position. Moreover, the overheating pressures in some countries translated into rising inflation and led to a real appreciation of their currencies, which in turn aggravated the external imbalances further.

To dampen the impact of the crisis, national authorities have adopted a number of policy measures, which however differed significantly across countries, depending on the room for manoeuvre to adopt supportive monetary and fiscal policies in the various countries.

SUBSTANTIAL EU AND ECB SUPPORT TO WEATHER THE CRISIS

The international and European community provided substantial financial support to some countries in the region. The EU supported some CEE countries via the medium-term financial assistance (MTFA) facility, in conjunction with the International Monetary Fund (IMF) programmes. This MTFA facility was substantially increased during the crisis and also the EU structural funds have helped to cushion the impact of the crisis.

It is also important to emphasize the support from the ECB, contributing to the stabilization of financial markets in the region. Many banks in the CEE countries are owned by euro area banks. Therefore, the CEE countries benefited strongly from the ECB's enhanced credit support policy and the unlimited provision of liquidity to euro area banks. On top of this, the ECB has offered some of the national central banks repo lines to meet euro liquidity needs.

NEED TO RETURN TO A SUSTAINABLE CONVERGENCE PROCESS

The financial crisis has clearly shown how important it generally is for any country in the EU to embark on policies aimed at sustainable growth paths. This includes sound economic policies, enhanced economic flexibility and the building-up of fiscal buffers in normal times. Also the regulatory framework for financial markets has to be adjusted at the national and supranational level such as to ensure economic and financial stability.

The need for such policies and the need for pursuing a regulatory reform agenda certainly applies to all EU countries, not just the CEE countries. That said, there have been some proposals that a rapid euro adoption could help the CEE countries to overcome the impact of the crisis more quickly. However, policies to overcome the financial crisis and the adoption of the euro are two distinct issues that need to be clearly separated.

On the one hand, policies to overcome the crisis – such as large fiscal measures – were clearly needed and have been put in place in all EU countries. Now that the worst of the financial crisis seems to be over, EU countries have to return to sustainable policies and must advance with the regulatory reform agenda as spelled out by the G20.

On the other hand, the financial crisis has not changed anything with respect to the procedure governing the euro adoption process. Before joining the euro area, countries need to ensure that the right accompanying policies are implemented and that the structure of their economies ensures a high shock absorption capacity. In particular, the economies need to be sufficiently flexible to cope with the more limited range of economic policy instruments once they enter the euro area. While the CEE countries have already made good progress in this respect before the crisis, further efforts are needed. The financial crisis has hit the CEE countries in a severe way and, therefore, required a forceful policy response. Once the crisis is over, a return to sustainable policies is absolutely essential for the further convergence process. A sufficient degree of sustainable convergence is crucial for the CEE countries, to be able to reap the full benefits of euro area membership. Otherwise, the single monetary policy of the euro area might not be suitable, thereby bearing the risk of boom–bust cycles and high inflation volatility in the country concerned.

All this underlines the importance of a credible euro adoption strategy. Therefore, entering the euro area prematurely – that is before reaching a sufficient degree of convergence and economic flexibility – would not be a panacea for the CEE countries to overcome the crisis impact. On the contrary, a premature entry into the euro area would deprive the countries from important adjustment tools and would therefore not be in the interest of the country joining.

A CREDIBLE EURO ADOPTION STRATEGY IS IMPORTANT

A credible euro adoption strategy helps stabilizing the economies, as it provides an important anchor for policymakers. As already mentioned before, a credible strategy requires in particular responsible macroeconomic policies and advancements in structural reforms.

One essential element of the countries' euro adoption strategies relates to the credibility of timetables. At the time of EU accession most countries had announced to join the euro area as soon as possible. However, this was based on assumptions at the time of the accession. The recent financial crisis has impacted the convergence progress and has moved euro adoption further into the future. Therefore, individual countries' timetables have to be carefully looked at and adjustments may be necessary.

An overly ambitious timetable for adopting the euro can be rather costly for the country concerned. This may encourage market participants to pursue strategies which may prove to be risky if the timetable turns out not to be achievable.

A LOOK BEYOND THE EU BORDERS

The financial crisis also took its toll outside EU borders. Many non-EU emerging European economies, including EU candidate and potential candidate countries, recorded a strong fall in external and domestic demand, amid mounting concerns over financial stability and increased uncertainty about the availability of external financing.

While policymakers in these countries currently focus rather on the entry into the EU and not on euro adoption, the need for sustainable convergence is still high on their agenda. Overall, non-EU emerging European economies are in the early stages of catching up in income levels with those of the EU. Ensuring a smooth process of real and nominal convergence is therefore a key priority in the region. Moreover, the risks of boom–bust cycles in credit or asset prices have been amply illustrated by the recent developments, whereby countries with sounder fundamentals were generally less affected by the crisis. Rapid and determined international policy actions, including support from European institutions via

Macro-Financial Assistance (MFA) and Instrument for Pre-Accession Assistance (IPA) funds have contributed to bringing confidence back.

Moreover, an issue of relevance for some economies in the region is the official, unilateral use of the euro. This unilateral euroization is, however, not in line with the provisions of the Lisbon Treaty. And as the recent intensive financial pressures experienced by the unilaterally euroized economies have also illustrated, the unilateral adoption of the euro is not the magic tool that automatically provides protection against the impact of external shocks.

CONCLUDING REMARKS

The CEE countries have already made significant progress with respect to their catching up with the euro area. However, some of the countries have been severely hit by the financial crisis. This clearly has an impact on the state of the convergence process of the CEE countries and has potentially moved euro adoption further into the future. The timetables of euro adoption have to be carefully assessed, given particularly the large uncertainties that are associated with the current economic and financial situation.

One thing, however, needs to be very clear. The financial crisis has not changed our policy for adopting the euro. Therefore, to prematurely adopt the euro, in particular if not accompanied by a sufficient degree of sustainable convergence, is certainly not a solution to overcome the impact of the crisis. Only a credible euro adoption strategy helps stabilizing the economies, also with respect to the crisis impact. Achieving sustainable convergence can be seen as an important anchor and an opportunity for the CEE countries to adopt economic policies that will eventually lead to the successful adoption of the euro, hopefully not in the too distant future.

NOTE

1.   Member of the Executive Board of the European Central Bank (ECB).

PART III

The euro area – a shelter?
Euro assets – a safe haven?

7. The euro area: a shelter? Estonia's perspective

Märten Ross

Can the euro area be a shelter for our countries from the turmoil of global financial and economic storms? And what kind of shelter would it be? After all, a shelter could be envisioned as a comfortable waiting room with a fireplace and free coffee. Or it could be the place for the homeless. So, the appeal of that shield would matter too. Furthermore, we could also ask if very small and open economies need any shelter at all in good times.

This chapter elaborates on whether the euro area is a shelter from Estonia's perspective. First, background information on the Estonian economy is given. Second, the trade channel and the financial channel are discussed. Finally, conclusions are drawn.

ESTONIA'S ECONOMY IN BRIEF

Estonia introduced a currency board arrangement in 1992, under which the exchange rate of the Estonian kroon is now fixed to the euro. The strong nominal anchor currency has greatly facilitated the flexibility of the public and private sector in terms of economic adjustment. At the same time, Estonia's trade and capital flow regimes have been among the most liberal in the world. For example, the exports of trade and services have been around 75 per cent of GDP. Thus, Estonia provides a good case for establishing the actual impact of globalization and free movement of capital on a very small economy.

It is also important to recall that from the late 1990s Estonia's banking sector has been practically fully integrated into the Nordic banking system. For example, over 90 per cent of the deposits are collected by the fully integrated subsidiaries or foreign branches of four Nordic banking groups that have comparatively high international ratings. The currency board arrangement means that Eesti Pank, Estonia's central bank, does not provide a classical lender-of-last-resort facility. Consequently, the liquidity management of the banks operating in Estonia has been strongly centralized and is group-based.

At the same time, Estonia's fiscal position has been among the most solid ones in Europe. At end-2008, public gross debt stood at a meagre 5 per cent. As the government itself had collected liquid financial assets in the amount of 12 per cent of GDP (mostly high-rated foreign assets), its net financial position has, in fact, remained positive.

To give a full picture of the playing field, it should be added that the Estonian product market is considered open and smoothly functioning. Moreover, Estonia's labour market has been described as one of the most flexible in Europe. So, the Estonian economy has been facing global storms with an open mind for many years already. Estonia has not been sitting idle and waiting for a shelter to open up. Therefore, it is not surprising that the economy has been handling the present crisis without any major public discussions about the need for a fundamental regime shift.

ESTONIA AND THE POST-LEHMAN CRISIS

In Estonia the global economic and financial boom happened to coincide with the accession to the European Union (EU). Consequently, Estonia's economic activity was boosted by the increasing profitability in the tradable sector, further opening of the labour market and the speeding up of financial integration. As a result, future income expectations picked up sharply and financial deepening evolved rapidly.

Unfortunately, as many mistakenly took this EU accession effect to be a more permanent positive shock to economic growth rather than a level shift, this led to overshoots in credit and real estate markets as well as pressures on the external accounts and inflation. However, it should be noted that due to a conservative policy framework and additional discretionary policy steps in fiscal and financial regulation, the adjustment of the convergence boom started already in 2007. Thus, by the time Estonia entered the post-Lehman period, economic adjustments were already on the way. Therefore, short-term growth expectations have been very low in 2008 and 2009.

The most dramatic impact of the late-2008 global crisis was passed on through the trade channel. The drop in Estonia's exports, although comparable in magnitude to the neighbouring countries, hit Estonia's economic performance and confidence hard. The previous domestic adjustment had only a gradual impact on unemployment, whereas the post-Lehman trade collapse conditioned rapid shrinkage in employment and had a more fundamental effect on the medium-term outlook of the household sector.

In many aspects, the effect of the global crisis on the Estonian financial system mirrored that of the so-called Russian crisis in the late 1990s. Emotions ran high, the credibility of the banking sector weakened temporarily and many foreign companies decided to close their foreign exchange positions. This raised the demand for hedging instruments, which, in turn, increased forward quotations. As a result, the cost of capital grew.

However, as euro interest rates started to fall in November–December 2008, the situation became rapidly more ambiguous. Most of the non-financial sector financing is in euros and often in flexible interest rates, which is why the fall in short-term euro interest rates was quickly passed through to the economy, easing the financial burden of firms and households considerably. The kroon interest rates remained at higher levels for somewhat longer, although never reaching the levels witnessed at the end of the 1990s.

By the fall of 2009, the situation had, in many respects, stabilized as elsewhere in Europe. Furthermore, as the government has decided to put the fiscal house in order as soon as possible, the fiscal position has stopped deteriorating and the government is currently still a net lender. Although the return to fiscal surplus may take some time, Estonia will exit the crisis with a very low debt burden. Thus, households need not worry about the impact of the exit strategy on their budgets in the distant future. It is also noteworthy that although the crisis of such magnitude inevitably increases loan losses, the level of losses incurred so far has been sufficiently low and the accumulated buffers so strong that the stability of the integrated banking sector does not raise any doubts. In other words, households are free to follow the signals generated by the overall growth environment, without having to worry about potential future tax rises.

So, before starting to assess whether the euro could be regarded as a shelter, we should not forget that life is also possible without the euro.

THE SHELTER IS ALREADY AVAILABLE TO SOME EXTENT

When analysing the role of the euro as a possible shelter for the non-euro area EU member states, one should not forget that the successful existence of the euro is already now influencing our performance. Estonia is directly affected by its neighbouring countries that belong to the euro area and also indirectly by the euro area as a whole. The recent crisis has taught us that a stable neighbour, such as the entire euro area, is a great blessing for Estonia, as it helps preserve the exchange rate stability necessary for trade and capital flows.

Furthermore, the relative calm of European economies, notwithstanding the scale of the global financial crisis, is partly the result of monetary stability that has been brought along by the introduction and stable functioning of the euro in most of the EU. Without that stabilizing force, the array of problems facing our financial landscape would have been notably more complex.

Last but not least, as the euro has performed as a cornerstone of stability, its interest rates have been able to reflect the magnitude of economic shocks. As mentioned above, the rapid lowering of interest rates has brought a considerable direct and indirect financial relief to firms and households also in the non-euro area countries, including Estonia. Therefore, the non-euro area countries are equally interested in the smooth functioning of the euro area.

THE EURO SHELTER AND THE TRADE SHOCK

The post-Lehman global trade collapse had a fast and direct impact also on Estonian exports. However, comparing the trade performance of Estonia with that of its Northern neighbours, both inside or outside the euro area, the differences appear to be either negligible or non-existent (see Figure 7.1).

This is not surprising as the recent shock hit the whole world and did not differentiate between countries on the basis of their monetary arrangement. The few differences observed have rather been related to the specialization of trade in countries and regions. True, the differences might have been bigger if trade financing had been the major factor behind the

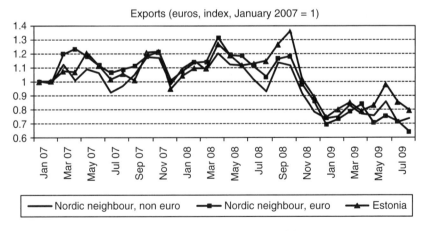

Figure 7.1   Exports in Estonia and its Nordic neighbours
(January 2007 = 1)

collapse of trade. Then the higher financial stability provided by the euro shelter would have, indeed, made a difference. However, although no major studies have been carried out on this matter, most of the existing surveys have not indicated financial constraints to be a major obstacle for export growth in Estonia.

Strategically speaking, it cannot be excluded that the stability of investment resulting from the shelter provided by euro area membership would have possibly influenced investment during the crisis and thus supported the long-term competitiveness of exporters. However, the data available on the second and third quarters of 2009 do not reveal a notable decline in the investment ability of the exporting companies. In a way, this can, of course, reflect the high level of integration of Estonia's exporting companies with the euro area, in particular the Nordic countries. All in all, the euro shelter as such most likely would not have made a big short-term difference for the export sector.

THE EURO SHELTER AND THE FINANCIAL CHANNEL

While the post-Lehman global trade crisis apparently did not have a disproportionately high impact on the non-euro countries, such as Estonia, the same cannot be said about the financial channel. The crisis actually caused a bigger differentiation between the euro area countries; thus, the effect for non-euro countries was clearly more severe.

In Estonia's context two aspects are relevant to explain this difference in reaction. First, while a small economy is by definition exposed to somewhat bigger volatility, size matters even more in a crisis, unlike the actual financial position. This is most likely to do with the information asymmetry between bigger and smaller economies. In other words, the smaller the role of investment in the large portfolios of investors, the higher the probability of bundling these positions together and liquidating them without giving much consideration to the fundamental factors. In bigger countries, good policies could preserve stability also in the time of crisis, whereas in smaller countries, like Estonia, even a strong banking sector and a sound fiscal position could not protect a country from the excessive bundling of all sorts of countries together and, as a result, indiscriminately selling its assets at the height of the crisis. Joining the euro area does not make countries bigger in size, but the safe haven of a stable currency area has, nevertheless, made a considerable difference in some states (see Figure 7.2).

The second aspect why the euro shelter matters is related to the different treatment of foreign currency and cross-border debt positions in 'normal'

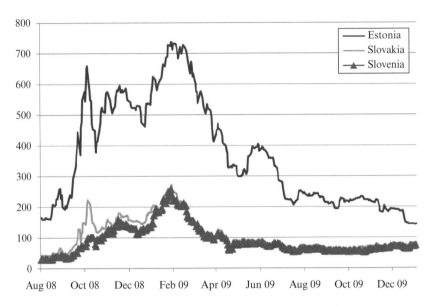

*Figure 7.2   5-year credit default swaps (CDS) premia in Estonia,
Slovakia and Slovenia*

times versus the time of crisis. As financial integration had already reached
quite a high level in Estonia, accompanied by the quite logical build-up of
stable financial positions between the headquarters and branches of Nordic
banking groups, this drew surprisingly many comments from the public
and stakeholders during the crisis. While a more specific analysis as well as
relevant *ex post* experience has not revealed any stability concerns related
to these positions (rather the contrary), the crisis appears to be exactly the
time when investors and analysts tend to overemphasize these risks.

As a result of this differentiation, the cross-border and currency positions that did not have much of a negative effect on the euro area countries
appeared to be a source of vulnerability for the euro area 'outsiders'. This
is even stranger, as accession of fixed-exchange-rate countries like *Estonia*
to the euro area per se has not been shown to improve the micro level
financial soundness of companies or households. But this is probably a
part of human psychology that cannot be escaped in this game.

CONCLUSIONS

Estonia provides an interesting case study on how the euro area could give
economic shelter to small open EU economies. Estonia has been mimicking

the euro area monetary arrangement as closely as possible while operating a very open trade already for decades. The Estonian banking sector is highly integrated with the Nordic countries, and Estonia's fiscal position is one of the soundest in the EU. Nonetheless, the relative distress generated by the post-Lehman trade and financial crisis has highlighted the benefits of being a member of the stable currency area.

The experience thus far shows that the immediate benefits of the shelter provided by euro area membership for Estonia's trade channel are limited, whereas the medium-term benefits are certainly there. At the same time, financial market linkages are probably much stronger and the effect of the euro shelter would be considerably bigger. Much of this effect is not directly related to the 'hard factors', such as the financial soundness of firms or households due to lower capital cost. Rather it appears that the information asymmetry and related herd behaviour during the crisis explains much of the difference.

8. Slovakia's experience with the euro

Ivan Šramko

The purpose of my contribution is to describe Slovakia's experience with the euro and I will also try to comment on the underlying history. By way of introduction, Slovakia's experience was relatively different from those of other countries insofar as we had a political consensus in Slovakia from the point when we first started the euro adoption debate. Why so? Perhaps because the lack of a positive image in the early 1990s had provoked the then incoming government to completely change this image, by joining NATO and the euro area, by tackling the range of problems Slovakia used to have. This included a show of political will and a political consensus to have the euro in our country. This was very important also because the first decision was taken and the euro introduction strategy was adopted back in 2003, which means that the period leading up to actual accession was longer than the usual term of government. It was of crucial importance that the new government coming in after the elections in 2006 would support this process, this long-term and successful economic project. This is why I can say that the complex project of introducing the euro in Slovakia was and still is a big success.

That said, it is necessary to make two notes: the first note is that to make a deep and serious assessment of this process or an analysis of this process we would need more time. It is not possible to make some preconclusion about the influence of euro adoption on the real economy now after the effect. Of course, there are some factors which we can describe even now, but it takes more time to produce conclusive evidence on the euro's impact on the real economy. There are some economists who say that the National Bank of Slovakia (NBS) needs a decade to be able to provide a serious analysis of the impact of euro adoption on the real economy. And of course, to provide conclusions or some results based on these months of development of our economy in relation to euro adoption is also not very easy because given the global financial turmoil and global recession the economies are experiencing a different type of stress. Much rather, the main problem of the economy is the global recession, such as the global setback in demand, because Slovakia is one of the most open economies in the Central and Eastern European (CEE) countries and fully dependent on the development in the euro area countries.

What were the main challenges in the past, or what were the key questions connected with euro adoption? Before euro adoption, there were several widely discussed challenges: the main challenges appeared to be the so-called impossible trinity, the problem of 'shooting a moving target', the so-called Balassa–Samuelson effect and the exchange rate pass-through. Impossible trinity means that a country with an open capital account cannot control both exchange rate and inflation. So, the NBS decided as a strategy on cutting our period of participation in ERM II as short as possible; presumably this is the conclusion at which policymakers at other central banks arrived as well: if it is necessary to join ERM II, do so for as short a period as possible. The NBS started in November 2005 and during the period of when the Slovak koruna was a part of ERM II. To give some answers to the questions which were not answered in the past – for example, how many times is it possible to change the central parity and so on? The NBS implemented an inflation targeting framework under the condition of ERM II; this means that the main goal of the NBS was inflation. The NBS started with inflation targeting in 2005, which means that inflation was still the main goal of the NBS, but the central bank also had to look after exchange rate stability. Observers of Slovakia's stay in ERM II will know that the NBS had, for example, to intervene at times to keep the exchange rate from becoming too volatile in 2005, 2006 and 2007. The second question or challenge in the convergence process is the so-called Balassa–Samuelson effect, which stands for higher price increases in the non-tradable sector, leading to higher headline inflation. But the estimates differ significantly. The NBS expected only a 0.7 percentage point contribution to headline inflation in the medium term due to several mitigation factors; taking into account the current domestic economic developments, reflecting the global economic crisis, the impact would be higher. However, the Balassa–Samuelson effect is not a short-term effect, and the medium-term outlook suggests a return towards the original estimates. Another challenge for a country with floating exchange rates like Slovakia is the so-called exchange rate pass-through, which explains the effect of the exchange rate on inflation and influences the long-term inflation sustainability. Especially the development of the Slovak koruna in 2007 confirms that the exchange rate appreciation had a very limited impact on *inflation*. The NBS's long-term estimates on exchange rate pass-through indicated that 1 percentage point of appreciation of the Slovak koruna exchange rate leads to a 0.16 percentage point decrease in overall inflation, depending on the different scenarios. The NBS estimates of exchange rate pass-through are between 0.13 and 0.20 percentage points.

The widely discussed threat of excess inflation after euro adoption did not materialize. Slovakia is recording the lowest level of overall inflation in history. Inflation and pass-through were some of the most open questions which were also raised in the statements of the European Central Bank (ECB) and the European Commission before the final decision was made. In fact, it was really the question of what would happen with inflation in Slovakia once the exchange rate had been irrevocably fixed.

Turning to the changeover effect, the complex consumer protection system contributed to a very low changeover effect that, based on our calculations, reached approximately only 0.15 percentage points. It is in line with the experience of other countries, for example 0.09 to 0.25 percentage points in original euro area countries, 0.2 percentage points in Cyprus, 0.3 percentage points in Slovenia and Malta. Notable price increases were recorded in transport services, veterinary services, maintenance of dwellings and restaurants. If the NBS took into account also items with decreasing prices, the range would be from -0.12 to 0.12 percentage points. So, on average, the NBS would have to conclude that the euro changeover effect is zero.

The euro changeover as such was successful and passed very smoothly, without any significant problems. A very high information level and the readiness of the business sector were based also on foreign know-how and experience, especially in the banking industry, with regard to the structure of the banking industry. As is well known, most of Slovakia's banks are owned by banking groups resident in the euro area. Several advantages of the euro adoption in Slovakia have already materialized, for example, the exchange rate stability, the high rating of the country. What was very important in this changeover process and in the aftermath? There was and still is very strong support of the general public for euro adoption, which is really exceptional. The general view in the other countries which adopted the euro, the latest research shows that there is very strong general support in Slovakia. More than 83 per cent of the population welcome the adoption of the euro. Moreover inflation developments are fully in line with the euro area average, and the risks which were presented before the adoption of the euro did not materialize.

What are the first results of the euro adoption in Slovakia? The euro brings stability. A few months after the conversion rate had been set, the exchange rate of the Visegrad group countries (Czech Republic, Hungary, Poland) started to depreciate strongly; for example, there were some currencies which depreciated by 35 per cent compared to the value at the beginning of 2008. The Slovak koruna remained stable in 2008. There was no reason to speculate with the currency before the euro adoption. The stable currency increases overall economic stability, and generates favourable conditions for long-term business decisions. Automatically, euro adoption and the development of the currencies of neighbouring countries opened the question about Slovakia's price competitiveness. In the context of a relatively large depreciation of exchange rates of the neighbouring countries, Slovakia's price competitiveness in the region has deteriorated; while labour costs have decreased in the Czech Republic, Poland and Hungary, labour costs have slightly increased in Slovakia, rising a little bit beyond the Visegrad group countries average at the beginning of 2009. The hourly labour costs were lowest in Hungary and Poland. Once the exchange rate of the neighbouring countries started to appreciate, the countries lost their advantages, so that the labour costs in Slovakia are again the second-lowest in the Visegrad countries and lower than the average of the Visegrad group countries. Currently, the hourly labour costs continue to be very stable.

Slovakia was practically the first country where inflation dropped after euro adoption. Of course, this is not only due to domestic reasons. The main factor behind this was really the global development of inflation in the euro area in other countries, but it is a fact that inflation was very much under control. Competitiveness is not just about the exchange rate, what is also important is the relation between labour costs and labour productivity. Slovakia still retains a favourable ratio between labour costs and productivity, and price competitiveness is just a part of overall competitiveness. Other factors, like the business conditions, are usually more important in this context. Slovakia is still in one of the best positions in the region.

Thanks to the euro adoption, rating agencies recognized Slovakia as the most reliable country in the region. The spread of the long-term government bond yields widened in the course of the financial crisis. The spreads increased to some extent for all CEE countries. However, the spread for non-euro area countries rose sharply during the first month of 2009, while the spreads of Slovakia remained stable. This should be good evidence for confidence warranted by the euro adoption. The impact on the real economy, despite euro adoption, did not shield Slovakia's economy from adverse effects of the global economic crisis. The negative effect of the global recession is significant. Slovakia witnessed the highest drop in industrial production among CEE countries due to the high openness of the economy and a large share of cyclical industries in the output. At the same time, Slovakia had the biggest fall in the first quarter compared with the last quarter of 2009; in the second and third quarters the Slovak economy was among the countries with the best performance or highest economic growth within the European Union (EU).

The direct effect of the credit crisis on the Slovak financial sector was limited. Why is this so? After all, we cleaned up the banking industry in 2000, Slovakia has restructured the banking industry, privatized the banking industry, and has transferred a huge portion of bad loans, also from the 1990s, to the special agencies. Following the clean-up of the banking industry, the banks then concentrated very strongly on the domestic market. The banks did not buy toxic assets abroad, they concentrated fully on the domestic market, and they never had problems with liquidity; the loan deposit ratio was very positive, with deposits covering 80 per cent of the loans.

The main conclusions from the above are that the euro changeover passed very smoothly in Slovakia, with high public support playing a very important role. The successful euro adoption brought several immediate benefits, and the euro has brought stability, it has made the economy less volatile and increased confidence. Slovakia enjoys the highest rating in the region, which has had a very positive impact on foreign direct investment (FDI) inward to the country. Of course, the country is not like the other countries, FDI rates are not very high. However, foreign investors coming to the country have typically listed the euro among the arguments why they chose Slovakia. Following the introduction of the euro, Slovakia experienced a temporary deterioration of price competitiveness, and the euro did not shield the domestic economy from the adverse effect of the global economic crisis, yet the economy is expected to recover relatively quickly given the structure of the economy. If there is a strong foreign demand, there will also be a positive impact on the Slovak economy.

9. Currency substitution in the economies of Central Asia: how much does it cost?

Asel Isakova

INTRODUCTION

Currency substitution, or the use of foreign currency to finance transactions, by domestic residents has been a widespread phenomenon in emerging market and transition economies. This chapter investigates the importance of currency substitution in a group of transition economies in Central Asia and estimates the degree of substitutability between domestic currency and foreign currency in these economies. This empirical analysis contributes to an understanding of the economic importance of currency substitution in three economies – Kazakhstan, the Kyrgyz Republic and Tajikistan. Moreover, the study examines the implications of currency substitution for seigniorage revenues of central banks and its welfare cost.

The countries of Central Asia have experienced important structural socio-economic and political transformation related to the demolition of old administrative systems and building new institutions of the free market (Gürgen et al., 1999). Building a market economy required economic liberalization, including price liberalization and gradual capital markets decontrol. Price liberalization resulted in an accelerated pace of inflation and rapid depreciation of newly introduced national currencies. The weak positions of domestic legal tenders and their decreasing purchasing power led to a flight from national money and to an increase in foreign currency holdings by residents. Currency substitution was a result of the general economic instability and undermined the credibility of the domestic money. Moreover, the rudimentary financial sector institutions were not able to provide households with reliable financial instruments for saving in domestic currency. Holding foreign currency (mostly US dollars) thus became a way to hedge against the risk of inflation and depreciation of the local currency.

Macroeconomic stabilization in Central Asian economies at the end of the 1990s brought down inflation rates and thus helped local currencies regain credibility. This has not, however, reversed the process of dollarization. There is no estimated measure of the cash holdings denominated in US dollars in Central Asia. The level of foreign currency denominated deposits is thus used to reflect the importance of currency substitution (see Appendix, Figures 9.A1 and 9.A2).

Dollarization and currency substitution in transition economies is an important issue to address for several reasons.[1] By influencing the monetary transmission mechanism and the money demand, dollarization makes the conduct of monetary policy more challenging (Sahay and Végh, 1995; Baliño et al., 1999; Havrylyshyn and Beddies, 2003; Feige, 2003). High levels of dollarization may bring more volatile exchange rates and a weaker interest rate channel as residents become less sensitive to changes in interest rates on domestic currency assets (Horváth and Maino, 2006).

Furthermore, dollarization affects the ability of governments to earn revenue from seigniorage. Bufman and Leiderman (1993) show that small increases in dollarization have resulted in large seigniorage losses in Israel. Harrison and Vymyatnina (2007) argue that currency substitution can also preclude a government from using an inflationary tax to finance its expenditure programmes, as the spending power is limited by the willingness of domestic residents to hold domestic currency.

In this chapter, currency substitution in Central Asia is examined in a dynamic optimization framework with a money-in-the-utility model with two currencies. Estimation of the structural parameters is based on estimating the Euler equations derived from the optimality conditions. This approach allows for explicit estimation of the main parameters of the model such as the level of dollarization, the elasticity of substitution between the domestic and foreign currency, as well as the magnitude of relative risk aversion and intertemporal substitution. Estimation of the non-linear equations is performed using a Generalized Method of Moments (GMM) framework (Hansen, 1982). This approach was employed by İmrohoroğlu (1994), who examines currency substitution in Canada, and Bufman and Leiderman (1993), who use a model of the same type to investigate currency substitution in Israel. In the context of transition economies, a similar framework is used by Friedman and Verbetsky (2001), who study dollarization in Russia, and Selçuk (2003), who investigates currency substitution in some economies of Central and Eastern Europe (CEE). The value added of this approach is that by explicitly estimating the parameters of the model, the implications of dollarization for seigniorage revenues and households' welfare can be analysed. Bufman and Leiderman (1993) examine how changes in the level of dollarization affect the seigniorage revenue of the Israeli government, while Friedman and Verbetsky (2001) examine seigniorage loss and changes in economic welfare due to changes in dollarization in the Russian economy. This approach will be used in this chapter to examine three Central Asian economies.

INSTITUTIONAL FRAMEWORK AND CURRENCY SUBSTITUTION IN CENTRAL ASIA

The dissolution of the Soviet Union at the beginning of the 1990s led to a deep socio-economic crisis in Central Asia: a severe output decline, general macroeconomic instability, and hyperinflation. Economic relations with other republics in the former Soviet Union were demolished. This had a negative impact on living standards and caused a deep recession in the economies of the region (Pomfret, 2006). Although the beginning of the transformation process appeared to be a painful experience for the countries of Central Asia, they managed to restore positive economic growth in the late 1990s and demonstrated impressive growth rates in the 2000s. High energy prices and increasing investments in the oil and gas sectors were the main factors that drove economic growth in Kazakhstan.[2] Two other economies have experienced relatively modest developments in comparison to their regional neighbour. Kyrgyzstan's growth was driven mainly by gold production and investments in the gold sector, while the economy of Tajikistan was dragged down by the effects of the civil war that persisted even after the peace accord was signed in 1997. Real economic recovery, therefore, did not start before 2000 (Pomfret, 2006).

A period of hyperinflation in the first half of the 1990s was a consequence of price liberalization and overall economic decontrol in Central Asian countries. Moreover, newly established central banks were heavily financing state enterprises' losses and government deficits. A rapid growth in money supply contributed to high levels of inflation in all countries. With the introduction of national currencies, the central banks in the region gradually took control of prices and could achieve price stability by the end of the 1990s. Economic developments of the 2000s stimulated rapid developments in the financial markets in Central Asian states. Large inflows of capital and foreign exchange into these economies in the form of export receipts, remittances, foreign direct investment, and external borrowing by banks have supported economic growth and financial market developments. Remittances have recently developed into an important source of foreign exchange for the Kyrgyz Republic and Tajikistan.[3] They have contributed to growth and poverty reduction, but also have turned into a policy challenge. One of the issues arising from large inflows of remittances is that the latter contribute to the growing inflow of foreign currency in the Central Asian economies that is beyond the control of monetary authorities.[4]

Central banks in the region have recently gained more importance and control, and the framework of monetary policy has evolved over the period of transition in these economies. In the earlier period, central banks' policies were characterized by targeting money growth by means of conducting a tight monetary policy to take control of inflation through managing the money supply. As local currencies continued depreciating in the late 1990s, the countries' policymakers became concerned with the external balances and the stability of local money relative to major currencies (mainly the US dollar). Gradual liberalization of exchange rate regimes and of the capital account increased exchange rate volatility. An important means of supporting stable exchange rates proved to be foreign exchange interventions. At this stage of development, currency substitution might largely impede the effects of the monetary policy in Central Asian economies, as large amounts of foreign currency in circulation increase the part of money supply that is not under the control of central banks. As this affects domestic money demand, exchange rates become more volatile. Such instruments as official interest rates have limited efficiency due to thin financial sectors and underdeveloped financial intermediation. It is worth reiterating the motives to hold foreign currency in the three economies. First of all, a memory of macroeconomic instability and high inflation explains people's concern about the stability of local currencies. This is particularly true for Tajikistan, where actual macroeconomic stabilization started only in the 2000s. In Kyrgyzstan, the political unrest in 2005 followed by a revolution undermined the building sentiment of credit to national policies and added to the feeling of uncertainty about future economic developments. Second, Kyrgyzstan and Tajikistan remain among the countries with the lowest income per capita. Labour emigration is a widespread phenomenon in these countries with remittances constituting an important source of foreign currency. Furthermore, underdeveloped financial markets and a lack of confidence in local banking institutions hinder households from taking their foreign cash holdings to a bank. In the Kyrgyz Republic, for example, only 5 per cent of the population have a bank account (EBRD, 2008). In Tajikistan, the situation is aggravated by the considerable size of the shadow economy (due to drug trafficking), where monetary transactions are most probably performed in a foreign currency.[5] The current situation in Kazakhstan differs as this country has a lot more developed financial markets and a high income per capita. Feige (2003), however, estimates that in 2001 a foreign currency accounted for about 95 per cent of the total currency holdings in Kazakhstan. Integration into world financial markets, presence of foreign banks and oil dependence do constitute the factors that drive dollarization though in a slightly different form, that is financial dollarization. All the countries in the region have recently seen important inflows of the foreign capital and foreign exchange (see Appendix, Table 9.A2).

A MODEL OF CURRENCY SUBSTITUTION

The model presented in this section is based on a standard money-in-the-utility function model with two currencies. This framework has been employed by several other studies which examine substitution between domestic and foreign currencies in different countries (Bufman and Leiderman 1993; İmrohoroğlu, 1994; Friedman and Verbetsky, 2001; Selçuk, 2003). In the model residents hold foreign currency as a simple and natural hedge against local inflation due to the motives and contexts described in the previous section. The foreign currency is thus assumed to be stable and trustworthy. Local and foreign currencies can be easily exchanged in the market at the market exchange rate. The model is rather standardized and simplified. There is no production activity in the economy. Agents receive an endowment every period that constitutes their wealth together with holdings of real balances that are unspent in the previous period, the interest rate earned on the bond, and a lump-sum transfer from the government.

The economy consists of a continuum of infinitely lived identical individuals with total measure one. A representative agent is assumed to derive utility from the consumption of a single good and from the liquidity services provided by holdings of domestic and foreign money. Thus, an agent maximizes the expected value of the discounted utility:

$$E_0 \sum_{t=0}^{\infty} \beta^t U(c_t, x_t), \qquad (9.1)$$

where β is a discount factor and c_t is consumption, and x_t denotes liquidity holdings. Money services are produced by using a combination of domestic and foreign real balances in a Constant Elasticity of Substitution (CES) production function:

$$x = [(1 - \alpha)m^{-\rho} + \alpha m^{*-\rho}]^{-\frac{1}{\rho}} \qquad (9.2)$$

where m_t denotes domestic real money balances and m_t^* denotes foreign money balances. Coefficient α is a share of foreign money balances in producing money services. Parameter ρ is used to compute the elasticity of substitution between domestic and foreign currency, and represents the substitutability between two currencies. The money services part of the utility function reflects the willingness of residents to diversify their money holdings portfolio to lower the risk of losing their monetary assets due to economic instability and inflation in home country. The budget constraint of a representative household is as follows:

$$c_t + m_t + m_t^* + b_t$$
$$= y_t + \tau_t + \frac{m_{t-1}}{(1 + \pi_t)} + \frac{m_{t-1}^*(1 + \varepsilon_t)}{(1 + \pi_t)} + \frac{b_{t-1}(1 + r_{t-1})}{(1 + \pi_t)}, \quad (9.3)$$

where r_t is a nominal interest rate on one period bonds between period $t - 1$ and t. Variables π_t and ε_t represent the inflation rate and rate of depreciation of the national currency, respectively. The nominal exchange rate is the ratio between the domestic price level and foreign price level: $E_t = P_t/P_t^*$. The residents care about the stability of the exchange rate and the relative value of the domestic currency to foreign currency. As they assume that the foreign currency is more stable, holding it gives them a certain confidence and conserves the value of their monetary assets. Each period every individual receives an endowment y_t, and a lump-sum transfer from the government, τ_t. Moreover, agents hold financial assets b_t, that give the nominal interest rate r_t between period t and $t + 1$.

The following form of the utility function is assumed:

$$U(c_t, x_t) = \frac{(c_t^{1-\gamma} x_t^{\gamma})^{1-\sigma} - 1}{1 - \sigma}, \quad (9.4)$$

where x is represented by equation (9.2).

Assumed specification of the utility function is used to derive the Euler equations, which are further rearranged in the following estimation equations:

$$\beta \left(\frac{c_{t+1}}{c_t}\right)^{\sigma(\gamma-1)-\gamma} \left(\frac{m_{t+1}}{m_t}\right)^{\gamma(1-\sigma)}$$
$$\times \left[\frac{1 - \alpha + \alpha\left(\frac{m_{t+1}^*}{m_{t+1}}\right)^{-\rho}}{1 - \alpha + \alpha\left(\frac{m_t^*}{m_t}\right)^{-\rho}}\right]^{\gamma(\sigma-1)/\rho} \times \frac{(1 + r_t)}{(1 + \pi_{t+1})} - 1 = d_{1,t+1}, \quad (9.5)$$

$$\frac{\gamma(1-\alpha)\left(\dfrac{c_t}{m_t}\right)}{1-\alpha+\alpha\left(\dfrac{m_t^*}{m_t}\right)^{-\rho}} - (1-\gamma)$$

$$\times \left\{ \left[1 - \beta\left(\frac{c_{t+1}}{c_t}\right)^{\sigma(\gamma-1)-\gamma}\right] \left[\frac{1-\alpha+\alpha\left(\dfrac{m_{t+1}^*}{m_{t+1}}\right)^{-\rho}}{1-\alpha+\alpha\left(\dfrac{m_t^*}{m_t}\right)^{-\rho}}\right]^{\gamma(\sigma-1)/\rho} \right.$$

$$\left. \times \frac{1}{(1+\pi_{t+1})} \right\} = d_{2,t+1} \qquad (9.6)$$

$$(1-\alpha)\left(\frac{m_t^*}{m_t}\right)^{1+\rho} - \alpha - \beta\left(\frac{c_{t+1}}{c_t}\right)^{\sigma(\gamma-1)-\gamma}\left(\frac{m_{t+1}}{m_t}\right)^{\gamma(1-\sigma)}$$

$$\times \left[\frac{1-\alpha+\alpha\left(\dfrac{m_{t+1}^*}{m_{t+1}}\right)^{-\rho}}{1-\alpha+\alpha\left(\dfrac{m_t^*}{m_t}\right)^{-\rho}}\right]^{\gamma(\sigma-1)/\rho} \times \left((1-\alpha)\left(\frac{m_t^*}{m_t}\right)^{1+\rho}(1+\varepsilon_{t+1}) - \alpha\right)$$

$$\times \frac{1}{(1+\pi_{t+1})} = d_{3,t+1} \qquad (9.7)$$

To improve the fit of the model, a specification of the utility function with habit formation is considered:

$$U(c_t, x_t) = \frac{((c_t - \delta c_{t-1})^{1-\gamma}x_t^{\gamma})^{1-\sigma} - 1}{1-\sigma}, \qquad (9.8)$$

where an introduced parameter δ measures the intensity of habit persistence in the consumption decision of the agent.

Hansen's (1982) GMM procedure is applied to estimate the parameters in the system of equations represented by equations (9.5–9.7). in this section. The instruments employed in the estimation are lagged values of the variables used in the estimation. The data used in the empirical investigation are of monthly frequency and span from 2000 to 2008 in the case of Kazakhstan and the Kyrgyz Republic, and only from 2002 in the case of Tajikistan. See Table 9.A1 in the Appendix for description of the data used in the study.

EMPIRICAL RESULTS

The estimation results for each country are reported in Table 9.1. The model is estimated with different interest rates as reported in the table. The parameter estimates for β are economically meaningful and are below unity for every country. Thus, households in these economies value future consumption less than consumption in the present period. The values of the estimates for γ vary from 0.01 to 0.18 among countries depending on the choice of the interest rate. Thus, the share of money in providing utility is significantly lower than the share of consumption.

The share of foreign money holdings in providing monetary services α is estimated between 0.46 and 0.59. This implies quite high efficiency of foreign money and therefore a high level of currency substitution in all three economies.

The elasticity of substitution parameter s is of particular interest. It is assumed to be positive from 0 to infinity. If it equals 0, then the two currencies are complements, but if it exceeds 0, then there is substitutability between the two currencies. Studying dollarization in Canada, İmrohoroğlu (1994) finds that the elasticity of substitution between the US dollar and the Canadian dollar is less than 1. The author explains that this implies little substitution between the two currencies, as the implicit demand for the US dollar does not appear to be responsive to the relative currency price. In the studies by Friedman and Verbetsky (2001) and Selçuk (2003) the elasticity is found to be greater than 1. In this chapter, the elasticity of substitution between the US dollar and local currencies significantly exceeds 1 several times. In the manner of İmrohoroğlu (1994), this implies that holding foreign currency is highly responsive to the relative currency price in Central Asia. In the Kyrgyz Republic and Tajikistan, the parameter ρ was estimated between -0.31 and -0.94, which implies that the elasticity of substitution between domestic and foreign currencies $s = 1/(1 + \rho)$ is between approximately 1.5 and 17. The parameter estimates for ρ could only be estimated in the restricted range of values for Kazakhstan when habit formation in consumption is assumed. The values of ρ vary between -0.70 and -0.87, indicating that substitutability between national and foreign currencies is similarly high in this country.

The relative risk aversion (RRA) parameter σ could not be estimated precisely in most cases and its estimates were sometimes negative. The negative parameter of RRA implies non-convexity of preferences, which poses a difficulty in interpreting results of the estimated model. The problem of negative values of RRA parameters and imprecision of its estimates has been studied in the economic literature.[6] This issue is, however, beyond the subject of the present discussion.

Table 9.1   GMM estimates (utility with habit formation for Kazakhstan)

(a) Kazakhstan

	Refinance rate	Treasury bill	Deposit rate	FFR
β	0.92***(0.00)	0.95***(0.00)	0.96***(0.00)	0.98***(0.00)
α	0.49***(0.00)	0.50***(0.00)	0.50***(0.00)	0.50***(0.00)
γ	0.10***(0.00)	0.12***(0.01)	0.10***(0.01)	0.07***(0.01)
σ	−0.12***(0.01)	−0.13***(0.01)	−0.11***(0.01)	−0.08***(0.01)
δ	0.79***(0.00)	0.78***(0.01)	0.78***(0.03)	0.78***(0.01)
ρ	−0.70***(0.06)	−0.87***(0.02)	−0.85***(0.02)	−0.87***(0.02)
J-statistics	8.49 [0.75]	7.28 [0.84]	7.28 [0.84]	7.85 [0.80]
No. obs	103	103	103	103

(b) Kyrgyz Republic

	Repo rate	MMR	Deposit rate	FFR
β	0.95***(0.00)	0.96***(0.01)	0.94***(0.00)	0.99***(0.00)
α	0.55***(0.01)	0.56***(0.01)	0.56***(0.01)	0.62***(0.03)
γ	0.05***(0.00)	0.06***(0.00)	0.06***(0.00)	0.02***(0.00)
σ	0.02 (0.03)	0.03 (0.08)	0.005 (0.03)	−0.04 (0.01)
ρ	−0.76***(0.08)	−0.72***(0.08)	−0.67***(0.06)	−0.31*(0.17)
J-statistics	5.87 [0.75]	6.60 [0.68]	6.16 [0.72]	5.91 [0.75]
No. obs	94	90	95	95

(c) Tajikistan

	Refinance rate	Interbank rate	Deposit rate	FFR
β	0.89***(0.00)	0.89***(0.00)	0.92***(0.00)	0.98***(0.00)
α	0.54***(0.00)	0.53***(0.00)	0.53***(0.01)	0.47***(0.01)
γ	0.08***(0.00)	0.07***(0.00)	0.06***(0.00)	0.01***(0.00)
σ	0.05 (0.04)	0.07***(0.03)	0.01 (0.03)	−0.02 (0.00)
ρ	−0.69***(0.01)	−0.68***(0.01)	−0.70***(0.01)	−0.94***(0.03)
J-statistics	5.63 [0.86]	5.26 [0.87]	4.97 [0.89]	5.78 [0.83]
No. obs	71	61	71	71

Notes: (a) Standard errors are in parentheses; *P*-values are in brackets; (b) β-discount factor, α-share of foreign money balances in producing money services; $s = 1/(1 + \rho)$-elasticity of currency substitution; (c) ***, ** and * stand for 1, 5 and 10 per cent significance level respectively.

   The habit formation parameter in Kazakhstan δ was estimated at 0.78, which indicates a strong persistence in consumption behaviour. In two other countries, introducing habit persistence did not change significantly the values of the model parameters.

The *J*-test statistic for testing the overidentifying restrictions of the model indicates that the data provide support for the considered model, and the instrumental variables are valid.

IMPLICATIONS FOR SEIGNIORAGE REVENUE

One of the concerns for policymakers is the decline in central banks' seigniorage revenue that is associated with currency substitution. Authors argue that this effect may be significant (Bufman and Leiderman, 1993; Friedman and Verbetsky, 2001). In the context of transition and developing economies the loss of seigniorage revenue is an important issue. Calculating average seigniorage rates during the 1960s and 1970s for a cross-section of countries, Fischer (1982) finds that seigniorage accounts for more than 10 per cent of total government revenue in many less developed countries, especially those with high inflation rates.

In this chapter, the implications for seigniorage revenue are derived from analysing a hypothetical steady state of the presented model. Steady states with different inflation rates π and dollarization α are compared. In the steady state, consumption and real money balances' holdings grow at some constant rate and the population in the home country is assumed to grow at zero rate. The real return on the market portfolio, R, is invariant with respect to both time and inflation rate. The government is assumed to return its seigniorage revenue as a lump-sum transfer to households. Under these conditions, the steady state demand for domestic real money balances can be derived using the optimality conditions from equations (9.5–9.7).

To compute the seigniorage, a monetary concept of seigniorage is used. This approach is suitable for the present model's setup and is simple in computation. In the steady state, the growth rate of money μ is equal to the steady state inflation rate π.

The following parameter values are assumed for simulation exercise: $\gamma = 0.07$ and $\beta = 0.98$. The parameter α will be given values from 0.4 to 0.7, and ρ is assumed to be -0.7. The ratio of consumption over income is assumed to be 0.8.[7] The RRA parameter σ is assumed to be 0, since it was not estimated precisely and its estimated value was negative in some cases. The underlying assumption of Purchasing Power Parity (PPP) is used to consider two scenarios of the domestic currency depreciation. In the first scenario, I assume that the foreign inflation rate $\pi^* = 0$ while the domestic inflation rate changes from 0.2 to 50 per cent. In this scenario, the depreciation rate, ε moves together with the domestic inflation rate and $\varepsilon = \pi$. In the second scenario, the foreign inflation rate is constant but equals

Table 9.2   Simulated seigniorage/GDP ratios

(a) Scenario 1: $\varepsilon = \pi$ ($\pi^* = 0\,\%$)

$\pi,\%$	α			
	0.4	0.5	0.6	0.7
0.2	0.48	0.28	0.11	0.03
0.5	0.98	0.53	0.19	0.05
1	1.42	0.67	0.22	0.05
2	1.58	0.61	0.18	0.04
3	1.41	0.48	0.14	0.03
4	1.19	0.38	0.1	0.02
5	0.98	0.3	0.08	0.02
6	0.82	0.24	0.06	0.014
8	0.59	0.16	0.04	0.01
10	0.44	0.12	0.03	0.007
20	0.16	0.04	0.01	0.003
30	0.09	0.02	0.006	0.001
50	0.05	0.01	0.003	0.0008

(b) Scenario 2: $\varepsilon = \pi$ ($\pi^* = 5\,\%$)

$\pi,\%$	α			
	0.4	0.5	0.6	0.7
0.2	0.62	0.59	0.49	0.28
0.5	1.36	1.27	1.01	0.52
1	2.25	2.03	1.48	0.66
2	3.3	2.75	1.67	0.6
3	3.83	2.91	1.51	0.48
4	4.07	2.81	1.28	0.37
5	4.15	2.61	1.07	0.29
6	4.11	3.37	0.9	0.24
8	3.86	1.91	0.65	0.16
10	3.51	1.53	0.48	0.12
20	2.03	0.65	0.18	0.04
30	1.31	0.38	0.1	0.02
50	0.76	0.21	0.06	0.01

Note: $\beta = 0.98$, $\gamma = 0.08$, $\rho = -0.7$, $\sigma = 0$, $c/y = 0.8$

5 per cent. This scenario implies that the domestic currency depreciates at a slower rate than does the domestic inflation rate.

Table 9.2 presents the results of the seigniorage revenue simulation. The simulated values are presented as the ratio to GDP in per cent. This ratio was calculated for different values of the domestic inflation rate π and for different values of the share of foreign money balances α.

The results in Table 9.2(a) show that the ratio of seigniorage to GDP increases with the rate of inflation, but only to a certain level of the inflation rate. The seigniorage revenue reaches its peak when the inflation rate is 2 per cent when the dollarization level $\alpha = 0.4$. After that it gradually decreases. This result is similar to that obtained by Friedman and Verbetsky (2001) who found that the government achieves its highest seigniorage revenue at an inflation rate of 1–3 per cent depending on the level of dollarization. More important is the relation between dollarization and seigniorage revenue. The results show that the latter is a decreasing function of dollarization. The higher α is the lower is the ratio of seigniorage revenue to GDP.

In scenario 2 (Table 9.2(b)), the ratio of government revenue from seigniorage-to-GDP is higher than in the first scenario for each level of dollarization and each inflation rate. The agents prefer to hold more domestic money when there is inflation abroad. Moreover, they hold more domestic currency when the domestic inflation rate is lower than the foreign inflation rate.

The findings in this section support the hypothesis that decreasing seigniorage revenue is caused by increasing dollarization level. For further analysis, actual seigniorage-to-GDP ratios were calculated using data from the countries' central banks. The actual seigniorage-to-GDP ratio was calculated using data on the monetary base following the monetary seigniorage concept. Results are presented in Table 9.3. Both simulated and actual ratio of seigniorage-to-GDP decrease when the dollarization level α increases. There is, however, no significant variation in actual annual seigniorage revenue over time.

ECONOMIC WELFARE AND DOLLARIZATION

By affecting the seigniorage revenues of the government and thus the amount of lump-sum transfers paid to the public, currency substitution impacts the welfare of households. Dollarization itself stems from several factors that have an effect on economic welfare, that is high rates of inflation, rapid depreciation of domestic money, and so on. Holding foreign money thus becomes a way for households to preserve their wealth.

In this section, the potential implications of dollarization and currency substitution for welfare are discussed. The baseline assumption is that the welfare of a household changes if dollarization α increases, that is $\alpha_0 < \alpha_1$ and $u(\alpha_0) > u(\alpha_1)$. To calculate the welfare costs of dollarization in a

Table 9.3   Actual and simulated seigniorage/GDP ratios (in per cent)

(a) Kazakhstan

Period	Inflation rate (in %)	Dollarization level, α	Simulated seigniorage/ GDP ratio	Actual seigniorage/ GDP ratio
2000	13	0.51	0.07	0.05
2001	8	0.64	0.02	0.05
2002	6	0.6	0.06	0.05
2003	6	0.47	0.35	0.06
2004	7	0.43	0.48	0.08
2005	8	0.42	0.46	0.06
2006	9	0.35	0.94	0.096
2007	11	0.32	1.07	0.07

(b) Kyrgyz Republic

Period	Inflation rate (in %)	Dollarization level, α	Simulated seigniorage/ GDP ratio	Actual seigniorage/ GDP ratio
2000	19	0.58	0.02	0.014
2001	7	0.59	0.06	0.005
2002	2	0.62	0.14	0.002
2003	3	0.64	0.08	0.003
2004	4	0.7	0.02	0.005
2005	4	0.73	0.01	0.005
2006	6	0.66	0.03	0.009
2007	10	0.52	0.09	0.0016

(c) Tajikistan

Period	Inflation rate (in %)	Dollarization level, α	Simulated seigniorage/ GDP ratio	Actual seigniorage/ GDP ratio
2002	12.3	0.49	0.1	0.01
2003	16.3	0.49	0.07	0.01
2004	7.1	0.6	0.05	0.003
2005	7.1	0.56	0.09	0.003
2006	10	0.7	0.007	0.004
2007	13.1	0.75	0.002	0.015

Table 9.4   Consumption compensation for increasing dollarization

π,%	ΔC/GDP, %	
	Scenario 1: ε = π	Scenario 2: π* = 5%
0.2	−0.56	1.56
0.5	−0.77	1.42
1	−1.01	1.17
2	−1.28	0.68
3	−1.42	0.24
4	−1.49	−0.11
5	−1.53	−0.4
6	−1.56	−0.62
8	−1.59	−0.93
10	−1.61	−1.12
20	−1.639	−1.47
30	−1.644	−1.56
50	−1.647	−1.61

Note: α changes from 0.5 to 0.6, β = 0.98, ρ = −0.7, γ = 0.08, c/y = 0.8.

steady state with a given rate of inflation, one needs to compute the percentage decrease in consumption per capita that would generate the same welfare change as that from moving from the original level of dollarization α_0 to a higher level of dollarization α_1. Or it is necessary to find such Δc that would return the household to its original level of utility: $u(c, \alpha_0) = u(c + \Delta c, \alpha_1)$.

The welfare loss is computed for a change in dollarization α from 0.5 to 0.6 for different rates of inflation. Two scenarios of exchange rate determination from the previous section are analysed. Table 9.4 presents the results of the simulated changes in welfare represented as percentage in GDP. Negative values of the consumption compensation imply welfare gains, while positive values imply welfare loss. These results reveal that dollarization in fact brings gains in welfare that can be as large as 1.65 per cent of GDP if the domestic inflation rate reaches 50 per cent in the case of zero foreign inflation. The welfare gain is an increasing function of inflation. This finding can be explained by the fact that an increase in foreign money holdings hedges households from losses due to depreciating domestic money. The higher the inflation rate, the higher the gain from an increase in foreign currency holdings. This also implies that the loss in seigniorage revenue due to increasing dollarization is exceeded by the gains from holding foreign currency.

In the second scenario, holding foreign money brings welfare losses if the domestic inflation rate is lower than the inflation rate in the foreign economy. In this scenario, holding dollars is not optimal since the domestic currency is stronger when foreign inflation exceeds inflation at home. Thus, the welfare loss occurs due to uncertainty about the foreign inflation rate and about the exchange rate between local and foreign currencies. The seigniorage loss is greater than the gain in household consumption as a result of switching to foreign currency. Hence, dollarization in an inflationary environment with depreciating local currency vis-à-vis foreign currency becomes welfare generating. The welfare cost depends on the ability of resident households to diversify their money holdings in such a way as to avoid the risk of sudden depreciation of either currency.

CONCLUSION

This chapter establishes good substitutability between domestic and foreign currencies in three economies of Central Asia – Kazakhstan, the Kyrgyz Republic and Tajikistan. Currency substitution and dollarization are shown to be of significant magnitude and importance in these transition countries. The analysis of the steady state implications of dollarization reveals decreasing seigniorage revenue of central banks due to currency substitution. An increase in dollarization index from 0.4 to 0.5, decreases seigniorage-to-GDP ratio by almost half.

The welfare analysis comprises the loss of seigniorage and a change in welfare due to switching to a foreign currency. The findings of the welfare analysis are sensitive to the scenario of domestic currency depreciation. If foreign inflation is zero per cent, then switching to holding dollars is a welfare generating decision. Though the government loses its revenues from money issuance, the overall effect of currency substitution can be positive. In the second scenario, however, holding dollars decreases households' wealth if inflation in the home country is lower than inflation abroad. Residents choose to hold foreign currency, which in fact has less purchasing power and depreciates at a higher rate than the domestic currency. Once the domestic inflation rate outpaces foreign inflation, switching to dollars starts bringing gains in welfare. Dollarization thus affects household wealth from two sides: decreasing lump-sum transfers from the government and hedging motives against domestic inflation.

Currency substitution and dollarization though negatively affecting seigniorage do not necessarily bring welfare loss. Governments willing to de-dollarize local economies should be primarily concerned with the stability of local currencies rather than with restricting foreign money holdings as foreign currency, will remain in demand as long as it brings a gain in welfare and is considered more stable than the local currency.

NOTES

1. Here, no formal distinction is made between dollarization and currency substitution, and the two terms are used interchangeably and refer to foreign currency holdings of residents.
2. IMF Staff estimates that in Kazakhstan oil accounts for more than 50 per cent of exports and 40 per cent of government revenues (IMF, 2009).
3. IMF (2007) estimates that Tajikistan has one of the highest remittances-to-GDP ratio among former Soviet Union economies.
4. IMF (2006) states that remittances are used to finance consumption and household construction rather than investment in productive capacity and therefore discourage savings. Large inflows of foreign exchange are difficult to measure and hamper monetary management.
5. Pomfret (2006) estimates trade in drugs and weapons to account for around 30–50 per cent of all economic activity in Tajikistan.
6. Negative and sometimes statistically insignificant values of the estimated parameter of relative risk aversion (RRA) and intertemporal elasticity of substitution (IES) have been obtained and discussed to different extents in studies on consumption behaviour through estimating the Euler equations by GMM. See, for example, Hansen and Singleton (1982), Hall (1988), Mao (1990), Holman (1998) and others. In his study, Pozzi (2003) proposed an explanation for the imprecision in estimating the RRA parameter and its estimates' negative values.
7. This is an average ratio of private consumption-to-GDP or total income across three countries and the period.

REFERENCES

Baliño, Tomás, Adam Bennett and Eduardo Borensztein (1999), 'Monetary policy in dollarized economies', *IMF Occasional Paper*, No. 171.

Bufman, Gil and Leonardo Leiderman (1993), 'Currency substitution under non-expected utility: some empirical evidence', *Journal of Money, Credit, and Banking*, **25** (3), 320–25.

European Bank for Reconstruction and Development (EBRD) Transition Report (2008), *Growth in Transition*, London: EBRD.

Feige, Edgar L. (2003), 'Dynamics of currency substitution, asset substitution and de acto dollarisation and euroisation in transition countries', *Comparative Economic Studies*, **45** (3), 358–83.

Fischer, Stanley (1982), 'Seigniorage and the case for a national money', *Journal of Political Economy*, **90** (2), 295–313.

Friedman, Alla and Alexey Verbetsky (2001), 'Currency substitution in Russia', *Economics Education and Research Consortium*, Working Paper, No. 01/05

Gürgen, Emine, Harry Snoek, Jon Craig, Jimmy McHugh, Ivailo Izvorski and Ron van Rooden (1999), 'Economic reforms in Kazakhstan, Kyrgyz Republic, Tajikistan, Turkmenistan, and Uzbekistan', *IMF Occasional Paper*, No. 183.

Hall, Robert (1988), 'Intertemporal substitution in consumption', *Journal of Political Economy*, **96** (2), 339–57.

Hansen, Lars P. (1982) 'Large sample properties of generalized method of moments estimators', *Econometrica*, **50** (4), 1029–54.

Hansen, Lars and Kenneth Singleton (1982), 'Generalized instrumental variables of nonlinear rational expectations models', *Econometrica*, **50** (5), 1269–85.

Harrison, Barry and Yulia Vymyatnina (2007), 'Currency substitution in a de-dollarizing economy: the case of Russia', *BOFIT Discussion Papers*, No. 3.

Havrylyshyn, Oleh and Christian H. Beddies (2003), 'Dollarisation in the former Soviet Union: from hysteria to hysteresis', *Comparative Economic Studies*, **45** (3), 329–57.

Holman, Jill A. (1998), 'GMM estimation of a money-in-the-utility function model: the implications of functional forms', *Journal of Money, Credit and Banking*, **30** (4), 679–98.

Horváth, Balázs and Rodolfo Maino (2006), 'Monetary transmission mechanisms in Belarus', *IMF Working Paper*, No. 06/246.

IMF (2009), 'IMF Country Report: Republic of Kazakhstan', No. 09/300, October, available at: http://www.imf.org/external/pubs/ft/scr/2009/cr09300.pdf (accessed January 2010).

IMF (2007), 'IMF Country Report: Republic of Tajikistan', No. 07/144, April, available at: http://www.imf.org/external/pubs/ft/scr/2007/cr07144.pdf (accessed May 2008).

IMF (2006), 'IMF Regional Economic Outlook for Middle East and Central Asia', September, available at: http://www.imf.org/external/pubs/ft/reo/2006/eng/02/mreo0906.pdf (accessed May 2008).

İmrohoroğlu, Selahattin (1994), 'GMM estimates of currency substitution between the Canadian dollar and the U.S. dollar', *Journal of Money, Credit and Banking*, **26** (4), 792–808.

Mao, Ching-Sheng (1990), 'Hypothesis testing and finite sample properties of generalized method of moments estimators: a Monte Carlo study', *Federal Reserve Bank of Richmond Working Paper*, 90–12.

Pomfret, Richard (2006), *The Central Asian Economies After Independence*, Princeton: Princeton University Press.

Pozzi, Lorenzo (2003), 'The coefficient of relative risk aversion: a Monte Carlo study investigating small sample estimator problems', *Economic Modelling*, **20** (5), 923–40.

Sahay, Ratna and Carlos A. Végh (1995), 'Dollarisation in transition economies: evidence and policy implications', *IMF Working Paper*, No. 95/96.

Selçuk, Faruk (2003), 'Currency substitution: new evidence from emerging economies', *Economics Letters*, **78** (2), 219–24.

World Bank (2008), 'Migration and Remittances Factbook 2008', available at: www.worldbank.org, March.

APPENDIX

Table 9.A1   Data description

Series	Time span	Source
(a) Kazakhstan		
Consumer Price Index	Jan 2000–Dec 2008	IMF
Deposits denominated in domestic and foreign currency (in million Kazakhstan tenge (KZT))	Jan 2000–Dec 2008	NBK
Industrial production (in million KZT)	Jan 2000–Dec 2008	ASRK
Refinancing rate of the National Bank (in per cent)	Jan 2000–Dec 2008	IMF
Treasury bill rate (in per cent)	Jan 2000–Dec 2008	IMF
Average deposit rate (in per cent)	Jan 2000–Dec 2008	NBK
Nominal exchange rate (KZT/USD) (in KZT)	Jan 2000–Dec 2008	IMF
(b) Kyrgyz Republic		
Consumer Price Index	Jan 2000–Mar 2008	IMF
Deposits denominated in domestic and foreign currency (in million Kyrgyzstan Som (KGS))	Jan 2000–Mar 2008	NBKR
Industrial Production (in million KGS)	Jan 2000–Mar 2008	NSCKR
Rate on repo operations of the NBKR	Jan 2000–Mar 2008	NBKR
Money market rate	Jan 2000–Mar 2008	IMF
Deposit rate	Jan 2000–Mar 2008	IMF
Nominal exchange rate (KGS/USD) (in KGS)	Jan 2000–Mar 2008	IMF
(c) Tajikistan		
Consumer Price Index	Jan 2002–Feb 2008	IMF
Deposits denominated in domestic and foreign currency (in million Tajikistan Somoni (TJS))	Jan 2002–Feb 2008	NBT
Industrial production (in million TJS)	Jan 2002–Feb 2008	NBT
Wages (in TJS)	Jan 2002–Feb 2008	NBT
Official rate of the NBT (in per cent)	Jan 2002–Feb 2008	NBT
Interbank rate (in per cent)	Jan 2002–Mar 2008	NBT
Deposit rate (in per cent)	Jan 2002–Feb 2008	IMF
Nominal exchange rate (TJS/USD) (in TJS)	Jan 2002–Feb 2008	IMF

Notes: NBK – National Bank of Kazakhstan; NBKR – National Bank of the Kyrgyz Republic; NBT – National Bank of Tajikistan; ASRK – Agency of Statistics of the Republic of Kazakhstan; NSCKR – National Statistical Committee of the Kyrgyz Republic; IMF – International Monetary Fund.

Table 9.A2   Capital inflows in Central Asia

	2000	2001	2002	2003	2004	2005	2006	2007	2008
Remittances* (million USD)									
Kazakhstan	122	171	205	147	166	178	187	223	192
Kyrgyzstan	9	11	37	78	189	322	481	715	1232
Tajikistan	–	–	79	146	252	467	1019	1691	2544
FDI** (million USD)									
Kazakhstan	1278	2861	2164	2213	5436	2123	6630	6900	10732
Kyrgyzstan	−7	−1	5	46	132	43	182	208	265
Tajikistan	24	10	36	32	272	55	66	160	190

Note: Data on FDI are estimates.

Source: * World Bank (2008) (data as updated in November 2009). ** EBRD Transition Report, 2008.

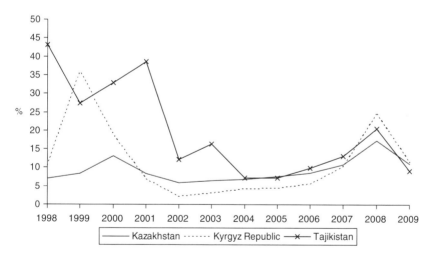

Note: Figures for 2009 are estimates.

Source: EBRD (2008).

Figure 9.A1   Inflation in Central Asia

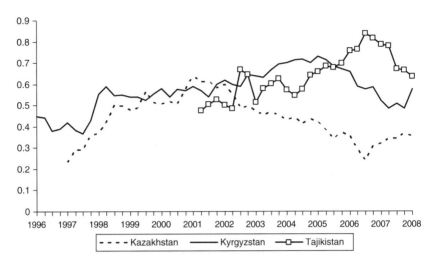

Note: Dollarization Index is computed as a ratio of foreign currency-denominated deposits to total deposits.

Source: Data from the websites of the central banks of the countries: National Bank of the Republic of Kazakhstan, National Bank of the Kyrgyz Republic and National Bank of Tajikistan.

Figure 9.A2   Dollarization in Central Asia

10. The euro as a safe haven asset in Central, Eastern and South-Eastern Europe

Helmut Stix[1]

10.1 INTRODUCTION

The ownership and use of financial assets denominated in foreign currency is considered to be a widespread phenomenon in some countries of Central and Eastern Europe (CEE) and South-Eastern Europe (SEE). In light of this fact, we analyse whether euro-denominated financial assets have been used as safe haven assets in this region.[2]

Why is this question important? Per se, de facto euroization has significant implications for economic policy – to name some examples: it constrains the effectiveness of monetary policy through the interest rate channel; it has implications on the choice of an exchange rate regime; it affects the extent of the pass-through of exchange rate movements on inflation through indexation; balance sheet mismatches might impair on monetary stability. From a fiscal policy perspective direct implications arise as the existence of substantial foreign currency cash balances has an impact on the size of unrecorded transactions and hence tax revenues, notwithstanding the fact that seigniorage revenues are lowered. While these problems are already significant in normal times, they are magnified in times of heightened uncertainty if agents tend to shift their financial portfolios towards save haven (foreign currency-denominated) assets.

For this reason, it is very important to unveil the extent of euroization and the various dimensions associated with it. This will help to better understand how monetary policy can best be conducted, how the financial crisis has affected the extent of euroization and how euroization is likely to evolve in the near future. The focus on the various dimensions of financial euroization is important, as the degree of impairment on economic policy that arises from financial euroization depends on many aspects associated with financial euroization. For example, the existence of high foreign currency cash balances raises different policy issues than the existence of deposits denominated in foreign currency.

Against this background, this chapter presents survey evidence on the extent and the determinants of euroization in CEE and SEE. This survey, commissioned by the Oesterreichische Nationalbank and entitled 'OeNB Euro Survey', has been conducted in 11 Central, Eastern and South-Eastern European (CESEE) countries and provides information which goes beyond previously available aggregate statistics: first, the survey allows for country comparisons based on harmonized data. Second, the survey contains information on the size of foreign currency cash (FCC) holdings as well as their currency composition. This allows presentation of direct estimates about the extent of currency substitution. Third, the survey provides information on the motives behind foreign currency-denominated asset holdings. Fourth, the survey provides information on various factors that have been shown or that are considered to be important determinants of the extent of euroization but for which information has only rarely been available previously – for example, agents' recollection of past economic turbulences, confidence in the banking system, expectations. The availability of such information allows providing micro-econometrically-based evidence on the causes of currency and asset substitution. Fifth, the survey contains information on how the crisis has affected plans of households and therefore allows us to derive some statements about how euroization will evolve.[3]

Using this information we structure the discussion along a temporal dimension: first, we analyse the extent and the causes of euroization during the years prior to the crisis (the breakdown of Lehman Brothers in September 2008). Then, we discuss how variables of central interest have evolved in the months after the heydays of the crisis. And finally, we use the information obtained about the behaviour of households and survey responses about portfolio plans to discuss how financial euroization is likely to evolve in the near future.[4]

10.2   DATA DESCRIPTION

The primary data source is the 'OeNB Euro Survey' which has been conducted semi-annually since fall 2007 (the latest data used in this chapter are from May/June 2009).[5] The geographical scope of the survey comprised 11 countries, namely six European Union (EU) member states (Bulgaria, Czech Republic, Hungary, Poland, Slovakia and Romania) and five EU candidate or potential candidate countries (Albania, Bosnia and Herzegovina, Croatia, Former Yugoslav Republic (FYR) of Macedonia and Serbia).[6] Slovakia has been dropped from the sample with the introduction of the euro. In each country and in each survey wave face-to-face interviews were conducted with about 1 000 persons aged 15+. The sample was selected via a multi-stage stratified random sample procedure, with the exception of Bulgaria, where quota sampling was applied. Results are representative of the respective population structure in all countries but Poland, where only the population of the ten largest cities was sampled (for further details, see Scheiber and Stix, 2009).

The most important questions asked in the survey pertain to the currency composition and amounts of FCC holdings and FCDs as well as to the motives for holding FCC and FCDs. Furthermore, the survey contains information on a number of other aspects which are of potential relevance for agents' decision to hold foreign currency-denominated assets: the perception of the economic situation and exchange rate and inflation expectations, the impact of the crisis and trust in the national currency and in various domestic institutions.

The questionnaire also contains several questions on the value of financial assets and answers will be used to project the aggregate amount of foreign currency circulating in a given country. Of course, caution is warranted in this context. First, due to the sensitive nature of these questions it can be assumed that underreporting regarding the size of asset holdings is very likely. Therefore, any results relating to amounts should be regarded as constituting a lower bound of actual figures.

Second, figures may be biased because of item non-response. On average across all countries, about 20 per cent of the respondents who report euro cash holdings refused to state the respective amount. Varying non-response rates could bias results if item non-response is not random.[7]

Third, the 'OeNB Euro Survey' focuses on individuals as opposed to households. Consequently, the questionnaire addresses personal holdings. This approach might constitute a problem in those cases for which it is difficult to distinguish between personal and household holdings (for example in the case of a couple with joint holdings). The questionnaire accounts for this issue by asking whether the interviewed person owns foreign currency holdings personally or jointly (together with a partner).

In light of these limitations – in particular underreporting and non-randomness of item non-response – it is advisable not to take the projected aggregate figures too literally and not to rely on a single indicator alone. Therefore, Scheiber and Stix (2009) have compared survey-based aggregate amounts with other survey evidence from neutral statements about the behaviour of fellow inhabitants, not involving any amounts. Reassuringly, the results from the projections and the results from the secondary evidence yield a rather consistent picture in a cross-country perspective. Furthermore, results from the 'OeNB Euro Survey' were also compared with other surveys, if possible. For example, some questions were formulated similar to questions contained in the Eurobarometer of the European Commission. A comparison shows that results from both surveys are highly correlated.

In summary, we think that, despite the likely presence of survey biases and the fact that the top of the wealth distribution will not be adequately represented in the survey results, the survey is very useful for cross-country comparisons. For the question asked in this chapter, namely whether euro assets have been used as safe haven assets, it is particularly informative because the survey unveils information about the behaviour of the broad public, which is of great relevance for policymakers.

10.3   BEFORE THE CRISIS: HIGH PERSISTENCE OF ASSET SUBSTITUTION

10.3.1   Extent of Currency Substitution Significant in SEE and Economically Irrelevant in CEE

The surveys provide evidence about foreign currency cash holdings from several dimensions. The first dimension concerns the dissemination of cash holdings among the population – focusing solely on the ownership of FCC without regard to amounts. Figure 10.1, which shows the share of respondents who answer that they hold EUR or USD cash, reveals two main results: first, the share of respondents who hold euro cash reaches substantial levels in some countries and varies considerably between countries. Second, euro banknotes clearly dominate in importance over USD banknotes.

In six countries at least every fourth respondent reports euro cash holdings, with the highest shares in FYR Macedonia (43 per cent), Serbia (39 per cent) and Albania (32 per cent). Still substantial, but slightly lower dissemination shares were obtained for Croatia, Slovakia and the Czech Republic (around 25 per cent). In the remaining countries, shares range from 9 per cent to 15 per cent. In contrast, US dollar cash only seems to play some role in Albania (7 per cent), Czech Republic and Poland.

For countries in the vicinity of the euro area and/or which are relatively rich, like the Czech Republic and Slovakia, it can be suspected that euro cash holdings do not serve as a store of value but rather to settle transactions in the euro area (travel activities) and accordingly amounts should be low in value and economically insignificant from the aggregate view of the respective economies.

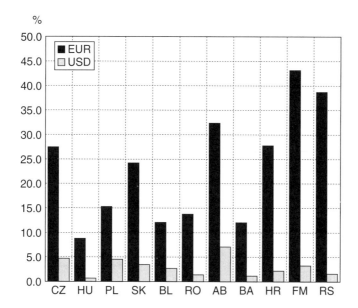

Notes: Data from 'OeNB Euro Survey' fall wave 2007 and spring wave 2008.
CZ: Czech Republic; HU: Hungary; PL: Poland; SK: Slovakia; BL: Bulgaria; RO:
Romania; AB: Albania; BA: Bosnia and Herzegovina; HR: Croatia; FM: FYR Macedonia;
RS: Serbia.

Source: Scheiber and Stix (2009).

Figure 10.1   Share of respondents holding EUR and USD

In order to analyse this conjecture, Figure 10.2 summarizes the relative importance of two motives behind euro cash balances.[8] The results support the view that motives differ across countries. In CEE, euro cash is mainly held to make payments in the euro area whereas the store of value function of cash is significantly less important. In SEE, results are detrimental, with the store of value function being more important than the transaction motive.

A similar picture can be obtained by analysing amounts (summarized in Figure 10.3) – those who answered that they hold euro cash where asked to indicate the amount (in categories). Nominal median euro amounts vary between EUR 90 in Slovakia to about EUR 734 in Serbia. In general, the results are in accordance with the contention that euro cash is being held for different reasons in CEE than in SEE. In the former group of countries the median is EUR 190 while in the later it is EUR 550.[9] Overall, this impression gets attenuated if median amounts are adjusted for differences

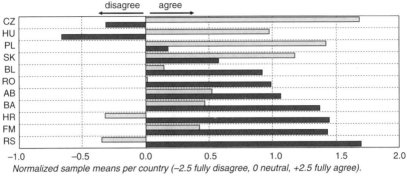

Note: Respondents who said they held euro cash were asked whether they agreed or disagreed on a scale from 1 (fully agree) to 6 (fully disagree) to a list of motives for holding euro cash (see legend). Data from 'OeNB Euro Survey' fall wave 2007 and spring wave 2008. CZ: Czech Republic; HU: Hungary; PL: Poland; SK: Slovakia; BL: Bulgaria; RO: Romania; AB: Albania; BA: Bosnia and Herzegovina; HR: Croatia; FM: FYR Macedonia; RS: Serbia.

Source: Scheiber and Stix (2009).

Figure 10.2   Motives for holding euro cash

using purchasing power parity (PPP) adjusted exchange rates as countries in SEE are relatively poorer than countries in CEE.

In preliminary summary, we note that a high proportion of respondents in SEE hold euro cash, and that the amounts being held are comparatively large. While the share of respondents holding euro cash is also considerable in CEE, the amounts reported are substantially lower. This leads us to the conclusion that the amount of euro cash in circulation is considerably higher in SEE than in CEE.

In order to assess the economic importance of euro cash holdings, Scheiber and Stix (2009) calculate a currency substitution index (CSI). This index expresses the estimated amount of foreign currency cash in circulation as a percentage of total currency in circulation (local currency in circulation plus foreign currency cash holdings, see Feige and Dean, 2004). Again, it should be noted that these projections are based on a series of simplifying assumptions and results should be treated as indicative only and focus mainly on cross-country differences.[10]

The results, summarized in Figure 10.4, confirm the substantial role of FCC in SEE countries. Projected foreign currency circulation ranges from 2 per cent to 22 per cent (Hungary, Romania) in the EU member states

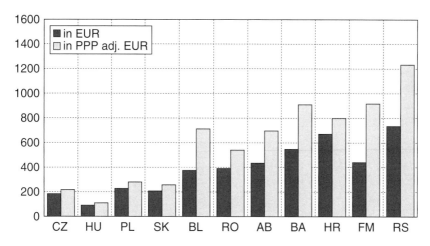

Notes: The chart shows median holdings of euro. Values are based on categorical answers. PPP adjustment using PPP exchange rates from the IMF. Data from 'OeNB Euro Survey" fall wave 2007 and spring wave 2008.
CZ: Czech Republic; HU: Hungary; PL: Poland; SK: Slovakia; BL: Bulgaria; RO: Romania; AB: Albania; BA: Bosnia and Herzegovina; HR: Croatia; FM: FYR Macedonia; RS: Serbia.

Source: Scheiber and Stix (2009).

Figure 10.3   Respondents holding euro cash (median)

and from 27 per cent to 76 per cent in the Balkan countries. Concerning the last group of countries the results suggest two clusters: FYR Macedonia and Serbia with shares higher than two-thirds and Albania, Bosnia and Herzegovina and Croatia with shares around 30 per cent – to put these figures into perspective: values of more than 50 per cent (about 33 per cent) suggest that the amount of foreign currency cash is higher than (about one half) the amount of local currency cash. These high shares of euro circulation in total currency circulation are striking, in particular, given the fact that the underlying figures result solely from survey answers (and in particular stated amounts). Given the assumed underestimation of survey-based amounts, the true degree of currency substitution can be suspected to be even higher.

10.3.2   Persistent Deposits Substitution

As the extent of deposit substitution in CESEE countries has been summarized in other places (for example, ECB, 2008), we do not want to inquire in great detail about country differences. In brief, private households hold

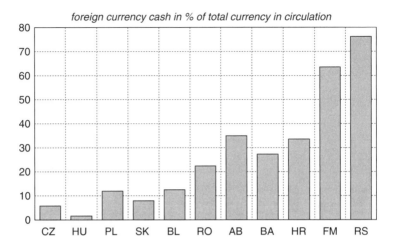

Notes: Data about foreign currency cash holdings from 'OeNB Euro Survey' fall wave
2007 and spring wave 2008.
CZ: Czech Republic; HU: Hungary; PL: Poland; SK: Slovakia; BL: Bulgaria; RO:
Romania; AB: Albania; BA: Bosnia and Herzegovina; HR: Croatia; FM: FYR Macedonia;
RS: Serbia.

Source: Scheiber and Stix (2009) and national central banks.

Figure 10.4   Currency substitution index

between 80 per cent and 90 per cent of their deposits in foreign currency in
Serbia and Croatia and between 40 per cent and 60 per cent in the remaining SEE countries. For the CEE countries these shares are substantially
lower, ranging from only 4 per cent to 15 per cent. For all countries, the
majority of these foreign currency holdings are denominated in euro.

Figure 10.5 depicts the temporal evolution of deposit substitution from
1999 to 2008. For the SEE countries, three observations are noteworthy:
first and foremost, although some temporal changes can be observed, it
is striking that the deposit substitution levels have remained very high
until 2008 – even for countries with very stable exchange rates and moderate inflation rates. As a case in point, even in Bulgaria and Bosnia and
Herzegovina which have a currency board arrangement, still between 50
per cent and 60 per cent of deposits are denominated in foreign currency.
Second, some countries saw an increase until 2001. This is likely to reflect
the euro cash changeover which led to inflows into the banking system.
Third, we stipulate that the increase in Serbia and Albania until 2005 has
been caused by a substitution of foreign currency cash holdings for foreign
currency deposits. This reflects growing trust into the banking system.

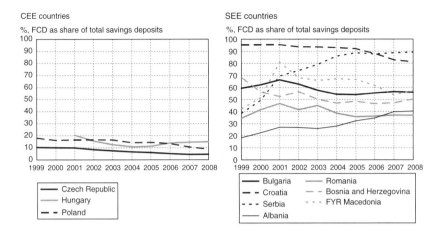

CEE countries

%, FCD as share of total savings deposits

SEE countries

%, FCD as share of total savings deposits

Czech Republic
Hungary
Poland

Bulgaria   Romania
Croatia   Bosnia and Herzegovina
Serbia   FYR Macedonia
Albania

Notes: FCD = foreign currency deposits. Entries for Bosnia and Herzegovina comprise savings deposits of both private households and the corporate sector. Deposits data for Hungary before 2001 are not available.

Source: National central banks.

Figure 10.5   Degree of deposit substitution in CESEE, 1999–2008

10.3.3   Structural Causes of Euroization and Reasons for High Cash Preference

The previous analysis has identified two striking results about financial euroization in some CESEE countries. First, the analysis of the temporal evolution of deposit substitution reveals a high degree of persistence in the sense that agents do only slowly adjust their portfolios to economic fundamentals. This is surprising given that the periods of economic and political turbulences happened already a while ago and that, in the years prior to the global financial crisis, the economic and political environment has stabilized in many countries, with rather low inflation rates and predictable economic policies. Nevertheless, euroization has continued to be present. This raises the question why agents continue to hold foreign currency deposits (and forego higher interest rates for deposits denominated in local currency)?

Second, cash – and in particular euro cash – holdings seem to be very important in some countries. How can this be explained (and why do agents forego interest rate earning at all)?

The literature has provided many important insights into the possible

causes for the observed euroization persistence. One strand of the literature highlights the role of network externalities and the role of transaction costs (Feige et al., 2003; Oomes, 2003; De Freitas, 2004; Reding and
Morales, 2004, for example). Accordingly, the more foreign currencies are
used by other people the lower are the associated transaction costs and
hence the lower the incentive to use the domestic currency. Another strand
of the literature has identified the lack of confidence in domestic money
or the lack of credibility of economic policy resulting from past periods of
turbulence as important (Feige, 2003; Nicolo et al., 2005). Accordingly,
euroization could be viewed as the 'collateral cost of low institutional
credibility' (Yeyati, 2006, p. 82). An alternative explanation highlights the
development stage of the financial system (Savastano, 1996; Duffy et al.,
2006). It has also been argued and empirically demonstrated that portfolio considerations play an important role for the extent of euroization
(Ize and Yeyati, 2003). This model predicts euroization persistence if the
expected volatility of inflation remains high relative to the volatility of the
real exchange rate – notably an explanation resting on forward looking
aspects.[11]

As the different (partly competing) explanations are difficult to test
empirically, it is not surprising that this issue is far from being settled – and
probably several explanations are applicable. In two papers (Scheiber and
Stix, 2009; Stix, 2009), I have analysed this issue closer and the evidence
suggests that the observed high euroization ratios prior to the economic
and financial crisis are to a significant extent the result of past periods of
turbulences. In some countries past turbulences might have caused some
hysteretic behaviour such that agents hold biased expectations about
the exchange rate or the inflation rate and, consequently, do not or only
very slowly react to economic fundamentals. Moreover, these past events
might have driven euroization at levels from which a reversal is difficult to
achieve because of network effects (Feige et al., 2003). As a consequence,
substantial progress towards stabilization during recent years did not
materialize in substantially declining euroization rates.

These results suggest that it can take a long time until people adjust their
behaviour and until network effects weaken. For policymakers this implies
that they can do little to change the extent of euroization in the short to
medium term. However, at the same time, our findings also suggest that –
in a first step – progress in economic normalization and in restoring trust
in institutions can lead to lower extent of currency substitution (a substitution of foreign currency cash holdings for foreign currency deposits), a
situation which is easier to handle from an economic policy perspective
than a situation with a high extent of currency substitution.

The second stylized facts – (euro) cash holdings seem to be of significant importance in some SEE countries – is of importance as a lower level of financial intermediation is thought to hinder efficiency and economic growth. A first presumption about the causes of high levels of currency substitution is that this is related to a low density of banking services, and in fact Scheiber and Stix (2009) present some evidence in favour of this argument. However, what is more intriguing, is that Stix (2010) reports a high cash preference even for those individuals who have already a bank account (for example to settle wage payments). How can this be explained?

In a series of regressions, controlling for several potentially important factors, we show that the extent of cash holdings is related to trust in banks and/or the perceived safety of deposits (Stix, 2010). Thus, this result is in line with the finding of Guiso et al. (2004) who detect a relationship between social capital (trust) and cash holdings in Italy. Moreover, people who report that they remember periods when access to savings deposits was restricted still have a higher likelihood of a cash preference than people who do not remember (although this effect is quantitatively small relative to effect of trust in banks). In addition, we find that regional factors also play a role which might be related to the effectiveness of tax authorities and the structure of the economy.

A direct policy implication from this finding is that it is of key importance to build up and to maintain a high level of trust in banks and in the safety of savings deposits. It is also interesting that we can still detect an effect of trust in banks although the banking systems of the SEE countries are modern and mostly in the hands of banks from Western European countries. Obviously, this implies that building up trust can take a considerable length of time.

10.4 DURING THE CRISIS: SOME DEPOSIT WITHDRAWALS

Given the not too distant experience of banking problems, households can be expected to react rather sensitively to changes in the perceived safety of deposits. Also, we think that the same applies to expected devaluations. Changes in the level of trust in banks and changes in the level of trust in the local currency affect two aspects of the portfolio choice: (1) the decision between savings in local currency versus foreign currency; and (2) the decision between deposit holdings versus cash holdings. In this section, we analyse how trust in banks and the perceived safety of deposits as well as agents' expectations of depreciations have evolved during the crisis.

10.4.1 Trust in Banks Deteriorated During the Crisis

In light of the finding from the literature, that trust in banks is very important for financial intermediation (for example, Guiso et al., 2004), the
question of whether the crisis has lowered trust in banks and whether the
loss is permanent has gained considerable attention (for example, Knell
and Stix, 2009; Sapienza and Zingales, 2009). For some of the countries
under analysis in this chapter, this question is of even greater relevance
than for the US or Austria, as banking crises and actual losses of depos-
ited money are still vivid in people's memories. Indeed, the findings from
the 'OeNB Euro Survey' reported in Dvorsky et al. (2009) reveal that
trust in banks diminished in all CESEE countries. In particular, Hungary,
Bulgaria, Romania and Serbia faced a noticeable drop. However, at the
same time, the comparison with values for the US reveals, rather surprisingly, that the loss in banking trust in five CESEE countries is of about the
same magnitude as in the US – and even in the countries with a stronger
decrease, the difference does not seem very sizeable.

Additional evidence can be derived from survey responses about the
perceived safety of savings deposits, which is obviously related to trust
in banks. Figure 10.6 shows the development of the perceived safety of
savings deposits over time. This indicator had recorded a decline at the
time of the fall wave 2008 as compared to the preceding survey wave for
almost all countries (with the exception of FYR Macedonia).[12] In contrast,
the May to June 2009 results of the 'OeNB Euro Survey' suggest a slight
recovery or at least a stabilization in most countries.[13]

We posit that the national and international stabilization efforts
have played a crucial role in stabilizing trust in banks. Also, the exten-
sions of deposit insurance schemes might have played a stabilizing and
trust-building role. Supportive evidence for this hypothesis is presented
in Prean and Stix (2009), who show for the case of Croatia that the
extension of deposit insurance coverage had an immediate, positive and
quite substantial impact on how Croatians assessed the safety of savings
deposits.

10.4.2 . . . and Some Deposit Withdrawals Occurred

An analysis of monetary statistics on household savings deposits confirms the conjecture that households in CESEE countries have reacted,
on average, more sensitively to a loss of trust in banks than have more
advanced economies. In eight out of ten analysed CESEE countries, outflows of household savings deposits occurred in October 2008. Although the
extent of withdrawals varied substantially across countries, this situation

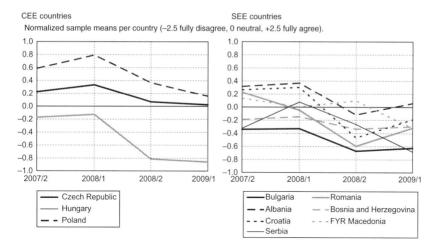

Notes: Respondents were asked whether they agreed or disagreed on a scale from 1 (fully agree) to 6 (fully disagree) to the statement above. In each year the data points refer to the first (spring) and second survey wave (fall). Data from 'OeNB Euro Survey'.

Source: Dvorsky et al. (2009).

Figure 10.6   Consent to the statement: currently, depositing money at banks is very safe

differed markedly from that in Western countries, for example Austria, for which no comparable withdrawals could be observed. However, for most EU member states of the sample, the reaction was considerably weaker and of only short duration as compared to non-EU member states. Figure 10.7 shows the development of total savings deposits of households since September 2007, both for CEE and SEE countries. When analysing the development over the months following October 2008, the changes in savings deposits are blurred by exchange rate movements. As a sizeable share of deposits is denominated in foreign currency, the observed devaluations vis-à-vis the euro (in some countries) inflate the value of foreign currency deposits when expressed in local currency. Therefore, Figure 10.7 presents the development of household savings deposits adjusted for exchange rate movements.

While in October 2008, deposit withdrawals were recorded in all but two of the CESEE countries analysed, developments in CEE and SEE countries differed sharply in the following months. In CEE countries, the great majority of households save in local currency. After September 2008, the growth rate of savings deposits accelerated from pre-crisis levels. This

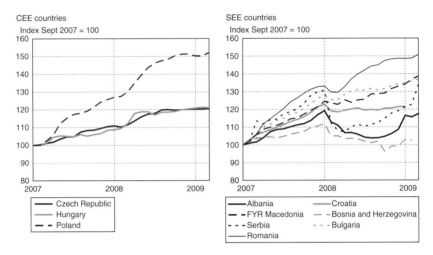

Notes: Data from national central banks. The constructed index keeps the exchange rate fixed at the level of the end of September 2007.

Source: Dvorsky et al. (2009).

Figure 10.7　Savings deposits of households at banks (exchange rate adjusted)

may partly reflect a portfolio shift from riskier assets to savings deposits as well as an increase in buffer stock savings or precautionary savings, much like in Austria. In the SEE countries, the initial drop in total savings coincided with the outbreak of the financial crisis. With trust in banks unsettled following the collapse of Lehman Brothers, households effected (partly substantial) withdrawals of savings deposits. The developments in the following months, however, took a highly heterogeneous path across the SEE region. A gradual normalization took hold in Romania, Bulgaria and FYR Macedonia – that is the withdrawals turned out to be temporary. Furthermore, in these countries private savings started to rise again, but compared to pre-crisis levels, the speed of capital accumulation has slowed. We stipulate that the decreased rate of accumulation of private savings is a consequence of the ongoing economic crisis influenced mainly by higher unemployment, lower growth rates of disposable income, and lower remittances. In other countries, particularly in Albania, Bosnia and Herzegovina, Croatia and Serbia, the return of withdrawn money to the banking system was not complete (or took longer) and the value of savings at banks seemed to have declined more persistently.

However, even in those countries where withdrawals were significant we consider it striking that the meltdown of deposits was not stronger – given the severity of the crisis and the countries' history. We think that this clearly shows that institutional credibility, and in particular credibility of banks, has indeed been built up in the years prior to the crisis.

10.4.3   Furthermore, Trust in Local Currencies Decreased

Another field in which agents can be considered to react rather sensitively in their portfolio decisions concerns exchange rate movements. The global financial crisis led to a significant depreciation of floating exchange rates in some CESEE countries (and put some stress on fixed peg regime countries) and to changes of inflation as well as of interest rates. These developments clearly might have repercussions on exchange rate expectations and on how agents view the stability of their currencies.

In fact, the results from the 'OeNB Euro Survey' show that in all countries surveyed, except for Bosnia and Herzegovina, a majority of respondents disagreed with the statement that the local currency was very stable and trustworthy, both for the current situation and for the coming five years (Dvorsky et al., 2009). From May/June 2008 to May/June 2009, the assessment turned from positive into negative territory for the Czech Republic, Poland, FYR Macedonia, and most markedly in Serbia. Furthermore, we observe still high shares of respondents expecting local currencies to depreciate further against the euro. This factor is likely to have a substantial impact on households' decisions with respect to the currency composition of their portfolio.

10.5   IN THE NEAR FUTURE: LIKELY NO DECLINE IN ASSET SUBSTITUTION

How will the situation evolve in the near future? Has the crisis affected the portfolio behaviour of households?

An indication about these questions can be derived from a direct survey instrument about whether the crisis has affected agents' assessment of the attractiveness of local currency versus foreign currency-denominated assets.[14] As summarized in Figure 10.8, the attractiveness of foreign currency-denominated assets has decreased only in two out of ten countries, in a further two countries it remained unchanged. In the remaining six countries the attractiveness of foreign currency-denominated assets increased – notably in those three countries which have already had the highest degree of euroization before the economic and financial crisis (Croatia, FYR Macedonia and Serbia).

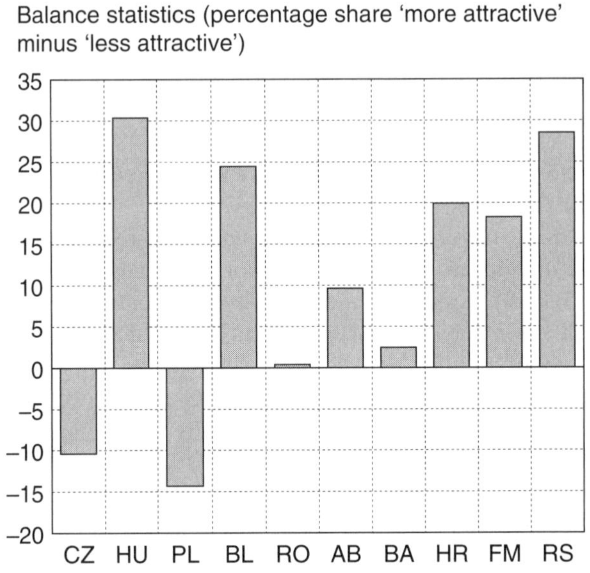
Balance statistics (percentage share 'more attractive' minus 'less attractive')
35
30
25
20
15
10
5
0
–5
–10
–15
–20
CZ HU PL BL RO AB BA HR FM RS

Notes: Recoded answers based on the question 'How has the global financial crisis changed your attitude towards the following types of savings . . . Have they become safer or less safe in terms of preserving the value of your savings?' Sample restricted to those who have savings and those who are older than 18.
CZ: Czech Republic; HU: Hungary; PL: Poland; SK: Slovakia, BL: Bulgaria; RO: Romania; AB: Albania; BA: Bosnia and Herzegovina; HR: Croatia; FM: FYR Macedonia; RS: Serbia.

Source: Own calculation based on 'OeNB Euro Survey' spring wave 2009.

Figure 10.8 Attractiveness of deposits in foreign currency vs deposits in local currency

On an individual level, one might suspect that answers to this question can be considered to reflect a surrogate of both current economic conditions as well as expectations about the future, in particular exchange rate expectations. A more thorough micro-econometric analysis confirms this contention: agents' assessment of the attractiveness of euro-denominated assets is significantly influenced by exchange rate expectations. However, we also find an indication of a habit persistence effect: the attractiveness has increased for those who held already euro-denominated assets during the crisis. One interpretation of this effect can be seen against the background of exchange rate depreciations during the crisis. Those who had euro assets were shielded off these depreciations, which reinforces the incentive to stick to euro assets in the future.

10.6 SUMMARY AND IMPLICATIONS

The question asked in this chapter is whether the euro has been used as a safe haven asset in CESEE. Based on the evidence presented in this chapter, the answer to this question differs according to the geographic region. In CEE countries, the ownership of euro-denominated assets is predominantly driven by transaction motives. Hence, the quantitative importance of euro asset holdings is small and its consequences for monetary and economic policy rather limited. In contrast, in SEE countries euro-denominated assets have been used as safe haven assets with the extent of both currency and deposit substitution being substantial.

We argue that the reasons why agents in SEE have held euro cash or euro deposits differ along a temporal dimension. Before the economic and financial crisis, the macroeconomic environment was relatively stable (in comparison to prior periods) and trust in institutions has been built up. Nevertheless, a high share of savings deposits was denominated in euro. We assign this observation to hysteresis effects – against the background of periods of economic and political turbulences in the 1990s agents continued to have biased expectations about the local currency. As a consequence, agents' portfolio choice did not fully reflect exchange rate and interest rate movements. This got manifested in very persistent euroization levels. We think that this episode bears the lesson that trust in local currencies and trust in institutions builds up only slowly. This implies that it might be very difficult to quickly and significantly reduce the level of euroization through sound macroeconomic policy. In this sense, policymakers are clearly constrained by past events.

Evidently, the arrival of the economic and financial crisis in SEE interfered with the pre-crisis stabilization efforts. Trust in banks fell and doubts about the local currencies evolved. Agents have reacted more sensitively to these two parameters than agents in Western European economies: deposit withdrawals occurred and euro cash holdings increased – a clear safe haven behaviour.

Although deposit withdrawals were substantial in some countries, we think that, given the extent of the shock, the reaction of households was not 'overly strong'. Furthermore, in those countries, which experienced stronger deposit withdrawals backflows into the banking system have occurred in the meantime. In our view, partly this reflects a success of the stabilization policy before the crisis which was able to build up trust in institutions in general and trust in banks in particular. Partly, it represents a success of economic policy and international coordination.

Nevertheless, the crisis caused an increase in expectations of exchange rate depreciations. This will clearly gauge the future role of the euro in SEE. Furthermore, habit persistence seems to be important: those who had euro assets plan to increase the share of euro-denominated assets. This existence of habit persistence and the fact that exchange rate expectations might be difficult to influence in the short run because of the entailed hysteretic component suggests that de facto euroization levels will not decline in the near future, especially in highly euroized economies.

NOTES

1. We thank Peter Backé, Sandra Dvorsky, Doris Ritzberger-Grünwald and Thomas Scheiber for helpful comments and suggestions. The views expressed in this chapter are strictly those of the author and do not necessarily reflect the views of the Oesterreichische Nationalbank. Excellent research assistance by Mariya Hake is acknowledged.
2. This chapter partly builds on work that I have conducted with Thomas Scheiber (Scheiber and Stix, 2009) and with Sandra Dvorsky and Thomas Scheiber (Dvorsky et al., 2009).
3. We will use the following terminology in this chapter: currency substitution will refer to the substitution of foreign currency cash (FCC) for local currency cash (LCC). Asset or deposit substitution – both terms will be used interchangeably – refers to the substitution of saving deposits denominated in foreign currency (FCD) for saving deposits denominated in local currency (LCD). Because the euro has a predominant role in the countries analysed, we will make use of the term euroization (instead of dollarization). Hence, financial euroization refers to the overall, and in our case unofficial extent of currency and asset substitution. This terminology differs from the literature in two aspects: first, currency substitution as we use it does not necessarily mean that FCC replaces domestic currency cash as a medium of exchange. Second, our use of the term asset substitution focuses only on saving deposits and neglects other financial assets.
4. Notice, that we focus only on the asset side and disregard the role of foreign currency loans.
5. For further details, see the OeNB's research platform on Central, Eastern, and South-Eastern Europe, available at: http://ceec.oenb.at
6. The survey does not cover Montenegro and Kosovo, which have unilaterally introduced the euro.
7. Non-response rates differ considerably across countries.
8. In particular, respondents who held euro cash were asked whether they agreed or disagreed with the statement 'I hold euro cash as a general reserve or as a means of precaution' or 'I hold euro cash to make payments abroad, for holidays'. Figure 10.2 shows the sample means for each country. A value of zero implies that, on average, people do neither agree nor disagree. A positive value means that people agree. A comparison of answers obtained for the two motives indicates the relative importance of motives.
9. Notice that results on median holdings are not only consistent with motives in a cross-country comparison but also across individuals. That is, if we compare individuals who answered that they hold their cash balances for expenses abroad with those who answered that they hold their cash balances as a store of value then we find that median holdings are lower for the former than for the latter.
10. First, the projections have been calculated without using imputation techniques – by simply ignoring non-responses. In particular, this assumes that those individuals who do not give answers are identical on average to those who do respond, an assumption

which is very strong. Second, the survey will very likely underrepresent individuals in the top of the wealth distribution.

11. Other explanations stress the interaction of deposit and loan euroization (Ize and Yeyati, 2003; Basso et al., 2007; Luca and Petrova, 2008).

12. The cross-country comparison for this variable for the 2008 fall wave is somehow constrained by the fact that the fieldwork periods differ across countries: in the fall wave 2008, the earliest fieldwork started in the first week of October while the last country was surveyed in the second week of November. Hence in some countries, respondents were asked only before the (announced) extension of deposit insurance schemes, in other countries the survey took place afterwards.

13. Compared with the 2008 fall wave, the perceived safety of deposits increased significantly in Albania, Croatia and Romania in May to June 2009. In the Czech Republic, Hungary, Bulgaria and Bosnia and Herzegovina, no significant change could be found. The only three countries where a significant decline of perceived deposit safety was recorded in the spring wave 2009 were the FYR Macedonia, Poland and Serbia.

14. 'How has the global financial crisis changed your attitude towards the following types of savings? Have they become safer or less safe in terms of preserving the value of your savings?'

REFERENCES

Basso, H.S., O. Calvo Gonzalez and M. Jurgilas (2007), 'Financial dollarization – the role of banks and interest rates', *European Central Bank Working Paper*, No. 748.

De Freitas, M. (2004), 'The dynamics of inflation and currency substitution in a small open economy', *Journal of International Money and Finance*, **23** (1), 133–42.

Duffy, J., M. Nikitin and R.T. Smith (2006), 'Dollarization traps', *Journal of Money, Credit, and Banking*, **38** (8), 2073–97.

Dvorsky, S., T. Scheiber and H. Stix (2009), 'CESEE households amid the financial crisis: euro survey shows darkened economic sentiment and changes in savings behavior', *Focus on Eastern European Integration*, 2009/4, 71–83.

ECB (2008), *Review of the International Role of the Euro*, Frankfurt am Main: European Central Bank.

Feige, E.L. (2003), 'Dynamics of currency substitution, asset substitution and de facto dollarisation and euroisation in transition countries', *Comparative Economic Studies*, **45** (3), 358–83.

Feige, E.L. and J.W. Dean (2004), 'Dollarization and Euroization in transition countries: currency substitution, asset substitution, network externalities, and irreversibility', in V. Alexander, J. Melitz and G.M. von Furstenberg (eds), *Monetary Unions and Hard Pegs: Effects on Trade, Financial Development, and Stability*, New York and Oxford: Oxford University Press, pp. 303–19.

Feige, E.L., M. Faulend, V. Sonje and V. Šošić (2003), 'Unofficial dollarization in Latin America: currency substitution, network externalities, and irreversibility', in D. Salvatore, J.W. Dean and T.D. Willett (eds), *The Dollarization Debate*, Oxford and New York: Oxford University Press, pp. 46–71.

Guiso, L., P. Sapienza and L. Zingales (2004), 'The role of social capital in financial development', *American Economic Review*, **94** (3), 526–56.

Ize, A. and E.L. Yeyati (2003), 'Financial dollarization', *Journal of International Economics*, **59** (2), 323–47.
Knell, M. and H. Stix (2009), 'Trust in banks? Evidence from normal times and from times of crises', *OeNB Working Paper*, No. 158.
Luca, A. and I. Petrova (2008), 'What drives credit dollarization in transition economies?', *Journal of Banking and Finance*, **32** (5), 858–69.
Nicolo, G.D., P. Honohan and A. Ize (2005), 'Dollarization of bank deposits: causes and consequences', *Journal of Banking and Finance*, **29** (7), 1697–727.
Oomes, N. (2003), 'Network externalities and dollarization hysteresis: the case of Russia', *IMF Working Paper*, No. 03/96.
Prean, N. and H. Stix (2009), 'The effect of raising deposit insurance coverage in times of financial crisis – evidence from Croatian microdata', Mimeo.
Reding, P. and J.A. Morales (2004), 'Currency substitution and network externalities', *University of Namur Working Paper*.
Sapienza, P. and L. Zingales (2009), 'A trust crisis', available at: www.financialtrustindex.com, (accessed 2 October).
Savastano, M.A. (1996), 'Dollarization in Latin America: recent evidence and some policy issues', *IMF Working Paper*, No. 96/4.
Scheiber, T. and H. Stix (2009), 'Euroization in Central, Eastern and Southeastern Europe – new evidence on its extent and some evidence on its causes', *OeNB Working Paper*, No. 159.
Stix, H. (2010a), 'Trust in banks, financial intermediation and the financial crisis – evidence from Central, Eastern and Southeastern Europe', Mimeo.
Stix, H. (2010b), 'Euroization: what factors drive its persistence? Household data evidence for Croatia, Slovenia and Slovakia', *Applied Economics*, July, 1–16.
Yeyati, E.L. (2006), 'Financial dollarization: evaluating the consequences', *Economic Policy*, **21** (45), 61–118.

PART IV

Lessons – from euro area divergences, and from the crisis

11. Economic divergence within the euro area: lessons for EMU enlargement

Agnès Bénassy-Quéré, Antoine Berthou[1] and Lionel Fontagné[2]

According to the optimum currency area theory (Mundell, 1961), the decision to form a monetary union should result from a trade-off between microeconomic gains and macroeconomic costs:

- Within a monetary union, uncertainty on bilateral foreign exchange rates as well as currency exchange transaction costs (bank charges associated with the exchange of goods and services, or capital transactions) disappear, and price transparency increases. An intensification of competition is expected, leading to price convergence and to an expansion of the volume of trade between members of the monetary union. The resulting welfare gains are all the more important as the extent of trade creation and price convergence is sizeable.
- Members of a monetary union by definition lose their monetary independence. This has no consequences if economic activity and price cycles are well correlated within the union. However, the loss of the monetary tool can be hard on countries affected by specific shocks. In this case, stabilization requires high international mobility of the production factors within the union, or a sizeable flexibility of relative prices, especially of real wages.

However, the pros and cons of forming a monetary union also involve political-economy arguments such as *coordination* and/or *credibility* effects. A single currency is expected to eliminate non-cooperative behaviour when the union is hit by a symmetric shock (beggar-thy-neighbour policies). In countries with an inflationary tradition, the banishment of devaluation is also expected to efficiently anchor inflation expectations, thereby reducing the costs of disinflation. The irreversible nature of monetary union is especially useful to this aim.

A last argument in favour of the single currency initially concerned the status of the euro and its capacity to compete against the US dollar as an *international currency*. The idea – never endorsed officially – was to put an end to the 'exorbitant privilege' of the United States which consists in trading and issuing debt in its own currency. A more diplomatic element was added to this economic issue: the idea that Europe would finally be able to make its voice heard on the international scene by establishing the euro as a key currency within the international currency system.

After ten years of operation, it seems that all the promises of the single currency – good or bad – have, at least partially, come true. The purpose of this chapter is to examine how these various benefits and costs have materialized during the first decade of the euro area, and to draw some lessons for the future. We find that what has been observed – including the sovereign debt speculative attacks – has to a large extent been a logical consequence of the policy framework put in place in 1999.

MICROECONOMIC GAINS: STILL SOME WAY TO GO

Economic research has long sought the expected gains from the single currency in the increase of trade within the monetary union. In reality, the question does not arise in these terms: it is not trade in itself that produces welfare gains, but the greater diversity of products accessible to consumers and producers, as well as their lower prices. The single currency, by facilitating access to the markets of the union and reinforcing competition between companies, must favour product diversity and price moderation. Berthou and Fontagné (2008a) have studied French trade data at the firm level provided by French customs at the product-level, with about 9 000 NC8 manufactured product categories. They have compared the evolution of French exports to the euro area with the evolution of trade to the rest of the EU-15, to the rest of Europe and to the rest of the world during the period 1998–2003 and decomposed it into:

- The variation of the number of export flows (extensive margin) which can be related to the number of exporters, destination markets or products exported by each individual firm;
- The variation of the mean value of exports for individual flows (intensive margin).

The results are summarized in Figure 11.1. The number of French firms exporting to the euro area decreased by 8.8 per cent between 1998 and

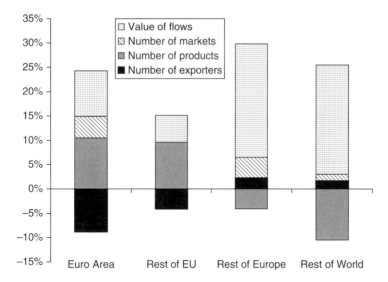

Source: Berthou and Fontagné (2008a).

Figure 11.1   Decomposition of growth in value of French manufacturing exports between 1998 and 2003 according to destination, in per cent

2003, the number of destination markets increased by 4.4 per cent, and the average number of products exported by a typical firm increased by 10.5 per cent. Combining all components, this 6.1 per cent increase in the extensive margin of French exports to the euro area has to be compared with a 9.4 per cent increase in the average value of exports by elementary, firm-product-destination flow. It thus appears that the increase in exports to the euro area primarily reflects an increase in the number of products exported by each firm on each market and an increase in the value of exports for each elementary flow.

Naturally, these changes are not only the result of the introduction of the euro. To isolate the effect of the single currency, it is necessary to resort to econometric analysis. A first estimation strategy (taking the rest of the world as a control group, and controlling for EU membership) reveals that the euro did increase the number of export flows towards euro area destinations: estimation results suggest a 6.5 per cent permanent increase in the number of trade flows targeting euro area destinations (extensive margin), as compared to non-euro area destinations. Conversely, the euro did not have any significant effect on the average value of individual flows (intensive margin).[3]

Second, the use of the individual dimension of the data on firms makes it possible to isolate the effect of the euro on the various components of this extensive margin (see Berthou and Fontagné, 2008b). The econometric estimation reveals that the adoption of the single currency had no significant effect on the decision of new firms to export to euro area destinations. However, results strongly confirm the intuition from descriptive statistics above, that incumbent exporters took the euro as an opportunity to export more product categories to euro area destinations. A weak but positive effect of the euro on the average value of exports by product-firm is found – for the 25 per cent most productive firms – when the sample of exporters is restricted to firms with more than 20 employees. All of these results together suggest that the lower transaction costs and the greater price transparency triggered by the euro further increased the competitive pressure for euro area destinations, and promoted trade volumes for most efficient firms.

This reinforcement of competition is observed in export prices. Based on the same dataset for the period 1995–2005, Martin and Méjean (2008) emphasize two effects of euro introduction. First, for the same product, the export price level to the euro area is, on average, slightly lower than for other OECD markets (the maximum gap is 2 per cent). Second, the euro reduced, within monetary union, price discrimination across markets. Before 1999, the average dispersion of prices was 5 per cent lower in the euro area as compared with other OECD markets; after the introduction of the euro, the difference in price discrimination between euro area and OECD markets almost reached 7 per cent.

Such pro-competitive effect recorded at the level of trade prices has however failed to foster further convergence in consumer prices across the euro area, as evidenced in Figure 11.2. Since 1999, consumption prices have significantly converged in the EU-27, but not within the EU-12 where there was already less divergence prior to the introduction of the euro, although still more than in the United States.

Such lack of convergence of prices at the consumer level despite enhanced competition at the firm level could tentatively be explained by a divergence in consumption tax rates. This explanation however falls short of evidence: standard VAT rates have converged in the euro area since 1999 (see Figure 11.3), so even without any convergence in pre-tax prices, after-tax prices should have converged.

Another explanation for the lack of price convergence at the consumer's level despite convergence at the firm's level is the lack of competition in the distribution sector. Figure 11.4 shows that most euro area countries retain highly regulated retail sectors and that progress has been slow especially since 2003.

These various pieces of evidence suggest that the euro has contributed

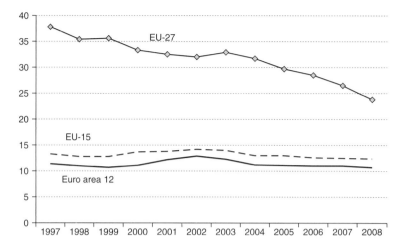

Source: Eurostat, structural indicators, available at: http://epp.eurostat.ec.europa.eu.

*Figure 11.2   Coefficient of variation of consumption prices, including
indirect taxes, in per cent*

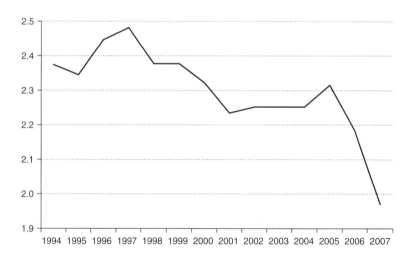

Source: Authors' calculations based on European Commission data (EC, 2007).

*Figure 11.3   Dispersion of standard VAT rates in the EU-12 (standard
deviation in per cent)*

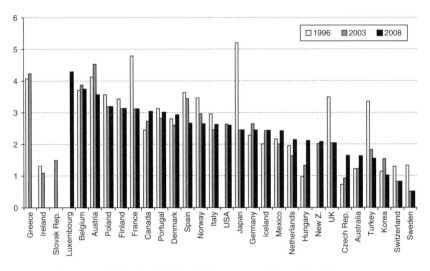

Source: Conway and Nicoletti (2006); OECD data, available at http://stats.oecd.org.

Figure 11.4   Regulatory conditions in retail distribution

to trade integration through a pro-competitive effect as well as a rise in the number of varieties available to the consumer. However the euro cannot substitute for a lack of structural reforms. These are a condition for consumers to reap the full gains of monetary union.

MACROECONOMIC DIVERGENCE

Starting on January 1999 (or even two years before), all European Monetary Union (EMU) members gave up monetary independence. Not only did their short-run nominal interest rates converge to the single policy rate, but their long-run rates also converged, before large spreads reappeared during the 2008–09 crisis. However inflation rates differed significantly across EMU members, from 1.7 per cent on average over 1999–2008 in Germany, to 3.2 per cent in Spain and 3.3 per cent in Greece (see Table 11.1). This resulted in substantial differences in real interest rates. For instance, the three-month real interest rate was negative in Spain during most of the period (see Figure 11.5). These low rates encouraged households and companies to get into debt in order to consume and invest, which reinforced the increasing pressure on demand, and therefore on consumer and especially asset prices.

*Table 11.1   Average consumer price index (CPI) inflation rates 1999–
2008, in per cent*

Greece	3.3
Spain	3.2
Ireland	3.0
Portugal	2.9
Luxembourg	2.8
Italy	2.4
Netherlands	2.4
Belgium	2.2
Euro area	**2.2**
France	1.9
Austria	1.9
Germany	1.7

Source: Eurostat, available at: http://epp.eurostat.ec.europa.eu.

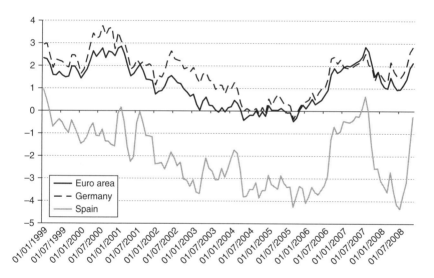

Note: Three-month interbank rate minus year-on-year CPI growth rate.

Source: Author's calculations from European Central Bank, Statistical Data Warehouse, available at: http://sdw.ecb.europa.eu/.

Figure 11.5   Three-month real interest rates in per cent

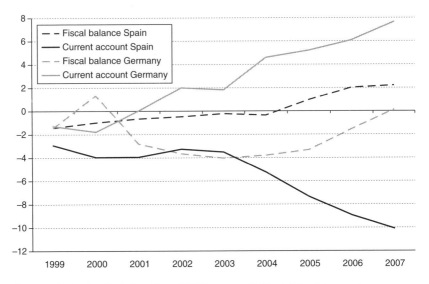

Source: Author's calculations from OECD data, available at: http://stats.oecd.org.

Figure 11.6   Fiscal and external current balances, in per cent of GDP

Thus, the single monetary policy proved to be destabilizing for the most inflationary countries some of which had significant real estate bubbles. These countries would have needed more restrictive regulatory and fiscal policies than those required by the stability and growth pact. In Spain, for example, even though the public budget was close to balance, the continuous increase in the current account deficit revealed insufficient private saving, which called for more restrictive policies (see Figure 11.6). Conversely, Germany infringed the stability pact several times, but this did not prevent it from recording increasing external surpluses. True, current-account imbalances are automatically financed in a monetary union through flows of money balances, and a member of a monetary union will no longer experience a balance-of-payment crisis. However the current account delivers relevant information on the savings-investment balance of each economy, hence on the type of tensions that may arise, either inflationary (through CPI or asset prices) or deflationary.[4] Additionally, as exemplified by the euro area crisis of 2009–10, the nation's saving-investment balance may prove more reliable than the government balance to assess public finance sustainability since the government may in fact be obliged to bail out part of the private sector, or it may abruptly lose economic growth and tax revenues due to the bust of an investment-leverage cycle.

The single monetary policy indeed caused macroeconomic divergences within the euro area, but more active fiscal policies, coupled with tougher regulations with regard to credit or to a correcting taxation in some countries, would have made it possible to attenuate these divergences. Like for microeconomic gains, the euro cannot be held responsible for the poor performance. The suspicion is more on accompanying policies: the government did not realize to what extent they had to reinvent national policies and their coordination when the euro was introduced.

THE EURO AND THE WORLD

By creating the euro, the Europeans could expect their currency to progressively play a similar role as the US dollar globally. More intensive use of the euro to denominate trade and investments would reduce the risk incurred by the residents of the euro area. Their foreign suppliers would also be incentivated to price in euro, which would attenuate the impact of exchange-rate variations on home-currency prices. Finally, higher liquidity would raise the attractiveness of the euro area for foreign investors. However, because changes in the international monetary system are generally very slow, such changes would only appear gradually. This is what happened.

The emergence of the euro as an international currency first materialized in the store-of-value function of the currency: the share of the euro rose significantly in international bond issuance, cross-border bank loans and official reserves (see Table 11.2). As a means of payment and unit of account, the euro also assumed a larger role. For instance, it was more intensively used for invoicing exports to non-euro partners. However the euro did not emerge as a vehicle currency (the US dollar remains the pivotal currency of the foreign exchange market and trade is generally not denominated in euro when it does not involve any euro member state). Neither did it emerge an official unit of account (for instance, few countries outside Europe peg their currencies to the euro). In short, the euro has not yet emerged as a genuine global currency, but more as a diversification currency and also as a regional currency (see Kamps, 2006; ECB, 2009).

As for the European voice in international fora, some progress has been made through the coordination of European views prior to international meetings. However, key questions such as the representation of the euro area in international organizations have remained unresolved, mainly because this would involve a loss in sovereignty for some of the member states. Here again, we see that further relinquishments will be necessary to reap the full gains of the euro.

Table 11.2   The international role of currencies: 1999 and 2008 compared

1999

Function	Dollar	Yen	Euro	Other
Trade with non-€ partner, 2001[1]				
• Exports	–	–	45.4	–
• Imports	–	–	44.4	–
Forex turnover, April 2001[2]	90.3	22.7	37.6	49.4
Outstanding amount of international bonds (extensive definition), end 1999[3]	45.9	18.7	21.2	14.1
Outstanding amount of international bonds (restrictive definition), end 1999[4]	48.9	16.0	20.7	14.4
Outstanding amount of cross-border bank loans (extensive definition), end 2008[5]	59.5	11.6	14.0	14.9

2008

Function	Dollar	Yen	Euro	Other
Trade with non-€ partner, 2007[1]				
• Exports	–	–	56.9	–
• Imports	–	–	46.7	–
Forex turnover, April 2007[2]	86.3	16.5	37.0	60.2
Outstanding amount of international bonds (extensive definition), end 2008[3]	39.8	14.2	29.5	16.6
Outstanding amount of international bonds (restrictive definition), end 2008[4]	44.7	6.8	32.2	16.3
Outstanding amount of cross-border bank loans (extensive definition), end 2008[5]	51.6	3.2	22.2	23.0

	1999				2008			
Outstanding amount of cross-border bank loans (restrictive definition), end 1999[6] / end 2008[6]	61.1	7.8	7.4	23.7	54.3	5.9	17.6	22.2
Cross-border bank deposits (extensive definition), end 1999[5] / end 2008[5]	60.0	4.7	20.8	14.6	59.3	2.1	22.4	16.2
Cross-border bank deposits (restrictive definition), end 1999[6] / end 2008[6]	66.5	6.2	13.9	13.4	52.3	3.2	21.7	22.8
Forex reserves, end 1999[7] / end 2008[7]	71.0	6.4	17.9	4.7	64.0	3.3	26.5	6.2
Forex pegs, June 2003[8] / April 2008[8]	31.3	0.0	13.6	–	45.4	0.0	18.6	–

Notes: [1] Unweighted average for eight countries; [2] Out of 200%; [3] Including domestic issues (for example, bonds in euro area); [4] Excluding domestic emissions; [5] Including loans/deposits to/from banks located in the USA, the UK, Switzerland and the Eurozone and denominated in their own currencies; excluding interbank loans/deposits; [6] Excluding loans/deposits to/from banks located in the USA, the UK, Switzerland and the euro area and denominated in their own currencies; excluding interbank loans/deposits; [7] Excluding unallocated reserves; [8] Share of currencies that are hardly or softly pegged, excluding the euro area.

Source: Bénassy-Quéré and Coeure (2010).

141

LESSONS FOR EMU ENLARGEMENT

For long, diversity will remain a key feature of the European monetary union. Differences in GDP per capita will justify inflation differentials that will translate into destabilizing differences in real interest rates, higher inflation countries enjoying lower real interest rates. Based on a linear convergence of consumer price levels in 30 years from 2006, Bénassy-Quéré and Turkisch (2009) have calculated that, with inflation at 2 per cent a year for a hypothetic euro area of 27, individual member-state inflation rates would range from 1 per cent (Denmark) to 5.2 per cent (Bulgaria). Such inflation differentials can theoretically be managed in a monetary union since they do not necessarily trigger cumulated losses in competitiveness in high-inflation compared to low-inflation countries.[5] However, the real interest-rate differentials they generate can cause credit booms with asset-price bubbles and busts. Because such imbalances involve a risk for other euro area members, they need to be closely monitored at the EMU level. The question then is how to design such monitoring.

Although financial stability is part of the ECB's mandate,[6] there are good arguments against the ECB trying to monitor asset prices aside from consumer prices. For instance, the Tinbergen rule states that one policy instrument (the interest rate) cannot reach two independent objectives simultaneously. Perhaps more convincingly, asset-price bubbles and credit booms were not a general feature of EMU member states before the 2008–09 crisis. Hence, stabilizing policies should be engineered at the national rather than EMU level, through regulatory, tax and fiscal measures. Given the strong risk of spillovers from boosting countries to the other EMU members, such reinforced counter-cyclicality of national policies should be closely coordinated at the Eurogroup level, either within an extended Stability and Growth Pact (that could include, for instance, assessments on private saving-investment imbalances and/or on real exchange-rate developments), or through the existing Broad Economic Policy Guidelines. The latter scheme was used in 2001 to recommend a tighter fiscal policy in booming Ireland, but the Irish government responded that it was already complying with the Stability and Growth Pact. With the experience of the 2008–09 crisis, it has become clear that monitoring more closely growing imbalances in individual member states would have considerably reduced both the severity and the length of the crisis in the euro area. One problem however is that calming booming economies without boosting deflationary ones would risk generating long-lasting anaemic growth in the euro area. Hence, a policy-coordination device would need to be symmetric.

Whatever the number and identity of countries in the euro area in the coming years, such renewed coordination will be key to manage fiscal adjustments and avoid new unsustainable imbalances. This implies that joining the euro area should de facto involve some loss in fiscal sovereignty, although surely not fully-fledged relinquishment. Perhaps this point was not enough stressed when the first group of countries initially rushed to meet the Maastricht criteria. And this lesson should be recalled to those EU countries that would like to join the euro to definitively escape balance-of-payment crises: being a member of the euro area will never be a free lunch.

NOTES

1. Agnès Bénassy-Quéré and Antoine Berthou, CEPII, France.
2. Lionel Fontagné, Paris School of Economics (Université Paris 1) and CEPII, France.
3. Results of a generalized least square estimation with random effects, with controls for market sizes, exchange rate volatility and the usual gravity variables (distance, common language), see Berthou and Fontagné (2008a).
4. Already in 2003 we had advocated a systematic use of current-account imbalances for guiding fiscal coordination within the Broad Economic Policy Guidelines set by the ECOFIN Council. See Bénassy-Quéré (2003).
5. In principle, price convergence occurs through a rise in the price of non-traded goods in catching-up economies (Balassa–Samuelson effect).
6. 'The ESCB shall contribute to the smooth conduct of policies pursued by the competent authorities relating to the prudential supervision of credit institutions and the stability of the financial system.' Art. 127.5 of the Treaty on the Functioning of the European Union.

REFERENCES

Bénassy-Quéré, A. (2003), 'The stability pact: two objectives, two rules', *La Lettre du CEPII*, No. 224, June.

Bénassy-Quéré, A. and B. Coeuré (2010), *Economie de l'Euro*, Paris: La Découverte.

Bénassy-Quéré, A. and E. Turkisch (2009), 'The ECB governing council in an enlarged euro area', *Journal of Common Market Studies*, **47** (1), 25–54.

Berthou, A. and L. Fontagné (2008a), 'The euro and the intensive and extensive margins of trade: evidence from French firm level data', *CEPII Working Paper*, No. 2008–06.

Berthou, A. and L. Fontagné (2008b), 'The euro effects on the firm and product-level trade margins: evidence from France', *CEPII Working Paper*, No. 2008–21, October.

Conway, P. and G. Nicoletti (2006), 'Product Market Regulation in non-manufacturing sectors in OECD countries: measurement and highlights', OECD Economics Department Working Paper No. 530.

European Central Bank (ECB) (2009), *Review of the International Role of the Euro*, Frankfurt-am-Main, June.

European Commission (EC) (2007), DOC/2108/2007.
Kamps, A. (2006), 'The euro as an invoicing currency in international trade', *ECB Working Paper*, No. 668.
Martin, J. and I. Méjean (2008), 'Trade prices and the euro', *CEPII Working Paper*, No. 2008–29, December.
Mundell, R. (1961), 'Theory of optimum currency areas', *The American Economic Review*, **51** (4), 509–17.
Treaty on the Functioning of the European Union, available at: www.aedh.eu/plugins/fckeditor/userfiles/file/Textes UE/Consolidated version_09_05_08.pdf.

12. Facts and lessons from euro area divergences for enlargement[1]

Zsolt Darvas

FACTS

1. Regarding the magnitude of divergence across euro area countries, and also temporal convergence/divergence of various indicators, euro area diversity is by and large similar to regional diversity in some sovereign countries, such as Australia, Canada, Japan, Poland, the UK and the US.
2. There are examples of successful economic catching up inside the euro area, but also of highly disappointing economic performances.
3. Booms that are characterized by a surge in credit, housing prices, construction and indebtedness are dangerous both in the run-up period to monetary union and inside.
4. The rise in manufacturing unit labour costs (ULC) is not inevitable during housing, construction and credit booms and structural features matter.
5. Regaining competitiveness via the so-called 'competitiveness channel' is a long-lasting and difficult process.
6. Crisis response: the euro is a shelter.

LESSONS

1. Fiscal policy, income policy, and bank regulation and supervision should aim to dampen huge housing and credit booms, that is, act in a counter-cyclical manner.
2. Measures improving the flexibility of product and labour markets should be implemented.
3. Efficient and transparent crisis management tools are needed.
4. Enhanced surveillance is needed.
5. Enhanced policy coordination is needed.

6. Euro area entry criteria are inadequate for judging the achievement of 'high degree of sustainable convergence', which they aim to assess.

12.1   INTRODUCTION

The tenth anniversary of the introduction of the euro in 2009 was over-shadowed by the deep impact of the global financial and economic crisis. While during the first phases of the crisis the euro gained in prestige – despite the wide diversity of crisis responses of euro area member states – largely due to the decisive and prompt response of the European Central Bank (ECB), market sentiment completely turned upside down in early 2010 due to the Greek debt crisis, which has even put the coherence of the euro area to a test in the eyes of many analysts. Pre-1999 critics of the euro project, who stressed its fragility due to the low level of labour mobility and the lack of fiscal and political union, now feel that their concerns have been vindicated. At the same time the general public's fascination with the euro has been seriously damaged in some solid euro area countries, such as Germany, which influences the policymakers of these countries.

It is against this background that this chapter will attempt to draw lessons from the divergent economic developments across current euro area member states for enlargement. While the Greek crisis is acute and currently overshadows any issue related to euro area enlargement, it should not obscure the proper interpretation of euro area divergences.

The Greek case is a very special one and does not have much relevance for potential newcomers.[2] The most frequently cited worries about Greece and other Mediterranean EU euro area member states include their huge current account deficit, their low domestic savings rate and their loss of competitiveness in the past decade. However, the primary reasons of the speculative attack against Greek bonds are its irresponsible fiscal behaviour, the recent credit downgrades of Greek government bonds, and the ECB's recent indication that it wishes to revert to its pre-crisis collateral policy by the end of 2010, implying that Greek government bonds may not be eligible for ECB refinancing after this date. These factors were coupled with the gloomy market sentiment against Greece, fuelled by its cheating to get into the euro area and to hide part of its government deficit since then, the huge new budget deficit figure for 2009, the weak fiscal track record, the prospect of exploding government debt[3] and the difficulties of adopting austerity measures in a country in which social unrest is wide-spread. It should not come as a surprise that Greek government bonds came under pressure after the ECB unveiled its collateral policy plans.

However, potential euro newcomers constitute a different world compared to Greece due to generally responsible fiscal policies in the past decade (with the important exception of Hungary) and rather low government debt ratios. Consequently, the lessons from the experience of other euro area catching-up economies, such as Finland, Ireland and Spain, and the lessons from Portugal, in which the prosperous pre-1999 catching-up halted after euro area entry, are much more relevant for potential euro newcomers.

There are a couple of divergent trends within the euro area and these trends are confined not only to some Mediterranean countries and Ireland. For example, from 1999 to 2007 the largest real house price increase was observed in France. Divergence within a monetary union is not necessarily bad and can indeed reflect benign developments. Other monetary areas, such as the US and other large countries are also characterized by regional divergences, and divergences are even warranted in a heterogeneous monetary union. For example, divergent economic growth may imply economic catching-up of less developed regions, and the ensuing higher regional inflation may simply reflect price level convergence that does not necessarily affect the competitiveness of the region. Similarly, capital flows across regions and consequently current account deficits and surpluses may simply reflect the better utilization of resources when capital moves to fast-growing regions to the benefit of the whole monetary union.

However, persistently low growth performance or the build-up of 'excessive' regional debt is undesirable. As a crucial warning signal, Figure 12.1 provides a historical overview of GDP per capita developments compared to the US in 11 euro area countries. The countries showed in the left-hand panel were catching-up with the US after World War II till about the early 1980s, when convergence stopped. Italy started to fall behind in the early 1990s and this process is expected to continue in the coming years, which is much more worrying in our view than the current Greek debt crisis. Among the countries shown in the right-hand panel Ireland clearly achieved an unprecedented convergence between the early 1990s and the recent crisis, but even its post-crisis GDP per capita level is expected to be among the highest within the euro area. Finland also did well after its crisis in the early 1990s, and its convergence is expected to continue in future years, while Spain and Portugal are expected to fall behind. Greece has converged in the past decade, but has not yet reached its per capita level compared to the US in the late 1970s, and, similarly to most other euro area countries, no convergence is seen in the coming years.

This chapter aims to establish six stylized facts and to draw six lessons from the divergent developments in current euro area member states for enlargement and also for the better functioning of the euro area. To this end, we first would like to offer an overview of the magnitude of the diversity across euro area countries in the light of within-country diversity of

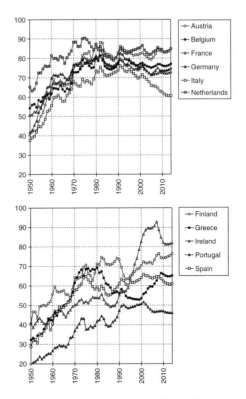

Source: October 2009a World Economic Outlook of the IMF.

Figure 12.1   GDP per capita at PPP (US = 100), 1950–2014

some sovereign states. We then establish the stylized facts and draw the lessons and close this chapter with some concluding remarks.

12.2   EURO AREA DIVERSITY

12.2.1   Diversity in Main Indicators in Light of Regional Diversity within Countries

How large is the diversity across euro area countries compared to regional diversity within sovereign countries? The answer is 'not too large', at least for those indicators that are available at a regional level, as indicated in the first five panels of Figure 12.2 and the comparison of Figures 12.3 and 12.4.

There are pitfalls in comparing cross-country diversity to cross-region diversity, as the number of regions as well as their sizes matter. When there are a large number of regions of which some are small, then some extremes may blow up measures of divergence. For example, when using data from 50 states and the District of Columbia, regional diversity seems much larger compared to the case when the nine broader regions defined by the US Census Bureau is used. We have used these nine US regions in order not to exaggerate regional divergences within the US and also the number of these broader regions is reasonably close to the number of countries that initially entered the euro area. For all other countries, for which we primarily used Territorial level 2 classification, we have merged regions with GDP below 1 per cent of the national GDP. For a similar reason we excluded Luxembourg from the calculation of euro area diversity measures, and considered the other 11 countries that joined in 1999/2001. The four countries that joined the euro area between 2007 and 2009 have spent too short a time in the euro area and are hence also excluded from the calculation of euro area diversity measures.

The first five panels of Figure 12.2 indicate that there are sovereign countries having higher cross-regional diversity than the cross-country diversity within the euro area in terms of some key indicators, such as GDP per capita, GDP growth, labour force participation rate and unemployment rate. Even in terms of inflation diversity shown in Panel 5 of Figure 12.2, which is available only for a few countries, after the convergence of inflation till the launch of the euro, the euro area's standard deviation was broadly in line with that of the US (for the US we used here the inflation rates of 24 key metropolitan areas).

While Figure 12.2 shows diversity between current euro area members, it is a different question how enlargement would modify diversity. From the perspective of the euro area aggregate the effect would be quite small, as all 12 new member states (NMS) of the EU constitute only about 9 per cent of the aggregate of the first 12 euro area members plus the 12 NMS (and four of the NMS have already entered the euro area). Hence, potential country-specific diversity after further enlargement is more important from the perspective of newcomers and these countries should learn the lessons from the current euro area members.

12.2.2   Real House Price Movements

Another cross-country difference is related to pre-crisis housing price developments (Figure 12.3), which played a crucial role in the boom and the consequent bust of certain euro area countries. Interestingly, France had the largest real house price hike among euro area countries.[4] Figure 12.4 highlights that regional real house price movements were more

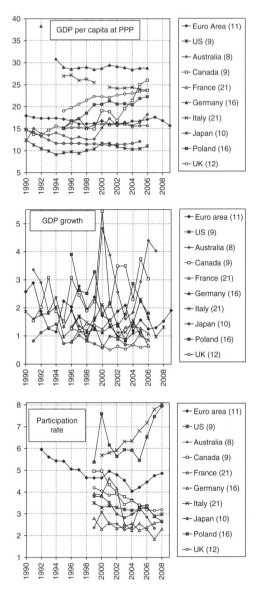

Notes: The number in brackets indicates the number of regions used to calculate standard deviation. GDP per capita is measured as national average = 100. All other indicators are measured in per cent. German inflation data are available for four regions for 1992–95, six regions for 1996–2000, nine regions for 2001–05 and 12 regions for 2006–09. In case of the euro area countries national definition of inflation rate was used for 1990–96 and the harmonized index of consumer prices since then.

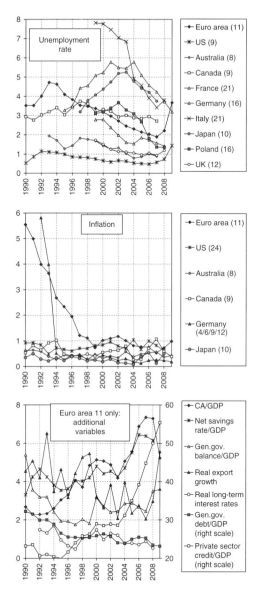

Source: OECD Regional Database, Eurostat, Statistics Canada, Australian Bureau of Statistics.

Figure 12.2 *Annual cross-country standard deviation in the euro area and cross-region standard deviation in selected countries of some key indicators, 1990–2009*

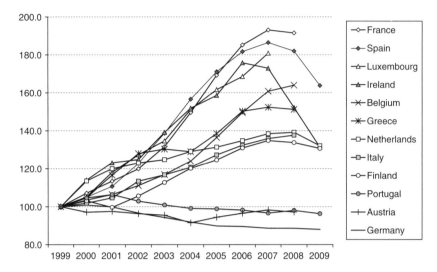

Note: Real house price index deflated with the GDP deflator. Data for 2008 and 2009 are not available for all countries.

Source: Using data from the ECB and AMECO, this figure extends Graph 33 of the European Commission (p. 31, 2009a).

Figure 12.3   Real house prices in euro area countries, 1999–2007 (1999=100)

diverse in the US and Canada than in the euro area, and were quite diverse within Australian capital cities and UK regions too.

12.2.3   The Interest Rate Scapegoat and Some Worrisome Divergences

Many other indicators are not measured at the regional levels of sovereign countries (for example, real interest rate, credit growth, current account balance, export performance, savings rate), or difficult to interpret due to fiscal federalism (for example, budget deficit and debt). Consequently, panel 6 of Figure 12.2 shows within-euro-area divergence trends for some of these indicators. The most serious divergence is observed for the balance of the current account and credit to the private sector, and hence Figures 12.5 and 12.6 depict individual country data of these two key indicators. Indeed, some countries had huge credit booms, most notably Ireland and Spain, but the level and growth of credit was substantial also in Luxembourg and the Netherlands. In contrast, neither France (which had the highest real house price increase, Figure 12.4), nor Belgium (where house prices rose almost as much as, for example, in Ireland) experienced a significant credit boom. Credit growth was modest in Greece compared to other euro area countries, yet Greece had the highest current account deficit before the crisis.

An important driver of booms in various indicators has been the difference in real interest rates. As Figure 12.7 indicates, real long-term interest rates (calculated with past inflation) have fallen in all European countries since the early 1990s, but again, both the initial level and the fall were diverse. In the early 2000s Ireland experienced the most dramatic fall in real long-term rates, followed by Greece, the Netherlands, Spain and France. The low real interest rates have likely contributed to credit booms and housing price increases, even though real interest rates calculated using past inflation likely overstate the relevant real interest rate, which is calculated with inflationary expectations. As ECB (Chart 3, p. 76, 2005) shows the dispersion of inflationary expectations measured by Consensus Economics inflationary forecasts was much less than the dispersion of actual inflation during 1999–2005. As a consequence, the standard deviation of real interest rates calculated with inflationary expectations was much less than the standard deviation of real interest rates calculated with past inflation after 1999, while interestingly in earlier years the relation was the opposite (Table 4, p. 69, ECB, 2005).

12.2.4 Competitiveness and Export Performance

While current account deficits are not necessarily bad, as discussed in the introduction, concerns are warranted when current account deficits are accompanied with a loss of competitiveness. Competitiveness is frequently measured by the real effective exchange rates, though these are misleading for catching-up countries. When the Balassa–Samuelson effect is in place, that is, when there is fast productivity growth in the tradable sector leading to wage rises both in the tradable and the non-tradable sectors, then total economy unit labour costs (ULC) rise. This rise, however, does not alter competitiveness if wage growth in the tradable sector keeps pace with productivity growth.

Therefore, it is crucial to look at sectoral differences in ULC developments. As Figure 12.8 indicates Ireland experienced an increase in total economy unit labour costs of around 30 per cent from 2000 to 2008, but the increases were confined to the construction sector and services, while manufacturing ULC has actually fallen. Hence, the key exporting sector of the country may even have gained competitiveness. Finland is quite similar to Ireland: massive ULC rise in construction and financial and business services and a fall in manufacturing ULC. Manufacturing ULC has also fallen in Germany and Austria, and remained broadly constant

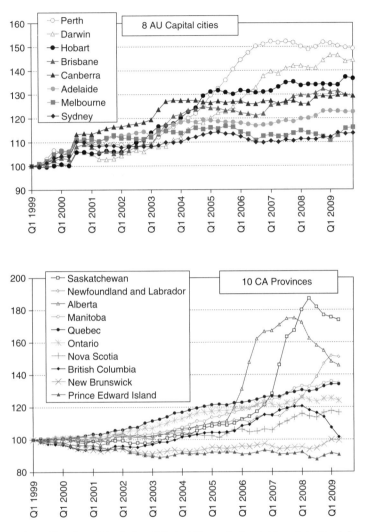

Notes: Australian data: Price Index of Project Homes in the eight capital cities deflated by city-specific all-items consumer price index. Canadian data: new housing price indexes deflated by province specific all-items consumer price index. UK data: price index of all properties deflated by UK average all-items retail price index. US data: US FHFA House Price Index: all transactions deflated by the US average all-items consumer price index.

Source: Australian Bureau of Statistics, Statistics Canada, Nationwide (UK), UK Office for National Statistics, US Bureau of Labor Statistics, Datastream.

Figure 12.4   Real house prices in regions of Australia, Canada, UK and US, 1999Q1–2009Q4 (1999Q1 = 100)

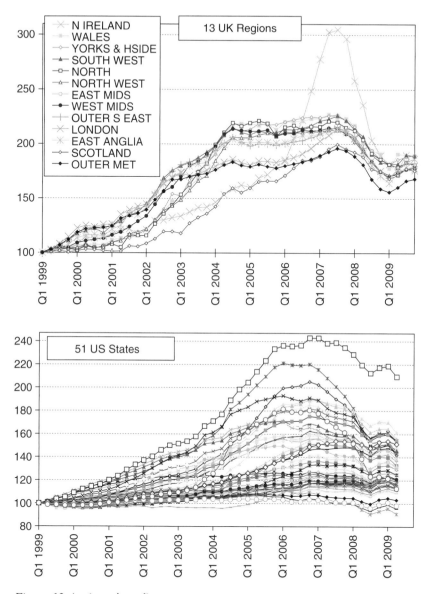

Figure 12.4   (continued)

in Belgium, France and the Netherlands. In contrast, in addition to other sectors of the economy, manufacturing ULC has also risen in Italy and Spain, and to some extent in Greece as well.

It is noteworthy that those four countries with manufacturing ULC

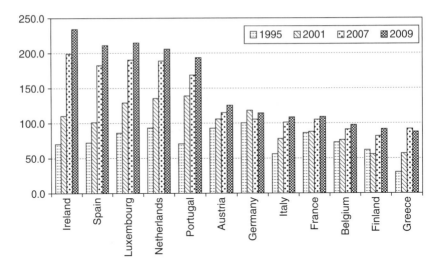

Source: IMF (2009b) International Financial Statistics. Credit data for 2009 refer to the latest available month (mostly between August and October 2009).

Figure 12.5   Credit to the private sector (in per cent of GDP), 1995–2009

decline had the highest shares of manufacturing in value added: 23.6 per cent in Finland and Germany, 21.9 in Ireland, and 20.2 in Austria (2007 data). It is also noteworthy these four countries in the order of Ireland, Germany, Austria and Finland were the top performers in terms of exports. The Netherlands, in which manufacturing ULC remained stable, has also outperformed to some extent the euro area average. The most disappointing export performance is shown by Italy. In Italy, Portugal, Spain, and in more recent years in Greece as well weak export performance was also accompanied by appreciating real effective exchange rates, and manufacturing ULC has also risen.

Germany is frequently blamed for the loss of competitiveness in other countries, as Germany (jointly, by the way, with Finland, Ireland and Austria) could achieve a reduction in nominal ULC in the manufacturing sector before the crisis. However, this blame is not well founded as there was a strong domestic component, that is, a rise in manufacturing ULC in the countries that have lost competitiveness. And in any case the euro area as a whole should gain competitiveness compared to other regions of the world if it intends to slow down the fall of its share in world output. Therefore, while Krugman (2010) is right in arguing that Spain's problem was not a fiscal problem, he is not fully right that a loss in competitiveness was inevitable. The examples of the three other countries having

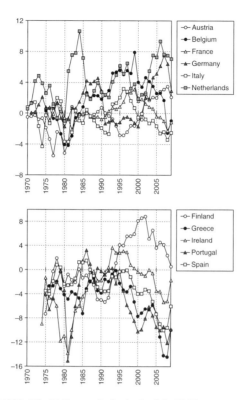

Source: October 2009a World Economic Outlook of the IMF.

Figure 12.6   Current account balance (in per cent of GDP), 1970–2014

huge house price booms (Ireland, France, Belgium) suggest that a surge in manufacturing ULC was not at all a necessity. Consequently, structural weaknesses of the Spanish labour market may explain the difference.

12.2.5   Labour Mobility

In terms of wage formation a crucial issue is labour mobility (see Ahearne et al., 2009). The literature on the optimum currency area (OCA) has established that a high degree of factor mobility is needed to make it optimal for a country to give up its nominal exchange rate as an instrument of economic adjustment in the face of asymmetric shocks (Eichengreen, 1991). In theory, an economic boom in a member of a currency union puts upward pressure on real wages as the demand for labour rises. Immigrants, attracted by improved employment prospects and higher wages, increase

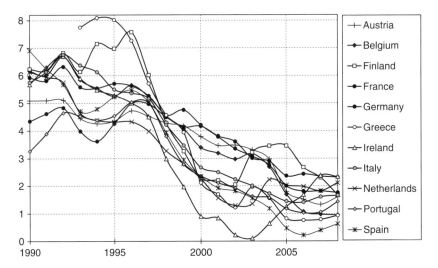

Note: In order to smooth year-to-year volatility, three-year moving averages are shown.

Source: AMECO.

Figure 12.7   Real long-term interest rates (using the deflator of private consumption), 1990–2008

the supply of labour, thereby containing inflationary pressures. During a downturn, net outflows of workers reduce the supply of labour, which eases the downward pressure on wages and softens the reduction in living standards for those residents who stay.

However, Krugman (2010) is not fully right blaming low European labour mobility for the Spanish ULC rise during the boom: labour mobility is indeed lower in Europe than in the US, but Spain (and also Ireland) has experienced massive inflows of migrants during the boom years. According to the European Commission (Table 4, p. 116, 2008b), the share of foreign nationals resident in Spain has increased from 6.6 per cent in 2003 to 11.8 per cent in 2007 (and there were strong inflows in the first years of the 2000s as well), while in Ireland the increase was from 7.5 per cent to 13.4 per cent during the same period. See also Ahearne et al. (Figure 7, p. 5, 2008) for annual inflows of migrants.[5]

Furthermore, one complication that is normally not considered by traditional OCA theory, but that may have particular relevance during the recent boom in some countries, is the effect of migration flows on the non-traded goods sector. While this may seem a small omission, developments in the non-traded sector, and the housing sector in particular, may be

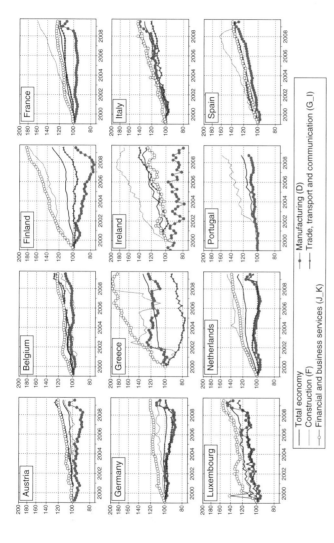

Notes: Ireland, Greece and Portugal: 2000Q1 = 100; all other countries: 1999Q1 = 100. Greek construction ULC has recently risen to 240, but for better readability of the figure, the vertical axis has a 200 cut-off.

Source: OECD: Unit Labour Cost – Quarterly Indicators (MEI).

Figure 12.8 Sectoral developments in ULC, 1999Q1–2009Q3

159

significant in explaining the recent migration experience in countries such as Ireland and Spain. Instead of reducing prices, large inflows of migrants could in fact push up demand and the price of non-traded goods, and real estate in particular. By affecting the dynamics of housing markets, migration may therefore have contributed to the booms and busts in housing markets witnessed in many countries over the past decade. The impact of migration on housing markets also gives rise to wealth effects associated with changes in house prices. While this caveat does not fundamentally call into question the beneficial impact of labour mobility, it does raise the issue of how governments should best respond to the build-up of real estate bubbles in a currency union (see Ahearne et al., 2008).

12.2.6   Crisis Response

Finally, the crisis also had a diverse effect on euro area countries. The actual fall of GDP in 2009 ranges between 1.1 per cent (Greece) and 7.5 per cent (Ireland). The response of unemployment was also diverse: the smallest rise is expected in Germany from 8.4 per cent in 2007 to 9.2 per cent in 2010, while in Spain the expected rise is from 8.3 per cent to 20.0 per cent and in Ireland from 4.6 per cent to 14.0 per cent (all data mentioned so far in this subsection is from European Commission, 2009b).[6] Both output and unemployment responses correlate reasonably well with pre-crisis credit growth, suggesting that credit booms contributed to pre-crisis overheating. In Spain and Ireland, the two countries with the fastest credit boom and the largest pre-crisis expansion of the construction sector, the burst of the bubble depressed particularly this sector and government revenues related to this sector.

On the other hand, crisis response does not seem to be related to pre-crisis current account imbalances. For example, Greece had the highest deficit (Figure 12.6), yet the Greek recession is the mildest among the first twelve members of the euro area. Using regression analysis covering various regions of the world, Mody (2010) also does not support the view that the current account imbalance is related to the downturn in GDP growth.

12.3   THE SIX STYLIZED FACTS AND THE SIX LESSONS

The data analysis of the preceding section and a survey of the literature allow us to establish at least six stylized facts and to draw six lessons which are relevant for euro area enlargement and also for the better functioning of the euro area.

12.3.1 Facts

Fact 1.   Regarding the magnitude of divergence across euro area countries, and also temporal convergence/divergence of various indicators, euro area diversity is by and large similar to regional diversity in some sovereign countries, such as Australia, Canada, Japan, Poland, the UK and the US, and some larger euro area countries.

This finding applies to some key indicators that are available at a regional level (GDP growth and per capita level, participation rate, unemployment rate, inflation, house price developments). Furthermore, house price developments, which are key factors behind the troubles of some current euro area members, were even more diverse across US States and Canadian Provinces than across euro area member countries. Consequently, neither the magnitude of current diversity, nor the mere fact that there was divergence in some indicators within the euro area, do necessarily question the long-run viability of the euro area. The potential arrival of new members would likely make the euro area more diverse than it is today, but as newcomers are quite small, it will not blow up diversity to an unmanageable level for euro area monetary policy.

Fact 2.   There are examples of successful economic catching-up within the euro area, but also of highly disappointing economic performances.

Finland and Ireland can be regarded as successful catching-up countries even when considering the impact of the current crisis. In the case of Ireland, which is in deep trouble now due to its huge pre-crisis housing and construction booms and the extraordinary expansion of the balance sheet of the banking system, it is frequently forgotten in current debates that parallel to these harmful developments a highly competitive export sector has been built-up, which outperformed all other euro area countries in terms of export growth. Irish per capita GDP is expected to remain one of the highest within the euro area as well as post-crisis growth.

On the sad side, Italy's fall in terms of GDP per capita started well before the launch of the euro and is most likely due to structural weaknesses.[7] Portugal's disappointing example is very relevant for potential newcomers, as it joined the euro area after a boom period in the mid-1990s fuelled by the fall in interest rates and the optimistic business climate. Fiscal policy, rather than counterbalancing the growth of credit, was expansionary. Competitiveness was eroded by inflation and several years of wage increases well in excess of productivity gains, leading to a widening of the current account deficit and a slowdown in output growth, averaging 1.1 per cent per year between 2001 and 2007, the lowest among euro area member states (growth in Italy and Germany was just about 0.1 percentage points higher). Investment then collapsed both because of a weakening of growth prospects and an excessive debt overhang created in the private sector during the boom years. The rate of unemployment has increased from 4.0 per cent in 2000 to 8.1 per cent in 2007 and fiscal problems have returned, as Portugal was under an excessive deficit procedure for most of the 2000s.[8]

Fact 3. Booms that are characterized by a surge in credit, housing prices, construction and indebtedness are dangerous both in the run-up period to monetary union and after euro area entry.

Portugal had such a boom in the run-up period to the euro and had a highly disappointing economic growth performance after entry as discussed in the previous point. Ireland and Spain had similar booms after these countries entered the euro area and these countries were severely impacted by the crisis and their pre-crisis seemingly benign fiscal situation has suddenly turned to be very fragile with huge budget deficits and a rapid increase in public debts, with all associated consequences.

Fact 4. The rise in manufacturing ULC is not inevitable during housing, construction and credit booms and structural features matter.

Spain lost competitiveness also in the manufacturing sector during the housing and construction boom, while Ireland gained, and the difference is most likely related to the structure of the labour markets and not necessarily to labour mobility, as both countries had a large intake of migrants during the boom years. Manufacturing ULC also remained stable in France and Belgium parallel with huge housing booms.

Fact 5. Regaining competitiveness via the so-called 'competitiveness channel' is a long-lasting and difficult process.

As discussed for example by the European Commission (2006), competitiveness deteriorates when inflation accelerates and wage awards exceed productivity increases. The consequent shift in the supply of tradable goods and net exports reduces growth and rebalances the cyclical divergence. Regaining the lost competitiveness subsequently via price and wage disinflation, or at least via lower wage growth than productivity growth,[9] is a slow process, yet within a monetary union this is the key channel. For Portugal, Blanchard (2007) suggested a coordinated decrease in nominal wages to get out of the trap – in particular, a relatively large initial wage decrease instead of gradual smaller wage decreases, as the latter may cause deflation expectations to rise for a prolonged period of time and hence push up real interest rates.

In Germany the boom that followed reunification eroded competitiveness and the real exchange rate became overvalued by the mid-1990s. It took

Germany about a decade to regain competitiveness, during which period economic growth was sluggish: annual GDP growth averaged 1.4 per cent in 1995–2005, which was the lowest rate among the first 12 euro area members (again, Italy is just 0.1 point higher); and manufacturing ULC dropped.

Fact 6.   Crisis response: the euro is a shelter.
The crisis has clearly revealed that euro membership helps through a credibility effect and also through ECB facilities at a time of drying-up of money markets. Even Denmark, a country which is regarded to have a credible exchange rate peg to the euro, was forced to raise interest rates while the ECB was cutting rates. Ireland and Iceland differ in many respects, including their size, but both countries had huge housing and credit booms, and the assets of the banking system relative to GDP have expanded to high levels in both countries. While Ireland also significantly suffers in the current crisis, Icelandic pains are some factors larger. Furthermore, some euro area members with worse fundamentals fared much better than some Central and Eastern European (CEE) countries outside the euro area with better fundamentals in the current crisis (see, for example, the brief comparison of Greece and Hungary in Box 1 of Darvas, 2009b, p. 11), and euro area members pay a much lower price for the same level of government debt and for the same level of net foreign debt than new EU member states outside the euro area (see Figure 6 in Darvas, forthcoming).

12.3.2   Lessons

Lesson 1.   Fiscal policy, income policy, and bank regulation and supervision should aim to dampen huge housing and credit booms, that is, act in a counter-cyclical manner.
The analysis of the Irish and Spanish case in Ahearne et al. (2008) also provides ample further evidence in supporting this conclusion. Lane (2010) discusses fiscal policy options and reports, after a broad survey of the literature, that fiscal policy can play a stabilizing role, yet there are serious political constraints and difficulties in implementation that limit the use of fiscal policy. He also suggests the use of subsidized savings schemes for cyclical stabilization in order to partly compensate the loss of independent monetary policy. Regarding banking regulation and supervision, the cross-border nature of European banking renders the solution of banking issues to the EU-level (Posen and Véron, 2009). In fact, uncoordinated country-level actions may have undesirable unintended consequences.

Lesson 2.   Measures improving the flexibility of product and labour markets should be implemented.

The contrast between the Mediterranean countries that have less flexible markets and have either lost competitiveness or were not able to gain in the pre-crisis period, and Ireland and Finland, two countries that have more flexible markets and have in fact gained competitiveness in their manufacturing sector despite their pre-crisis booms, along with the voluminous literature, suggest that product and labour market flexibility are essential for a successful performance within a monetary union.

Lesson 3.   Efficient and transparent crisis management tools are needed.
During the recent global crisis the ECB has swiftly implemented decisive measures to alleviate liquidity problems within the euro area and has gained prestige. However, many other crisis management tools were implemented in largely ad hoc manners at the country level, though joint decision and coordination emerged later. The arrival of the Greek debt crisis has highlighted an additional weakness of euro area governance as there was no provision for the emergence of a serious default risk of a euro area member state. At the time of writing this chapter (February 2010) it is not yet clear how the Greek crisis will evolve and what would happen if market financing dries up. Unfortunately there is a non-negligible chance for an ad hoc solution risking failure and the creation of moral hazard and hence the first best solution is calling in the International Monetary Fund (IMF) (see Pisani-Ferry and Sapir, 2010). In the medium term, efficient and transparent emergency tools (Münchau, 2010), including the resolution of eventual sovereign defaults, should be designed and consistently implemented.[10]

Lesson 4.   Enhanced surveillance is needed.
It has long been recognized that surveillance should be strengthened, see for example, Ahearne and Pisani-Ferry (2006), European Commission (2008a), Pisani-Ferry et al. (2008) and the crisis has thrown a new light on this matter.

Lesson 5.   Enhanced policy coordination is needed.
The euro area is indeed a monetary union without fiscal union and without binding economic policy coordination, yet with limited labour mobility. While the accumulation of private debt, which was frequently associated with housing and credit booms and persistent current account deficits has long been recognized, due to political reasons and also to the difficulties in disentangling 'benign' and 'harmful' processes, not much was done at the euro area level and individual countries were left to maintain full sovereignty in managing their own situation unless they fell under an excessive deficit procedure. The deep trouble of previous booming countries and

the pain of countries aiming to regain competitiveness naturally highlight the serious flaws of this institutional set-up. Dullien and Schwarzer (2009) rightly call the attention that debt accumulation is dangerous and domestic economic policies, such as the tax treatment of real estate in Spain, have contributed to such developments. Yet there are a lot of question marks around the proposal of an 'External Stability Pact' that these authors put forward, which would render current account balances (both deficits and surpluses) below a certain level, such as 3 per cent of GDP. First, excessive debt accumulation, and not the current account deficit itself, is dangerous, and even the different treatment of FDI financing of the current account does not address well this issue. Second, the key reason behind harmful debt accumulation (and hence persistent current account deficits) lies predominantly in domestic policies. Spain imported so much because its competitiveness position has deteriorated and there was an excess demand within the country largely due to the housing boom. Without these developments other countries in excess supply, such as Germany, the Netherlands and Finland, would not have been able to export so much to Spain and instead should have looked for other export markets. The close to zero euro area current account balance should not be regarded as a certainty, and it would not be wise to constrain current account surplus countries in gaining more competitiveness when Europe is loosing grounds on the global stage. Having said that, there is a strong rationale for coordinating demand policies, also taking into account the indications of an enhanced surveillance process, to avoid the repetition of situations when countries enter a debt trap at a weak competitive position à la Portugal at the time of euro entry. Italy has long been in a similar situation and the so far seemingly prosperous Spain and Greece may well enter such a situation now.

Lesson 6.   Euro area entry criteria are inadequate for judging the achievement of 'high degree of sustainable convergence', which they aim to assess.
An unpleasant implication of divergences within the euro area is that it has been a rule rather than the exception that euro area members have violated the entry criteria since becoming members. On average, more than half of euro area member countries violated at least one criterion between 2000 and 2007, and all countries are expected to do so in response to the crisis (see Figure 14 in Darvas, 2009a, p. 17). This fundamentally calls into question both the economic and moral foundations of the future application of the current entry criteria and clearly highlights that the criteria are inadequate for judging the achievement of 'high degree of sustainable convergence'.[11]

The reform of the criteria could be achieved at three levels. First, the inflation and the interest rate criteria are benchmarked on the 'three best-performing member states of the EU in terms of price stability', which have been interpreted in a special way. The Maastricht Treaty, as well as later treaties of the EU, do not specify how to determine the 'three best performers', and in practice this has been defined as the three EU countries having the lowest non-negative inflation rates. (See Box 12.1 for a confrontation of US metropolitan areas with this criterion.) Nothing would prevent the European Commission and the ECB from interpreting it differently, for example, the three countries that have inflation rates closest to the average of the euro area as we suggested (Darvas and Szapáry, 2008; Darvas, 2009a). Second, there is a way to reform the measurement of the four criteria within the framework of the current Treaty on the Functioning of the European Union with a unanimous decision of the Council and a good solution would be to relate all criteria to the euro area average and at the same time to extend the compliance period from the current one year to two or three years in order to be able to better measure sustainable convergence (see Darvas, 2009a). And third, a formal Treaty change would allow a more fundamental revision, which seems politically extremely difficult, so that the first two options seem more promising. Two decades after the criteria were designed and one decade since the euro was launched it is time to reform the criteria and to strengthen their economic rationale. This should be done, of course, parallel with enhanced surveillance and economic policy coordination (also ideally with the reform of the Stability and Growth Pact) to ensure a smooth functioning of the euro area.

BOX 12.1   CONFRONTING US WITH MAASTRICHT

We have calculated the Maastricht inflation criterion for the US metropolitan areas under the interpretation currently adopted for euro area entry decisions (average of the three lowest non-negative inflation rates plus 1.5 percentage points). Figure 12.9 shows that there were frequent violations of this hypothetical criterion during the almost 100-year period for which data are available. The key exceptions are those years when there was deflation. On average, 30 per cent of the metropolitan areas violated this criterion between 1916 and 2008. Considering recent periods, in the 1970s and 1980s, on average, 53 per cent of the metropolitan areas violated this criterion, but even 32 per cent of them, on average, have violated between 1990 and 2008, when inflation was lower and less variable than before. We have also calculated hypothetical violations of our suggested criteria, when the 1.5 percentage points are added to the average inflation rate. In this case the average violation for 1916–2008 is 11 per cent, for 1970–89 10 per cent and for 1990–2008 4 per cent. Thus US metropolitan areas would reasonably well satisfy our suggested criterion, but seriously violate the method currently used in the euro area.

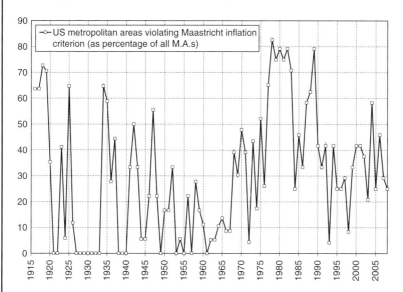

Notes: Number of metropolitan areas for which data is available: 11 for 1916–18, 17 for 1919–35, 18 for 1936–61, 19 for 1962–65, 22 for 1963, 23 for 1966–78, and 24 since 1979.

Source: Author's calculation using data from Bureau of Labour Statistics.

Figure 12.9   US metropolitan areas violating Maastricht inflation criterion (as percentage of all metropolitan areas), 1916–2008

12.4   CONCLUDING REMARKS

While within euro area diversity is well in line with the diversity within the US and other major monetary areas, the euro area is a monetary union without political and fiscal union and without a single economic policy, and its labour and product markets are less flexible. The crisis, the first real test of the euro, has harshly revealed the weaknesses of the euro area and underlined that it must be renewed if it is to rise from the current crisis and the loss in medium-term prosperity.

Yet the bottom line of lessons that we have drawn from the divergences within the euro area is that it is not impossible to manage economic catching-up within the euro area, especially if the policy lessons from current member states are drawn and followed. It is a different question, however, whether it is wise to join the euro area for countries currently outside, or whether they had better wait and opt for a floating exchange rate till a higher level of real convergence is achieved. In an earlier paper (Darvas and Szapáry, 2008) we arrived at the conclusion that although most of the new member states of the EU comply with the OCA criteria quite well, inflation targeting with floating rates is better suited than hard pegs to manage the economic catching-up process. This is because the needed structural price level convergence can be absorbed by the nominal exchange rate and not (or less) by inflation and hence all distortions (including low real interest rates) caused by inflation could be eliminated. However, the difficulties to manage the convergence process under inflation targeting with floating exchange rates should not be underestimated either. The experience of Iceland also underlines that a flexible exchange rate is not a panacea (Lane, 2008). Among the new EU member states with flexible exchange rate regimes, the Czech Republic and Poland were quite successful in the pre-crisis period in containing inflation and the build-up of vulnerabilities and these two countries were able to follow counter-cyclical fiscal policy during the crisis. However, Hungary and Romania were much less successful before the crisis and paid a huge price for that. The crisis therefore has highlighted the crucial implications of macroeconomic policies and the devastating consequences of the loss of credibility.

Consequently, catching-up countries that did gain credibility may have an interest in maintaining their flexible exchange rate systems for a while, but countries that entered a trap with high risk premia and low credibility might be well advised to join sooner and adopt appropriate provisions to avoid the mistakes of the Mediterranean euro area members. A more careful analysis of these issues is left for further research.

NOTES

1. Acknowledgement: Juan Ignacio Aldasoro and Kenneth Iversen provided excellent research assistance. Bruegel gratefully acknowledges the support of the German Marshall Fund of the United States for research underpinning this investigation.

2. Potential euro newcomers are those eight countries that joined the EU in 2004 and 2007, but have not yet entered the euro area. Denmark and UK have a formal opt-out and Sweden does not enter the ERMII in order not to meet the exchange rate criterion, because Sweden's membership was rejected by its voters in a referendum.

3. According to the European Commission (2009b), Greek government debt would reach almost 200 per cent of GDP by 2020 assuming no consolidation other than the withdrawal of fiscal stimulus, and about 180 per cent of GDP in the case of an annual consolidation of half percentage point of GDP, which is minimally required by the Stability and Growth Pact for countries under an excessive deficit procedure.

4. Still, France experienced just a modest increase of the building and construction sector in gross value added (from 5.1 per cent in 1999 to 6.3 per cent in 2007). The highest increase occurred in Spain (from 7.9 per cent in 1999 to 12.1 per cent in 2006) and in Ireland (from 6.6 per cent in 1999 to 10.2 per cent in 2006).

5. Obviously, an even larger inflow could have mitigated more the rise in wages.

6. Note that crisis response of output and unemployment also varies within the US. Forecasts for 2010 are not available, but the rise in the unemployment rate from 2007 to 2009 ranges in 1.1 percentage points (from 3.1 to 4.2 per cent in North Dakota) to 7.0 percentage points (from 4.7 to 11.7 per cent in Nevada).

7. See, for example, Buti (2009).

8. The experience of Portugal is analysed in detail in Blanchard (2007).

9. Obviously, all measures that boost productivity growth are crucial, but the wish for productivity increases is easier said than done.

10. Obviously, due to the difficulties in designing euro area level rescue operations, the medium term solution could be the transparent proclamation that any euro area country in trouble should turn to the IMF for emergency funding.

11. Other key reasons for reform that the criteria have been applied 'flexibly' in the past (in particular with regard to the debt criterion and the exchange rate criterion); the inflation criterion has become tougher as the EU grew from 15 to 27 members and hence keeping the same rules in an expanded EU violates the equal treatment principle; the inflation criterion (as well as the interest rate criterion) is benchmarked against all EU countries and not just against euro area member states; the 'Balassa–Samuelson effect' is expected to be much stronger in newcomers than it was in the first 12 euro countries and hence the joint achievement of low inflation and stable exchange rate is practically impossible (see details in Darvas, 2009a).

REFERENCES

Ahearne, Alan, Herbert Brücker, Zsolt Darvas and Jakob von Weizsäcker (2009), 'Cyclical dimensions of labour mobility after EU enlargement', Bruegel Working Paper, No. 2009/3.

Ahearne, Alan, Juan Delgado and Jakob von Weizsäcker (2008), 'A tail of two countries', Bruegel Policy Brief, 2008/4.

Ahearne, Alan and Jean Pisani-Ferry (2006), 'The euro: only for the agile', Bruegel Policy Brief, 2006/1.

Blanchard, Olivier (2007), 'Adjustment within the euro: the difficult case of Portugal', *Portuguese Economic Journal*, **6** (1), 1–21.

Buti, Marco (ed.) (2009), *Italy in the EMU – The Challenges of Adjustment and Growth*, Basingstoke and New York: Palgrave Macmillan.

Darvas, Zsolt (2009a), 'The Baltic challenge and euro area entry', Bruegel Policy Contribution, 2009/13.

Darvas, Zsolt (2009b), 'The EU's role in supporting crisis-hit countries in Central and Eastern Europe', Bruegel Policy Contribution, 2009/17.

Darvas, Zsolt (forthcoming), 'The impact of the crisis on budget policy in Central and Eastern Europe', *OECD Journal on Budgeting*.

Darvas, Zsolt and György Szapáry (2008), 'Euro area enlargement and euro adoption strategies', *European Economy – Economic Papers 304*, Directorate-General for Economic and Financial Affairs, European Commission, Brussels; in Marco Buti, Servaas Deroose, Vitor Gaspar and João Nogueira Martins (eds) (2010), *Euro – The First Decade*, Cambridge and New York: Cambridge University Press, pp. 823–69.

Datastream, http://online.thomsonreuters.com/datastream (accessible to subscribers only).

Dullien, Sebastian and Daniela Schwarzer (2009), 'The euro zone needs an external stability pact', *Stiftung Wissenschaft und Politik* (SWP) Comments No. 9, http://www.swp-berlin.org/common/get_document.php?asset_id=6125.

Eichengreen, Barry (1991), 'Is Europe an Optimum Currency Area?', NBER Working Paper, No. W3579.

European Central Bank (ECB) (2005), 'Monetary policy and inflation in a heterogeneous currency area', ECB Monthly Bulletin, May 2005, 61–77.

European Commission (2006), *The EU Economy 2006 Review, Adjustment Dynamics in the Euro Area, Experiences and Challenges*, Brussels: Directorate-General for Economic and Financial Affairs of the European Commission.

European Commission (2008a), 'EMU@10 – Assessing the first ten years and challenges ahead', *Quarterly Report on the Euro Area*, **7** (2), Brussels: Directorate-General for Economic and Financial Affairs of the European Commission.

European Commission (2008b), 'Employment in Europe 2008', Brussels: Directorate-General for Employment, Social Affairs and Equal Opportunities of the European Commission.

European Commission (2009a), 'Competitiveness developments within the euro area', *Quarterly Report on the Euro Area*, **8** (1), 18–49, Brussels: Directorate-General for Economic and Financial Affairs of the European Commission.

European Commission (2009b), 'European economic forecast – autumn 2009', *European Economy* 10/2009, Brussels: Directorate-General for Economic and Financial Affairs of the European Commission.

International Monetary Fund (2009a), 'World Economic Outlook 2009', Washington, DC: International Monetary Fund.

International Monetary Fund (2009b), 'IMF International Financial Statistics – December 2009', CD edition.

Krugman, Paul (2010), 'The making of a euromess', *New York Times*, 15 February.

Lane, Philip (2008), 'Iceland: The future is in the EU', http://www.voxeu.org/index.php?q=node/2521, 6 November.

Lane, Philip (2010), 'External imbalances and fiscal policy', IIIS Discussion Paper No. 314, Institute for International Integration Studies, Trinity College Dublin.

Mody, Ashoka (2010), 'Who fell in 2009: those with current account deficits or with extra froth?', http://www.voxeu.org/index.php?q=node/4507, 21 January.

Münchau, Wolfgang (2010), 'What the eurozone must do if it is to survive', *The Financial Times*, 31 January.

OECD (2010), 'Unit Labour Cost – Quarterly Indicators (MEI)', Paris: OECD.

Pisani-Ferry, Jean, Philippe Aghion, Alan Ahearne, Marek Belka, Jürgen von Hagen, Lars Heikensten and André Sapir (2008), *Coming of Age: Report on the Euro Area*, Brussels: Bruegel Blueprint.

Pisani-Ferry, Jean and André Sapir (2010), 'The best course for Greece is to call in the fund', *The Financial Times*, 2 February.

Posen, Adam and Nicolas Véron (2009), 'A solution for Europe's banking problem', Bruegel Policy Brief, 2009/3.

13. Revisiting the European financial supervisory architecture – lessons from the crisis in emerging Europe*

Erik Berglof and Franziska Ohnsorge[1]

In spite of the immense magnitude of the global financial shock that hit emerging Europe the region avoided a traditional emerging market crisis – normally a combination of currency collapses, systemic bank runs and spikes in inflation. Given the depth of trade and financial integration, with economic growth funded by very large capital inflows and much of the banking systems controlled by foreign banks, the impact should have been much greater. Understanding the crisis and its impact in the region carries important lessons for the global debate of financial integration.

It was not like emerging Europe was unaffected. The region experienced the worst output collapse since the great 'transitional recession' following the end of communism (see Figure 13.1). On average, real GDP contracted by about 6 per cent in 2009, and the recovery promises to be slow and fragile. Emerging Europe was the region in the world that suffered most in terms of output decline (see Figure 13.2a), in large part due to its deep trade integration with advanced countries. Especially during the first quarter of 2009, exports collapsed by 12–25 per cent across the transition region. In a sample of 12 mainly Eastern European countries, we estimate that the contraction in external demand during the first quarter of 2009 accounted for almost one half of the 6.5 per cent contraction in real GDP.

But capital flows did not suddenly reverse as in emerging market crises in the past. In fact, if Ukraine and Russia are excluded, capital outflows from emerging Europe in the first two quarters of 2009 were less than any other emerging market region in the world (relative to the size of external assets see Figure 13.2b). While bond markets and markets for syndicated loans virtually disappeared, bank lending through the strategic banks held up remarkably well in light of the region-wide output decline.

Most of all, emerging Europe avoided the region-wide banking crisis

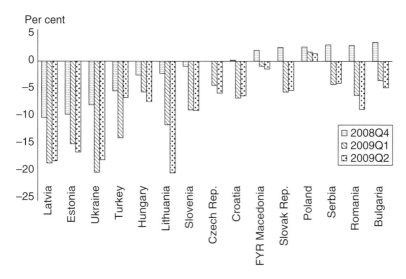

Source: National Statistical Offices, ISI Emerging Markets and staff estimates.

Figure 13.1   *Real GDP growth, 2008Q4–2009Q2 (quarter-on-quarter, seasonally adjusted, in per cent)*

that seemed almost inevitable in the spring of 2009. At the time there was great concern that Western European taxpayers would not allow bank support programmes to benefit Eastern European subsidiaries. Had such discrimination taken place it is very likely that authorities in Eastern Europe would have retaliated by 'ring-fencing' foreign subsidiaries or through other means preventing capital from flowing out of their domestic banking systems. The banks themselves also knew that debt levels in the region would have to come down in response to a lower demand for credit and a changing attitude to risk. While the banks as a collective had an interest in 'managed deleveraging', each individual bank would be better off being the first to withdraw from the region. The likely outcome seemed to be a 'run for the exits' with disastrous effects for the financial systems of the region.

THE TWO FACES OF INTEGRATION

Why was emerging Europe saved from this calamity? Ironically, the same deep integration (see Figure 13.3) that made the region particularly vulnerable to the global financial crisis also helped mitigate its impact. Financial

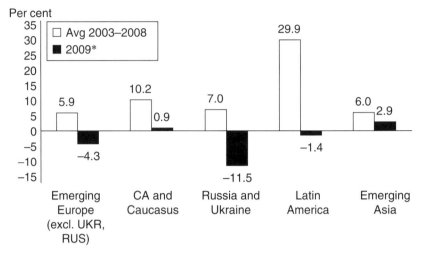

Note: * 2009 data are estimates.

Source: IMF, World Economic Outlook April 2010.

Figure 13.2a   Real GDP growth, 2003–09 (per cent)

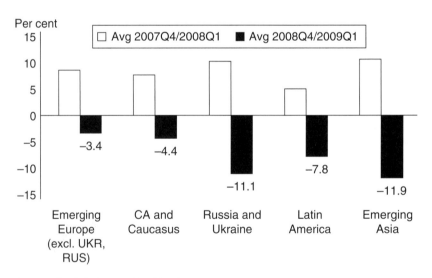

Source: Bank for International Settlements.

Figure 13.2b   Percentage changes in external assets of BIS-reporting banks

Figure 13.3   Cross-border bank linkages

integration, in particular, had two faces: one positive side promoting eco-nomic growth and mitigating the impact of the global financial crisis and another side creating vulnerability to the same crisis.

During the boom years, financial integration fuelled credit and asset price booms but also fostered much-needed financial development and provided the foreign savings that funded growth. With some important exceptions – particularly Asian developing countries, which have tended to be capital exporters – capital has flowed downhill from richer countries to poorer countries in the last 20 years. This was especially pronounced within Europe. However, in most developing countries and emerging markets, these capital inflows have not benefited growth. Emerging Europe was the exception: during 1994–2008, additional capital inflows to emerging Europe of 1 percentage point of GDP were associated with higher growth in GDP per capita by about one-third percentage point. The critical question is whether this relationship was causal.

The 2009 Transition Report of the European Bank for Reconstruction and Development (EBRD) makes an effort to establish the direction of causality in the relationship between capital inflows and growth. Two approaches are used:

- A standard growth regression exploits the time dimension in a panel regression to establish causality; and
- A sectoral approach estimates the link between inflows and industry-level growth depending on the degree to which industries can benefit from inflows.

The growth regressions add various measures of financial integration to those used in standard growth regressions. These include the current account deficit and the change in net foreign assets but also the share of foreign banks in banking system assets and in the number of banks. The panel regressions, estimated using a Generalized Method of Moments (GMM) model for a sample of 56 emerging markets during 1994–2008, use past values of financial intermediation to control for reverse causality running from growth to financial integration. The results for the financial intermediation variables are mixed. However, when the measures of financial integration are interacted with an emerging Europe dummy, the interaction is typically significant with the correct sign (see Table 13.1). In particular, overall, foreign bank ownership significantly increased growth in emerging Europe: for example, a 10 percentage point increase in the share of foreign banks in bank assets or in the number of banks raised growth in emerging Europe by 0.4–0.5 percentage point.

The sectoral approach is more powerful in eliminating the reverse causality running from growth to financial integration and eliminating omitted variable bias (by including an extensive set of dummies). Sectors which are more dependent on external finance should in principle benefit disproportionately from capital inflows. But did they actually grow faster in the presence of greater inflows? To address this question, Friedrich et al. (2010) use 4-digit level industry data for a sample of 26 emerging markets in Europe, Latin America, Asia, and Africa during 1998–2005.

The difference between emerging Europe and other emerging markets is stark. For non-European emerging markets, the authors find no significant correlation between various measures of financial integration and industry-level growth. An emerging Europe dummy, however, differentiates significantly between the European and non-European sample. For the European sample of emerging markets, the authors find that output in manufacturing firms with average financial dependence grew significantly faster (about 1.5 times) in the highest-quartile capital inflow countries than in the lowest-quartile capital inflow countries. For foreign bank ownership specifically, the growth differential between heavily externally financed and own-financed firms was 1.3–1.4 percentage points higher in countries with the greatest share of foreign bank ownership than in countries with the least foreign bank ownership. Foreign bank ownership

Table 13.1   Country-level evidence on growth effects of financial integration

(Regression coefficients; *p*-values in parentheses; dependent variable: average growth in country GDP, 1994–2008)[1]

Variable	Financial integration (FI) measure[2]				
	CA	ΔNFA	GFI	Banks (a)	Banks (b)
Growth effect of financial integration (non-CESE+ countries)[3]	0.121 (0.44)	0.269 (0.001)	0.001 (0.822)	0.010 (0.572)	0.006 (0.823)
Differential growth effect in CESE+ countries[4]	−0.544 (0.078)	−0.014 (0.955)	0.029 (0.008)	0.028 (0.243)	0.045 (0.125)
Memorandum item: total growth effect in CESE+ countries	−0.422 (0.110)	0.255 (0.234)	0.031 (0.025)	0.039 (0.019)	0.051 (0.018)
Observations	213	209	209	194	194
Number of instruments	39	39	39	39	39
Hansen test *p* value	0.13	0.22	0.11	0.14	0.14
Number of countries	56	55	55	51	51

Notes:

[1]   The table shows results from five statistical models for each sample. The models differ in terms of the financial integration measure used, and are otherwise identical. Following Prasad et al. (2007), the following control variables were included (not shown in the table): initial GDP per capita, life expectancy, initial trade policy, fiscal balance to GDP ratio, as well as a measure for institutional quality (International Country Risk Guide (ICRG)). The magnitude, sign and significance of the additional control variables is similar to the ones obtained by Prasad et al. (2007) and related studies. Panel estimation using five 3-year non-overlapping averages, 1994–2008. Estimation using GMM, using past values of the measures for financial integration, log of the initial GDP per capita, life expectancy, fiscal balance, trade openness and institutional quality as instruments.

[2]   CA: average current account over period (share of GDP, in per cent); ΔNFA: change in net foreign asset position over period (as share of GDP, in per cent); GFI: level of gross financial integration (foreign assets + foreign liabilities, in per cent of GDP); Banks (a): share of foreign bank assets in total assets of banking system; Banks (b): proportion (number) of foreign banks in banking system.

[3]   Non-transition country sample obtained by starting with all countries and eliminating countries with (i) 1994–2008 average of purchasing power adjusted GDP per capita higher than US$ 20 000; (ii) area below 30 000 sq. km and island economy; (iii) average value of oil exports in per cent of GDP from 1994 until 2008 was higher than 10 per cent of GDP; and (iv) countries whose average developmental aid from 1994 until 2008 has been higher than 15 per cent of GDP.

[4]   The CESE+ group is composed of the CEB and SEE countries, Turkey and Ukraine.

Sources: IMF World Economic Outlook (current account, initial PPP-GDP per capita and fiscal balance); Claessens and Van Horen (2007) (foreign bank asset shares); Lane and Milesi-Ferretti (2006) and Abiad et al. (2009) (other financial integration measures); World Bank World Development Indicators (life expectancy); and Wacziarg and Welch (2003) (initial trade regime); Political Risk Services (ICRG – institutional quality).

clearly allowed externally-financed firms to grow faster than their own-financed peers.

Foreign bank presence supported growth in emerging Europe and also mitigated some of the capital outflows that were the hallmarks of previous crises. During the height of the current crisis, in the fourth quarter of 2008 and the first quarter of 2009, banking outflows from emerging Europe (excluding Russia and Ukraine) amounted to 3.5 per cent relative to assets, as compared to 12 per cent in, for example, emerging Asia. Outflows from Russia and Ukraine, countries whose banking systems were mainly domestically owned, rivalled those from emerging Asia.

But financial integration also produced vulnerabilities – particularly in the context of a very benign external environment. Foreign bank inflows contributed to rising private sector debt, and foreign bank presence increased the share of foreign currency lending. These vulnerabilities made many countries in emerging Europe more susceptible to external shocks. In fact, by most macroeconomic measures (external debt, current account deficits, credit and capital inflow booms), the countries in the region were more vulnerable to external shocks than East Asia was at the onset of the 1997 crisis.

INTERNATIONAL SUPPORT WAS CRITICAL

Without international support the impact of the global crisis on emerging Europe would have been much more severe. Integration – trade, financial and political – helped mobilize this support. The International Monetary Fund (IMF) and the European Commission (EC) provided unprecedented balance of payments support (see Figure 13.4). Coordinated crisis response was focused and large – but also ad hoc. The large bank support packages and fiscal stimulus in Western Europe benefited emerging Europe. Political integration also contributed to mature, non-protectionist domestic policy responses in both Western and Eastern Europe.

These elements came together in an unprecedented effort to coordinate public and private crisis responses through the so-called Vienna Initiative focussing on the large international banking groups in emerging Europe. Under the initiative, host authorities of subsidiaries of these banks committed to sound macroeconomic and financial policies, appropriate liquidity support and deposit insurance coverage. Home authorities, on their part, allowed access to their national bank support packages for Eastern European subsidiaries. Banks committed to remain in the region and avoid uncoordinated deleveraging. To back up these commitments, the IMF and the EC promised balance-of-payments support, and the

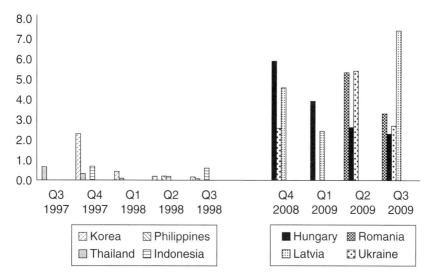

Source: IMF Members' Financial Data by Country and staff estimates.

Figure 13.4 Official support (per cent of GDP)

multilateral development banks committed to increase investments under the Joint International Financial Institutions (IFI) Action Plan. So far five countries have benefited from the Initiative: Hungary, Romania, Serbia, Bosnia and Herzegovina, and Latvia. Still, more than a year into the current crisis, the commitments are being observed.

TOWARDS A NEW EUROPEAN FINANCIAL SUPERVISORY ARCHITECTURE

The key lesson from the crisis in emerging Europe is that financial integration, if it is to be maintained at a similar or even higher level, requires a supporting regulatory and supervisory framework. The home-country model – leaving supervision of cross-border financial institutions solely to home authorities – failed to prevent the build-up of vulnerabilities to external shocks. The model also lacked an effective mechanism for crisis management *ex ante* (although *ex post* the degree of cross-country coordination of crisis management measures was impressive in Central and South-Eastern Europe, not least thanks to the Vienna Initiative).

The experience of emerging Europe demonstrates that the home country model needs to be amended. Home country authorities simply do not sufficiently take into account the interests of host countries. During the crisis, the Vienna Initiative has helped sharpen home country authorities' incentives for supervision of their resident banks' subsidiaries abroad by establishing the principle that, ultimately, home country authorities are responsible for supporting the banking group. The Initiative has also helped make collaboration between home and host supervisors more meaningful. The challenge is to establish a transition from this crisis response to a resilient regulatory architecture in the post-crisis world.

The alternative to home country regulation and supervision cannot be full-blown host country regulation and supervision. Surely, host countries must have scope for regulating and supervising financial institutions operating within their jurisdiction, but on its own this is not a satisfactory complement to the home country model. To begin with, most host countries are too small or insufficiently resourced to carry out meaningful supervision of global banking organizations. Even in countries with realistic capacity to meaningfully supervise, the prospect of host country intervention would most likely curtail entry or follow-up investment. Yet, without a legitimate complement to the pure home-country model, the risk is substantial that political pressures will generate a wave of host country regulation and supervision, potentially unravelling cross-border banking globally.

Take, for example, the emerging recognition of a need to manage risks from foreign currency exposures – a key vulnerability of the region (see Figure 13.5). Many borrowers in the region are exposed to foreign currency risk as they borrow without corresponding income in foreign currency. Regulatory initiatives to reduce these open exposures have taken several prongs in home and host countries: some to tighten prudential requirements as part of an effort to curb credit/asset price booms; some to achieve incorporation of indirect credit risks of foreign currency borrowing into banks' credit risk calculation of unhedged borrowers; and others to require the full disclosure of these risks to the borrowers. The EC has suggested in a public consultation penal capital requirements to discourage excessive mortgage lending in foreign currency, but this particular proposal has met with much public resistance. The dilemma is, of course, that in many countries long-term mortgage funding in local currency is not available, or at least not at attractive rates. Separately, the EC is expected to publish a study of various forms of disclosure in spring 2010. Many have urged a focus on preventing lending booms to begin with rather than changing incentives away from any particular form of lending. Several national European supervisors – both home and host supervisors – are considering their own regulatory initiatives to discourage foreign currency lending to unhedged borrowers (Austria, Hungary and Poland). This

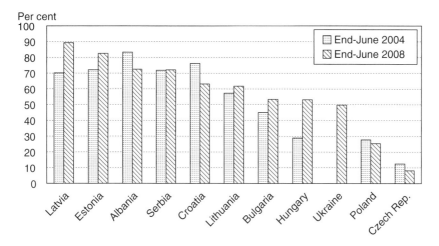

Source: ISI Emerging Markets.

Figure 13.5   Foreign currency lending in per cent of total lending (incl. exchange rate indexed local currency lending)

multitude of initiatives calls out for coordination that ensures the effectiveness of each country's measures.

The crisis has triggered rethinking of the European financial architecture, and important trailblazing reforms in supranational regulation and supervision are under way. In February 2009, a report was published that recommended a wide range of supervisory responses, including an overhaul of the European supervisory architecture (De Larosière et al., 2009). It recommended a revision of Basel II prudential requirements to raise both the quality and amount of capital (especially for trading books), encourage the build-up of counter-cyclical buffers, strengthen liquidity risk management, harmonize definitions of capital and tighten rules on off-balance sheet items. Many of these recommendations were echoed in the Financial Stability Board's recommendations endorsed by the G20 in Pittsburgh in September 2009 (FSB, 2009).

For the European Union (EU), current plans envisage that, in future, *macroprudential* supervision will be supported by a European Systemic Risk Council (ESRC). The ESRC will pool and analyse all information on macroeconomic, macrofinancial, and macroprudential developments. It will issue risk warnings, recommendations to address these risks, and monitor implementation of recommendations. Its members will be from the ECB, individual supervisors and the EC. However, important questions regarding enforcement and relations with other supranational bodies remain as yet unresolved. For example, who will be the recipient of these recommendations and will compliance be mandatory? What will be the ESRC's relationship with the ECB and with the European System of Financial Supervision, charged with micro-prudential supervision?

Responsibility for *micro-prudential* supervision will remain with national supervisors, organized in the European System of Financial Supervision (ESFS). The ESFS encompasses national supervisors, three overarching European Authorities (one each for Banking, Insurance and Occupational Pensions, and Securities), and a coordinating Steering Committee. Day-to-day supervision of financial institutions will remain the task of national supervisors. Supervision of cross-border financial groups will be coordinated by enhanced 'colleges of supervisors', consisting of home and host supervisory authorities of bank groups. The European Supervisory Authorities will arbitrate, coordinate and promote the harmonization of the rulebook. Technical standards will be endorsed by the EC. The ultimate arbiter will be the Court of Justice. But again, important questions remain regarding both the enforcement and the fiscal implications of bank resolution. As in the case of the ESRC, it has not yet been decided to what extent the decisions of the European Supervisory Authorities will be binding and what their scope will be. The fiscal implications of cross-border crisis resolution mechanisms also remain to be decided.

While questions of enforcement and fiscal implications of crisis resolution are being resolved, some pressing short-term issues have arisen while some longer-term issues risk being neglected. These short-term concerns include addressing foreign currency mismatches and re-igniting lending to support a recovery. As part of a longer-term strategy, supervisory relationships and crisis management between the EU and its neighbouring states need to be discussed. An important part of crisis management has been the ECB's coordinated quantitative easing that has effectively extended well beyond the euro area or even the EU borders through the extensive geographical reach of euro area-based cross-border bank groups. The ECB has also provided swap facilities against local currency collateral to two non-euro area EU member states, Denmark and Sweden. It will be important to extend these to similar EU member states in our region (for example Poland, Hungary) not only as part of crisis management but also as a mechanism of support to countries that credibly commit to euro area membership.

Progress in addressing these architectural issues as well as the specific vulnerabilities highlighted by the crisis is essential for the stability of the European economy. Most of emerging Europe is facing the prospect of a slow, drawn-out recovery. Western European demand for East European exports is unlikely to pick up very quickly. Access to credit will also remain curtailed as 'managed deleveraging' of the Western bank subsidiaries in Eastern Europe will continue for some time. If the regulatory and supervisory framework is not strengthened, the banking systems of emerging Europe are unlikely to resist the next global financial crisis as well as they have this one.

NOTES

*   We are grateful for comments from Jeromin Zettelmeyer and Piroska Nagy. Katrin Weissenberg provided excellent research assistance.
1.   European Bank for Reconstruction and Development.

REFERENCES

Abiad, Abdul, Daniel Leigh and Ashoka Mody (2009), 'Financial integration, capital mobility, and income convergence', *Economic Policy*, **24** (4), 241–305.

Bank for International Settlements, *Locational Banking Statistics*, Basel.

Claessens, Stijn and Neeltje Van Horen (2007), 'Location decisions of foreign banks and competitive advantage', World Bank Policy Research Paper, No. 4113.

De Larosière, Jacques et al. (2009), *The High-Level Group on Financial Supervision in the EU*, Brussels.

European Bank for Reconstruction and Development (EBRD) (2009), *Transition Report 2009: Transition in Crisis?*, London.

Financial Stability Board (FSB) (2009), *Improving Financial Regulation, Report of the Financial Stability Board to G20 Leaders*, Basel.

Friedrich, Christian, Isabelle Schnabel and Jeromin Zettelmeyer (2010), 'Financial integration and growth: is emerging Europe different?', *EBRD Working Paper*, forthcoming.

International Monetary Fund (IMF), *IMF Members' Financial Data by Country*, Washington DC.

International Monetary Fund (IMF), *World Economic Outlook*, Washington DC.

ISI Emerging Markets, *CEIC Data database*, New York.

Lane, Philipp R. and Gian Maria Milesi-Ferretti (2006), 'Capital Flows to Central and Eastern Europe', *Emerging Markets Review*, **8** (2) 106–23.

Political Risk Services, *International Country Risk Guide*, New York.

Prasad, Eswar, Raghuram Rajan and Arvind Subramanian (2007), 'Foreign capital and economic growth', *Brookings Papers on Economic Activity*, Economic Studies Program, The Brookings Institution, **38** (2007–1), 153–230.

Wacziarg, Romain and Karen Horn Welch (2003), 'Trade liberalization and growth: new evidence', NBER Working Paper, No. 10152.

World Bank, *World Development Indicators*, Washington DC.

14. Overconfidence as a cause of crisis: the case of Ukraine

Vladimir Dubrovskiy[1]

In the 'post-Lehman' worldwide economic meltdown, Ukraine was hit hard and lost about 28 per cent of its GDP of Q3 2008 within the next two quarters, or 20.3 per cent year-over-year. The crisis thus wiped out all growth gains made since Q3 2004 whereas the EU-27 was propelled back to 2006, and Latvia back to 2005 levels (see Figure 14.1). At the same time, Ukraine experienced the sharpest currency depreciation in the region: the Hryvnya fell by more than 80 per cent in just three months. Why this sharp setback after the apparently strong performance following post-transition recovery since 2000? Was Ukraine indeed just a victim of the

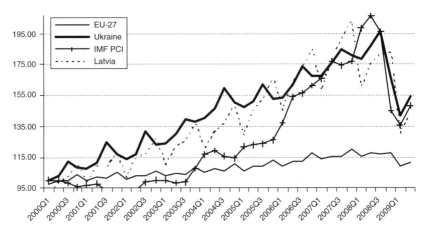

Sources: For EU and Latvia – Eurostat; for Ukraine – DerzhComStat[4] (Ukrainian statistic authority); for the PCI – IMF; Author's calculations[5]

Figure 14.1 *Quarterly indexes of GDP growth (Q1, 2000 = 100) for the EU-27, Latvia, and Ukraine in comparison with the IMF's Primary Commodity Index (PCI) recalculated to Q1, 2000 = 100.*

world economic crisis, as the government says, or did the domestic causes play an equally strong – or even more important – role?

The burst of the commodity price bubble (Figure 14.1), which drove prices down by even more than 30 per cent in the same period, provides some hints. No doubt, this directly affected Ukraine's commodity exports, which had constituted 24.2[2] per cent of GDP in 2008 but subsequently dropped almost twofold. All together, in the first quarter of 2009, total exports declined by 35.4 per cent year over year. But this is still only part of the story, because imports (54.9 per cent of GDP in 2008) plunged by 44.5 per cent in the same period. Therefore, the aggregate contribution of the trade factors should rather have mitigated the decline. Moreover, the downfall in construction started already in early 2008, and the run on Prominvestbank, which triggered all of the subsequent troubles in the banking sector, began already in September (hence, before Lehman) as a result of raiders' attacks. All of this suggests that the external shock not only affected the country's economy immediately, but caused the domestic bubble to burst as well. For example, the development of housing prices in Kyiv (see Figure 14.2) certainly reflected the latter.

The pre-crisis situation in Ukraine very much resembled a speculative bubble. Bubbles are commonly defined as a price component supported by expectations of a future appreciation not justified by fundamentals.[3] There is evidence that not only prices but also many other important market indicators, such as ratio of domestic credit to GDP and monetization (M2/GDP), grew far above their fundamental values. Moreover, macroeconomic imbalances were mounting, and the inflation rate became unsustainable long before the meltdown. These unhealthy developments were overlooked by the government as well as by private investors, both foreign and domestic. Just as market players in the bubble, they should have observed the warning signals, but they stuck to their beliefs that everything would go well.

In the literature, such 'overconfident' behaviour is considered to be one of the plausible causes of speculative bubbles. According to the psychological literature, overconfidence is a necessary part of normal human behaviour, although its revelation depends on the complexity of the task, and the amount at stake. Johnson and Fowler (2009, p. 7) show how people might have become overly confident, and they also conclude that the higher amount at stake, and the higher the degree of uncertainty, the higher the premium on overconfidence is. Naturally, investment businesses should attract and reward overconfident people. Scheinkman and Xiong (2003) have in turn demonstrated one of the ways in which unevenly distributed overconfidence can result in a speculative bubble, regardless of the transaction costs of trading. They modelled a so-called 'greater fool'

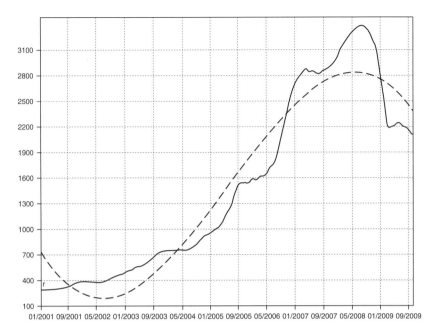

Note: Dashed line is the polynomial trend.

Source: Copy-pasted from www.domik.net, real estate agency Planeta Obolon'.

Figure 14.2   Average price of 1 sq. m. of an apartment in Kyiv (bid price) in 2001–09.

hypothesis: each buyer of an already overpriced asset expects to be able to find an even greater fool (a more overconfident person) who will buy this asset at an even higher price.

Extrapolation can be another plausible mechanism that is likely to transform overconfidence into a bubble, as it happened in Ukraine. 'Unrealistic optimism', itself based on overconfidence,[6] makes investors as well as experts and government ignore the warning signals 'as long as Titanic keeps sailing'. Being overly confident in their cognitive abilities based on past experience, or in their forecasting models, they miss the moment to exit the bubble.

Note that overconfidence seems to be an inherent trait not only of stock traders, but also of individuals who tend to extrapolate their career advances, while at the same time being unrealistically optimistic about potential unemployment or wage cuts. Such people, among other things, tend to take out risky loans based on their current temporary well-being, or even future prospects. If they typically meet equally overconfident credit managers who either underestimate the risks and share the optimism of clients, or are overly confident in current market trends and extrapolate collateral values accordingly, then the whole banking system is at risk.

Moreover, once a bubble has emerged, the very process of its creation rewards (thus selects) overconfident players. The 'optimists' who invested in the already overvalued but still rising assets get a profit, whereas those who are rationally afraid of the possible crash refrain, and therefore screen themselves out of the game. Thus, even if overconfidence does not prevail in the initial set of players (as in the experiments of Levine and Zajec (2007) who observed bubbles even in the absence of uncertainty and over-confidence), only the overconfident ones would remain after the bubble starts inflating.

At the same time, overconfidence ('a false sense of security') of state authorities is mentioned as a source of institutional underdevelopment in the literature devoted to the so-called 'resource curse'. In particular, Gylfason (2001, pp. 21–2) admits that overconfidence related to the resource abundance, along with Dutch disease, rent seeking and neglect with education, causes the resource-rich countries to develop slower than average. The speculative bubble in world commodities markets from 2005 to 2008 should have aggravated all of the adverse effects of resource abundance because it magnified the related rents.

But a false sense of security is not a phenomenon limited to the resource-rich countries. Policymakers tend to overlook threats until the problems are at the gates. Even more so (and for understandable reasons) are they reluctant to start reforms until they become unavoidable. The notorious overconfidence of the US financial authorities[7] can be mentioned as one of the causes of the global crisis. Of course, one can argue that the government should express confidence in order to maintain trust in society. However, while putting up a bold front, a good government should at the same time promptly react to the threats it observes. Otherwise, optimistic statements just reveal its overconfidence.

All of this does not deny the validity of other plausible causes of bubbles, such as positive feedback leading to self-amplification, herd behaviour, limited rationality, and so on. Most probably, in the real world all of these (and possibly other) causes act together. Ukraine seems to be a good case for the validity of overconfidence as one of such causes. Besides, it illustrates one of the ways in which beliefs and psychological peculiarities can transform into macroeconomic imbalances.

There are some theoretical reasons why in Ukraine, as well as in some other post-Soviet countries, overconfidence should be an important factor of economic behaviour.

Regarding the private sector, Johnson and Fowler (2009) suggest that overconfidence should prevail if the rewards are at least twice as high as costs, and uncertainty is sufficiently high. While in a mature market economy such conditions can be found only in some specific sectors, mostly on Wall Street or at least in Silicon Valley, in the post-Soviet countries virtually any kind of business met these criteria in the 1990s. Even now the extremely high risks and returns are observed in many industries. Moreover, politics and public service (including law enforcement) are very often corrupt and intertwined with business, which means high risks and returns in these spheres too. Therefore, overconfident people have advantages in the process of selecting political leaders and even some categories of bureaucrats.

Furthermore, as Babanin et al. (2002, pp. 126, 131) admitted, the Ukrainian elites were used to natural rents during the final 20 years of the USSR's existence. Ukraine does not possess large exportable oil deposits that are most often associated with distorting rents, but is abundant with ore, coal, uranium, fertile soils and other resources. Moreover, the institutional memory of the Soviet times still influences the culture of elites. Therefore, the Ukrainian government should also have had good reasons for overconfidence in the Gylfason sense.

Finally, people had little experience with living in a market economy. In particular, they had never actually seen cyclical crises. Like in Thailand of 1997, most people were used to economic growth, which was among the highest in Eastern Europe from 2000 to 2008, after the country had lost 60 per cent of its alleged initial GDP during the extremely deep and long recession of the 1990s. The factors that caused the meltdown in 2008 were distinct from the sources of the 1990s recession, so people did not have a chance to learn from their own experience.

All this created the ground for the bubble based on overconfidence. The suggested mechanism was as follows (see Figure 14.3).

Above all, the government would need to be blamed. It used the extra revenues generated by the export boom and augmented by capital inflows mostly for current consumption. No stability funds were created, and the National Bank of Ukraine accumulated only modest foreign currency reserves (about USD 37 bn in equivalent, while total indebtedness in the foreign currency constituted over USD 100 bn, of them about one-third short-term). Admittedly, a large part of the government debt accumulated earlier was repaid, but the budget remained in deficit, and borrowing continued, especially by state-owned companies.

Being overconfident in bright future prospects, the government took on burdensome social liabilities. Of course, it was important to restore household incomes, which had suffered severely during the recession of

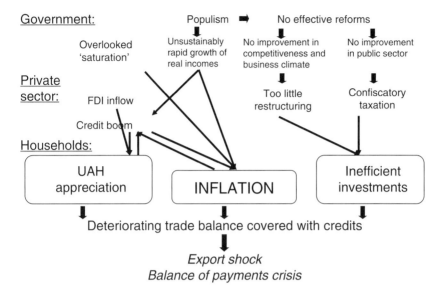

*Figure 14.3   Interconnections between the primary and immediate causes
of the currency crisis and GDP downfall in Ukraine of
2008–09*

the 1990s. It is also quite natural that incomes increased slightly faster
than GDP. Moreover, populism is a well-known 'child disease' of young
democracies. But, all in all, the rate of growth of household incomes consistently outpaced GDP growth since 2004, and this growing discrepancy
has been clearly unsustainable (see Figure 14.4).

Another revelation of overconfidence – 'unrealistic optimism' – has
been especially clear. As late as on 16 October 2008, the Ukrainian Prime
Minister Yuliya Tymoshenko said: 'Despite the swirling global financial
crisis, and despite the dramatic decline of GDP in other countries, our
economy, on the contrary, exhibits systematic growth'.[8] And these were
not just words. Even when the decline had already reached about 10 per
cent of GDP, Tymoshenko's Cabinet submitted and successfully pushed
through Parliament its budget for 2009 based on the assumption of small
but still positive growth.[9]

What is worse is that, unlike in the previous eight years of decline,
Ukraine did not implement successful economic reforms during the whole
period of economic growth. The business climate remained unfavourable
(142 out of 183 in the World Bank's 'Doing Business' report[10]), taxation
remained burdensome and confiscatory (181 of 183, ibid), and market
institutes facilitating efficient allocation of investments (such as equity

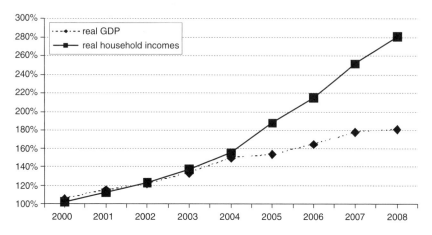

Source: DerzhComStat, author's calculations.

*Figure 14.4   GDP and real household incomes in Ukraine of 2000–08
            (index, 2000 = 100 per cent)*

market) remained weak. Along with rents from commodity exports, these factors hampered enterprise restructuring, and plausibly made the allocation of credit and investments inefficient.

The private sector, both domestic and foreign, appeared overconfident too.

First of all, in Ukraine's export-oriented industries most firm owners did not care much about efficiency as long as they made high profits given the unprecedented price boom. As a result, their business costs are among the highest, if not the highest, among competitors. Finally, Ukraine is the world's leader in using obsolete open-hearth furnace technology for steelmaking.[11]

Large foreign investments and credit inflows (see Figures 14.5 and 14.6), which tripled annually after 2004, were not used for modernizing and restructuring the economy. The inflows came despite very little, if any, improvement in business and investment conditions, being attracted instead by high returns, the large and growing domestic market, and alleged prospects of EU accession. The hopes for EU accession generated by the Orange revolution of 2004 evaporated, however, very soon. The returns, in turn, were mostly based on either the rents originated from the bubbles (in domestic housing or worldwide commodity prices), or households' overconfidence (see below). Finally, the rapid expansion of the domestic market was not supported by productivity growth. As well as many other investors and creditors all over the world, those who invested in Ukraine or lent to Ukrainian banks had underestimated the risks.

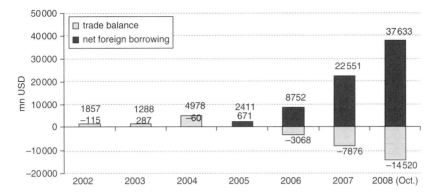

Sources: DerzhComStat, The National Bank of Ukraine (NBU).

Figure 14.5   *Trade balance and net foreign liabilities of the Ukrainian banks before the crisis (in 2002–Oct. 2008), mn USD*

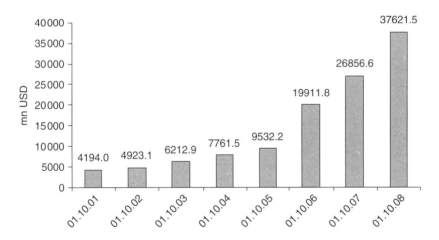

Sources: DerzhComStat.

Figure 14.6   *The stock of gross direct foreign investments in the Ukrainian economy*

Besides, both the private sector and the Ukrainian government over-looked the 'saturation' of the Ukrainian economy, first of all in terms of financial depth, namely monetization and domestic credit.

After the hyperinflation of the early 1990s and subsequent disinflation, the level of monetization (measured as the M2-to-GDP ratio) was as low

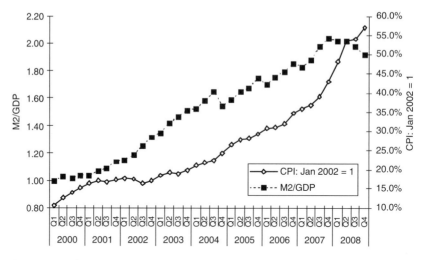

Source: DerzhComStat, NBU.

*Figure 14.7   Inflation (CPI: Jan 2002 = 1) and monetization (M2/GDP)
in Ukraine in 2000–08*

as 10 per cent in 1998 and increased up to 17 per cent in 2000. When the
economy started to grow, it absorbed the money very well, so even annual
increases in the monetary base by 40 per cent did not initially push up
inflation to dangerous levels (see Figure 14.7). However, this favourable
situation could not last for long. Inflation started to grow already in
2003, hit the two-digit level in 2004, and eventually reached 22.3 per cent
(December to December) in 2008. At its peak, at the end of 2007, the M2/
GDP ratio approached 54.3 per cent (45.1[12] on average for the whole year),
which was at this moment as high as in most CEE countries (46.9 per cent
in Estonia, 45.3 per cent in Poland, 40.6 per cent in Latvia). Meanwhile,
Ukraine lagged behind these countries in terms of fundamentals for financial depth, such as protection of property rights, trust, institutional development of the financial system, and so on.

   Therefore, the level of monetization alone could not increase further at
the same pace for long. The financial authorities should be given credit
for recognizing this fact. From the very beginning of 2008 they started
to contract the money supply. But this meant that the bubble was going
to burst, regardless of external shocks. However, this warning signal was
overlooked. In particular, the credit boom continued (see Figure 14.8)
even despite the simultaneous setback in construction.

   The story was similar for domestic credit (see Figure 14.8). Starting from

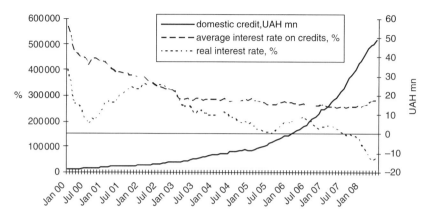

Source: DerzhComStat, NBU.

*Figure 14.8 The credit boom in Ukraine: domestic credit (in UAH mn)
and interest rate, nominal and real, per cent.*

very low levels in 2000 domestic credit rose by 73.7 per cent (on average for
the whole year) in 2008, which was higher than in the Czech Republic (52.5
per cent), Poland (49.9 per cent), Lithuania (62.7 per cent) and most other
CEE countries but Latvia and Estonia. The fundamentals for such high
levels were weak, let alone the risk associated with such rapid growth of
credit. Borrowers had little time to develop credit scores whereas lenders
had equally insufficient time to develop experience and skills necessary for
screening of applicants; and the institutional development of the banking
system lagged behind. For instance Ukraine still lacks a nationwide database of collateral and credit scores. These high risks were reflected by
nominal interest rates. But as long as 55 per cent of loans were made in
hard currency,[13] borrowing abroad at the European rates and giving mortgages at 15 per cent or more seemed to be good business, especially for
those who believed in extrapolated current trends in the housing market.
But who was going to take out such mad loans?

The population, while contributing to the bubble, should be blamed
the least. People were either passive, or rationally seized the opportunities
provided by banks and retailers. Furthermore, there is no reason to expect
consumers to be able to predict a crisis – a task that the absolute majority of experts, including the author, failed to accomplish. Extrapolation
of their raising incomes (see Figure 14.4) along with other trends, such as
appreciation of the Hryvnya, increase in real estate prices, and so on, was
the best they could do.

But at least a small but important self-selected part of the population

appeared overly confident and made important contributions to magnify-
ing distortions. Many upper-middle class Ukrainians became real estate
speculators. Their profits remained large despite the high interest rates
they had to pay. They largely contributed to the development of the real
estate bubble and to the credit boom. Permanently rising values of their
real estate assets gave them (as well as their creditors) a false sense of security. Of course, when the bubble burst, most of the loans they had taken
out became a risk. At the same time, for many of those who just bought
housing for dwelling (or land for development), it made perfect sense to do
so, as the apartment rents they had to pay did not differ that much from
mortgage payments.

At a certain moment, consumer credit and mortgage growth became
self-propelling. Initially, the consumer credit market had been severely
underdeveloped even given the overall weakness of banking in Ukraine;
in 2005 total liabilities of the household sector were three times below
those of private corporations. Yet of the amount of domestic loans issued
to households between 2005 and October 2008, as much as 44 per cent
were consumer loans and mortgages. Rapid credit expansion and a steady
loosening of lending conditions (increase in time and decrease in down
payment) supported the price growth. In turn, the latter made it rational
for households to take out a loan and buy an apartment or land as early as
possible. Once the rates were decreasing very slowly, if at all, while prices
went up, the sooner one buys, the lower the mortgage payments would
be.

Although there were some rational reasons for the credit boom in the
real estate market other than overconfidence, few would explain the large
part of consumer loans taken out at high rates. New car sales doubled from
2005 to 2007,[14] mostly because improved credit conditions made them
affordable despite unreasonably high and still increasing prices. Besides,
most of the loans were taken out in hard currency, mostly in US dollars.
This was rational for the borrowers, because interest rates in USD were
about one and a half times lower than in UAH, while the exchange rate
remained stable or even appreciating. At the same time, most of the borrowers earn their incomes in domestic currency, thus incurring a currency
risk for many years ahead. Of course, people did not expect any further
declines in incomes. At the same time, there is virtually no job security for
employees paid above-average wages (about EUR 200 at the pre-crisis
exchange rate), let alone for self-employed people and entrepreneurs.

At the macroeconomic level the above described developments led to
inflation combined with appreciation of the Hryvnya, and accumulation
of large private foreign indebtedness denominated in hard currency.

Inflation went up for a number of reasons.

Monetary expansion was hard to stop, as the National Bank had to buy increasing volumes of hard currency stemming from export revenues (which, in turn, kept rising due to the world commodity price bubble) and capital inflows (FDI and credits that were converted to the national currency). Should it stop doing so, as it had to in 2008, the Hryvnya would appreciate in nominal terms, with devastating consequences for the competitiveness of domestic producers.[15] Raising interest rates was also politically difficult for the authorities, despite actually negative real interest rates observed since August 2007, more than a year before the crisis started. Besides, an even higher interest rate could attract even more capital inflows, which would further aggravate the problems.

Increasing household incomes along with consumer credit had boosted demand beyond supply increases. Development of the latter was restrained by poor business conditions exacerbated with the real appreciation of the Hryvnya. Meanwhile, the government did not reform health care, education, insurance, or communal utilities, which would make these sectors able to provide more paid services of decent quality for middle-class customers, and in such a way increase the supply. At the same time, despite WTO accession, increase in imports was still restrained by numerous barriers.[16]

Finally, market concentration remained high (OECD, 2007), and probably even increasing. In particular, this factor could have made inflation less sensitive to some tightening of monetary policy in 2008.

Combined with a stable or even increasing UAH/USD exchange rate (although still some depreciation in respect to the euro) such a high inflation resulted in the appreciation of the real exchange rate. However, the latter reduced neither exports, nor capital inflows. Commodity exports remained competitive due to rapidly increasing prices. Capital inflows went to consumer loans typically used to buy imported goods, which, in turn, became even more attractive as the domestic currency appreciated.

Real exchange rate appreciation naturally led to mounting trade imbalances (see Figure 14.5), which were, however, more than covered by capital inflows until the second half of 2008. The sudden reversal of the latter in the fall of 2008, and the simultaneous contraction of exports due to the bursting of commodity price bubble triggered a 'hard landing' of the overheated economy. The sharp depreciation of the Hryvnya, in turn, caused a bank run, since individuals and firms tried to stabilize their savings by converting them into hard currency. The export industry setback was accompanied by a turn to extremely conservative credit policies motivated by high risks along with profits that banks made in currency markets during depreciation, which exacerbated the decline in investment.

Admittedly, high current account deficits covered by capital inflows have been typical for most CEE countries. Should these capital inflows be used to modernize the domestic economy (in this case imports would consist of predominantly investment goods, like equipment), the real exchange rate appreciation would eventually be justified by raising domestic competitiveness. Then, the imbalances, while still risky, would be sustainable. This was likely to be the case for Poland, which suffered remarkably little from the crisis, and some other CEE countries. But in Ukraine the seemingly similar macroeconomic picture actually reflected quite different microeconomic processes, which, in turn, were driven by different institutional patterns. One of the main reasons for these differences can be found in the institutional memory of elites that used to have overconfidence in rents during the Soviet times.

NOTES

1. Senior Economist, CASE Ukraine – Center for Social and Economic Research, Ukraine. The author is grateful to CASE Ukraine's team for help in data collection, and to Professor Janusz Szyrmer for fruitful discussion and advice.
2. Here and after, unless specially noted, the data are based on the national statistics provided by DerzhComStat (the Ukrainian national statistic authority) and NBU (the National Bank of Ukraine), in some cases with author's calculations.
3. 'Bubbles are commonly defined as a price component supported by expectations of a future appreciation not justified by fundamentals (Joseph Stiglitz, 1990; Karl E. Case and Robert J. Shiller, 2003; Markus Brunnermeier, 2008)', quoted by Bucchianeri (2008).
4. The data from DerzhComStat and NBU are published periodically, and are routinely added to the database and cross-checked by the CASE Ukraine staff. This database is then used for various purposes, including this chapter. It is impossible therefore to provide an exact reference to the particular data sources. Moreover, as long as the DerzhComStat provides only a limited number of tables and does not have the on-line tools for making custom enquiries (as, for example, Eurostat does), a full reference, to, say, an 8-year monthly time series would consist of about 100 individual URLs. Some older data may also appear unavailable.
5. The data on Ukraine were recovered from quarterly year-over-year data by rebasing all quarters in 1995 to 100.
6. 'Unrealistic optimism seems a robust behavioural feature when people have to evaluate their own risk to become victims of unfortunate life-events, compared to the average population (Hoorens and Buunk, 1993; Perloff and Fetzer, 1986; Weinstein, 1980)' quoted by Hoelzl and Rustichini (2005, p. 1).
7. 'The banking system is healthy', The Recent Financial Turmoil and its Economic and Policy Consequences, Ben S. Bernanke (2007), Federal Reserve Chairman, 15 October, available at: http://www.federalreserve.gov/newsevents/speech/bernanke20071015a.htm.
8. Opening speech at the Cabinet's Session of 16 October 2008. Quoted by *Ukrayins'ka Pravda*, in news article 'Tymoshenko again boasted that she has everything allright, better than anybody else in the World', available at: http://www.pravda.com.ua/news/4b1aa1e6af7bc/.
9. Notably, the Minister of Finance Victor Pynzenyk refused to present this budget, and soon resigned.

10. World Bank, 'Doing Business' report, available at: http://doingbusiness.org/economyrankings/.
11. 'Open-hearth furnace', available at: http://en.wikipedia.org/wiki/Open-hearth_furnace.
12. Here and after in this and two subsequent paragraphs data are taken from the World Bank's 'World Development Indicators' (WDI).
13. By October 2008.
14. Golovin (2008). The data provided by Auto-Consulting.
15. For a number of reasons that go beyond the scope of this chapter, the government failed to sterilize these capital inflows.
16. Apart from tariff and non-tariff barriers, Ukraine was ranked 139 by the World Bank 'Doing Business' in the nomination 'trading across borders'.

REFERENCES

Babanin, O., V. Dubrovskiy and O. Ivaschenko (2002), 'Ukraine: the lost decade . . . and a coming boom?', the country paper within GDN's 'Explaining Growth' Global Research Project, Alterpress, Kyiv, available at: http://www.eerc.ru/default.aspx?id=176 (accessed 12 May 2010).
Bernanke, Ben S. (2007),'The Recent Financial Turmoil and its Economic and Policy Consequences', 15 October, available at: http://www.federalreserve.gov/newsevents/speech/bernanke20071015a.htm (accessed 12 May 2010).
Bucchianeri, Grace Wong (2008), 'The anatomy of a housing bubble: overconfidence, media and politics', manuscript, available at: http://real.wharton.upenn.edu/~wongg/research/bubble.pdf (accessed 12 May 2010).
DerzhComStat (various years), http://ukrstat.gov.ua/
Eurostat (various years), http://epp.eurostat.ec.europa.eu/portal/page/portal/statistics/search_database
Eurostat, 'The quarterly data on GDP', available at: http://appsso.eurostat.ec.europa.eu/nui/setupModifyTableLayout.do (accessed 12 May 2010).
Golovin, Vlad (2008), 'A car becomes a luxury' (The media article), *Ukraine Wholenational Magazine*, available at: http://ukraine.webstil.info/news.php?action=newsdescription&target=337 (accessed 12 May 2010).
Gylfason, T. (2001), 'Nature, power, and growth', CESinfo Working Paper, No. 413.
Hoelzl, Erik and Aldo Rustichini (2005), 'Overconfident: do you put your money on it?', *The Economic Journal*, **115** (April), 305–18.
IMF Primary Commodity Price Index, available at: http://www.imf.org/external/np/res/commod/externaldata.csv (accessed 12 May 2010).
Johnson, Dominic D.P. and James H. Fowler (2009), 'The evolution of overconfidence', manuscript, available at: http://arxiv.org/ftp/arxiv/papers/0909/0909.4043.pdf (accessed 12 May 2010).
Levine, Sheen S. and Edward J. Zajac (2007), 'The institutional nature of price bubbles', SSRN Working Paper, No. 960178, available at: http://ssrn.com/abstract=960178 (accessed 12 May 2010).
OECD (2007), 'Economic Assessment of Ukraine 2007', the country survey, available at: www.occd.org/eco/surveys/ukraine.
'Open hearth furnace', available at: http://en.wikipedia.org/wiki/Open-hearth_furnace (accessed 12 May 2010).
National Bank of Ukraine (NBU) (various years), http://bank.gov.ua/

Scheinkman, Jose A. and Wei Xiong (2003), 'Overconfidence and speculative bubbles', *Journal of Political Economy*, **111** (6), 1183–219.

Ukrayins'ka Pravda, 'Tymoshenko again boasted that she has everything allright, better than anybody else in the World', news article, available at: http://www.pravda.com.ua/news/4b1aa1e6af7bc/ (accessed 12 May 2010).

World Bank, 'Doing business', available at: http://doingbusiness.org/economyrankings/ (accessed 12 May 2010).

World Bank, 'The World Development Indicators', access provided by the Global Development Network, available at: http://wdi.gdnet.ws:9999/ext/DDPQQ/member.do?method=getMembers&userid=1&queryId=6 (accessed 12 May 2010).

PART V

Post-crisis business models of banks in CEE

15. The Russian banking sector one year after the crisis began

Nataliya Orlova

RUSSIA AS A SAFE HAVEN

Since 2000, the Russian banking sector has undergone a period of rapid growth associated with the economic expansion that resulted from rouble devaluation after the 1998 crisis. Russia's corporate loan book demonstrated a strong average annual growth rate of 46 per cent, while retail lending grew at an average rate of 88 per cent. Growth in Russian corporate loan portfolios was primarily driven by capital inflows, which in turn were generated by high international commodity prices. With the government-managed stabilization fund sterilizing the impact of increased export-generated capital inflows, the market perception of Russia's macro stability improved, and access to international capital markets emerged. Additionally, these capital inflows had a significant impact on the Russian banking sector. Directly, these inflows increased the Russian banking sector's foreign debt from USD 9 billion in 2000 to USD 164 billion in 2007. Indirectly, international borrowing by Russian companies increased from USD 22 billion in 2000 to USD 249 billion in 2007, which has contributed to substantial increases in real sector liquidity. Altogether, increases in corporate accounts and foreign debt financed approximately 55 per cent of the increase in banking assets during the period of 2000–07.

In spite of an absolute increase in retail savings of USD 194 billion, the retail base as a percentage of GDP remained at a modest level of 16 per cent even in 2007. With inflation outstripping nominal interest rates, the resulting negative real interest rate environment created disincentives for retail deposit savings. As a result, some potential savings were reallocated to direct investments in the real estate sector and modest investment in the financial markets. These investments provided a much higher rate of return and represented an additional reason to push banks toward foreign debt instead of relying on retail savings.

However, on the lending side, the retail lending segment was unsurprisingly the key area of boom. Since 2003, fears of mounting competition with foreign banks have driven Russian banks to penetrate the retail lending market. While the retail loan book was virtually non-existent in 2000, it had reached USD 120 billion by 2007. The majority of these loans were short-term consumer finance and personal loans and thus boosted private consumption. In spite of the risk of overheating inherent in a rapidly expanding retail loan portfolio, the low saturation of the Russian economy with financial services had established the Russian banking sector as a safe haven by the time the first wave of the global crisis emerged in 2007.

The low penetration of banking services was the key reason why Russia remained little affected by the subprime crisis of 2007. With corporate loans equal to 30 per cent of GDP, retail loans equal to 10 per cent of GDP, and mortgage loans equal to 2.5 per cent of GDP, the Russian lending market was considered to have very strong growth potential. At the same time, Russian banks had very little exposure to financial markets, with securities comprising a mere 10 per cent share of total assets. In addition, the majority of this exposure was in the form of simple financial instruments, such as bonds or equity shares, while the exposure to complex structured instruments was highly limited. Finally, the 2003 upgrade of Russia's sovereign debt rating to investment grade further strengthened the country as a destination for foreign investment, significantly expanding the universe of potential portfolio investors. With Russia's fiscal position expected to remain strong on the back of robust commodity price growth, most notably of oil, this upgrade helped ensure continued and substantial access to capital markets for Russian banks.

Only with the collapse of Lehman Brothers did the crisis finally hit Russia in the fall of 2008. This event, combined with the deterioration in the outlook for oil prices, delivered a deep shock to the Russian financial sector. Even though macro stability was secured by the stabilization funds, Russia was ultimately plagued by financial turmoil in much the same way as many other countries. The deterioration in the global economic environment resulting from the financial sector shocks in major Western markets and continued global economic imbalances has left the Russian economy facing reduced demand and concomitant sharp price falls for key commodity exports, especially oil, as well as serious constraints on external financing. The Russian banking sector has suffered from a severe economic contraction in the Russian market, resulting in a liquidity crisis, rising non-performing loans (NPLs) and deteriorating capital ratios.

FINANCIAL TURMOIL IN THE SECOND HALF OF 2008

By the second half of 2008, these constructive developments in the Russian banking sector were under threat, most notably from the onslaught of the global financial crisis. However, even a month before the crisis hit Russia, Russia's conflict with Georgia served as a preliminary test of the durability of Russian markets. Although Russia's oil wealth could easily cover the cost of this conflict, the economy was vulnerable to other associated financial shocks: as a result of the conflict, the cost of insuring debt in the credit default swap (CDS) market rose; additionally, concern emerged over whether the conflict would frighten away foreign investors, thus affecting longer-term capital inflows amidst a global credit market already drained by the Western credit crunch.

When the financial crisis hit Russia in the fall of 2008, the liquidity crisis was further intensified by fears of rouble depreciation and foreign currency flight. Over the course of several months, oil prices declined from USD 130/bbl to USD 40/bbl, which had the cumulative effect of reducing the monthly current account surplus from USD 10 billion in September 2008 to USD 3 billion in the fourth quarter of 2008. The contraction of industrial output that began in October 2008 provided reason to believe that the current account deterioration was only temporary and would gradually recover to a sustainable level of surplus through import contraction; however the capital account deteriorated significantly.

The pressure on the capital account was fundamentally guided by a belief that the Russian economy was relying too heavily on short-term external debt. With regard to Russia's USD 480 billion in total foreign debt, the Central Bank of Russia (CBR) expected the level of debt redemption to fall between USD 100–120 billion in 2009. This amount exceeded the country's annual current account surplus and illustrated the dependence of Russian banks and companies on the financial markets.

Another cause for concern were the negative changes taking place in the banking sector. A combination of the sharp collapse in the Russian equity market, which lost 78 per cent in 2008 alone, and a drop in bond markets resulted in a crisis on the Russian interbank market. When KIT-Finance Bank, one of the largest market participants, became unable to meet its obligations, a crisis of confidence paralyzed the entire banking sector. This development fuelled expectations of a rouble drop and liquidity injections.

The interbank crisis was further exacerbated by an outflow of retail deposits from the Russian banks. Although the Russian Deposit Insurance

Agency was responsible for covering up to USD 20 000 – assuring coverage of roughly 70 per cent of banking sector deposits – Russian banks experienced an 8 per cent outflow of retail deposits from September to October 2008. This outflow largely reflected expectations of rouble depreciation, which prompted households to convert rouble-denominated deposits into foreign currency savings. As bank accounts were drained of foreign currency savings, these savings were not immediately returned, and instead remained in the form of dollar- or euro-denominated cash under mattresses.

The combination of the interbank crisis and the deposit outflows led banks to substantially increase their demand for the CBR's refinancing option. The CBR's most commendable achievement was its ability to thoroughly deal with the liquidity crunch. When Russia was torn into the financial turmoil of 2008, the system of refinancing facilities was essentially limited to repo operations based on state or municipal bonds. Taking into account the decline in Russian sovereign debt the previous year, it is clear that the size of this market was insufficient to guarantee large-scale refinancing support. Another important issue was that state bonds were mostly held by large state-owned banks. The low return on these state bonds made them largely unattractive for private banks, giving the latter limited access to refinancing facilities.

In September/October 2008, the CBR oversaw an unprecedented series of changes in the refinancing system. After defining a list of around 120 banks which possessed appropriate risk profiles, the CBR began offering unsecured loans with a 3–6 month maturity. At the end of fall 2008, the CBR started providing refinancing for corporate loans to banks' large borrowers. In a record short period, the CBR supplied banks with RUB 3.5 trillion (USD 100 billion or 6 per cent of GDP) in liquidity support, which played an important role in stabilizing the banking sector.

However, the CBR was faced with some immediate difficulties when this liquidity support failed to prevent a contraction in available lending. The reasons for this were twofold. First, the substantial injection of rouble liquidity fuelled expectations of rouble depreciation, resulting in a USD 131 billion net capital outflow in the fourth quarter of 2008. Household purchases of foreign currency accounted for USD 30 billion of this, outflows of foreign investment capital from the Russian market accounted for USD 20 billion, and the remainder reflected an accumulation of foreign currency among banks and companies. A second reason was the collapse in industrial growth, which contracted from growth of 6 per cent year-on-year in September 2008 to −10 per cent year-on-year by December of the same year. This development raised concerns about the quality of loan books. Anticipating the inability of companies to service their loans, banks stopped lending, instead choosing to focus their energies on the buy-back of bonds and securities. Despite economic contraction, the CBR decided to increase its interest rate in order to stabilize the exchange rate market.

The substantial liquidity injection and the gradual rouble depreciation that resulted delivered a huge blow to local confidence in the rouble. Consequently, dollarization gained importance. The share of foreign currency-denominated retail deposits increased from 13 per cent in the summer of 2008 to 30 per cent by the beginning of 2009. In mid-2009, the share of foreign currency-denominated deposits was virtually unchanged. On the corporate side, foreign currency-denominated deposits jumped from the pre-crisis level of 20 per cent to 50 per cent by the beginning of 2009. This loss in domestic confidence in the rouble appears to be the major negative impact from the global financial crisis: the 2009 statistics show that while inflows of international capital can resume fast enough, domestic deposits in foreign currency are not yet declining.

THE QUALITY OF THE LOAN BOOK

A greater threat to Russia's banking sector is the question of non-performing debt that looms on the horizon. This debt is particularly dangerous for Russian banks because they do not have experience working with bad loans. In the 1990s, all banking sector activity was focused on the currency market and later shifted to the state bond market. Prior to 1998, loans accounted for only 40 per cent of bank assets – compared with the current level of 60 per cent – and were concentrated on interconnected borrowers. Thus, in 1998, bad loans in a number of cases reflected the decision by bank owners to sacrifice their banking business in order to save the productive assets of the group.

In 2009, however, Russian banks were vulnerable to one overarching risk – the palpable decline of economic activity that is affecting all sectors of the country's economy. Russia's GDP is expected to drop 8–9 per cent year-on-year in 2009, and in the first six months of 2009, it dropped by 10.4 per cent year-on-year. The current economic downturn means that all banks will see an increase in non-performing loans to one degree or another. Exporters are suffering from the decline in global demand and the unavailability of foreign capital, so they will certainly face liquidity problems. Furthermore, the decline in the country's construction sector suggests that the credit quality of companies operating in the manufacturing, transportation and trade sectors will deteriorate. The dramatic drop in equity and real estate prices has reduced the value of collateral used by borrowers. Retail clients will also have trouble servicing their long-term debt.

The obvious concern is the short maturity of Russia's debt. Companies needed to redeem around USD 220 billion in 2009. Half of this amount was denominated in foreign currency, which imposes an additional financial burden considering the significant depreciation of the rouble since September 2008. The USD 220 billion debt figure is equal to roughly 20 per cent of Russia's current GDP. Given today's environment of declining global and local demand, it is indeed difficult to imagine that the real sector of the economy would be able to generate the necessary revenue flows to service its outstanding debt. As bad debts have multiplied, the situation has been further aggravated by the fact that a large number of these loans are foreign currency-denominated, since it was cheaper to borrow in foreign currencies during the period when the rouble was appreciating.

Because USD 220 billion in debt has to be paid in 2009 a level of bad loans of 15 per cent seems to be inevitable, and a 'domino effect' of bad debt could push non-performing loans up to 30 per cent. Banks are clearly working to reduce their exposure to troubled borrowers in order to keep bad loans in check. This, in turn, is exacerbating the situation for struggling companies that face severe liquidity problems, making it likely that some will become insolvent.

During periods of economic trouble, the issue of corporate governance often comes to the fore. If financial markets remain closed for a long time, borrowers may decide to restructure the principal part of their debt without making any effort to honour the initial schedule or play by the rules of the market. For this reason, creditors readily agree to almost any proposed restructuring scheme in order to keep the company from entering bankruptcy, which could result in a very low recovery ratio. Needless to say, this leads to the appearance of 'ghost' companies that continue to exist without performing any economic activity.

Another obvious risk is a decline in the transparency of Russian banks. In the first half of 2009, the largest Russian banks restructured around 5–10 per cent of their loan book in response to clients' liquidity problems. These loans were usually restructured ahead of their maturity date and so were not reported as NPLs and did not require additional provisions. However, with companies' liquidity problems turning quickly into solvency problems, these hidden NPLs must now be detected through stress tests performed by the Russian regulator. Thus, the second wave of the banking crisis could also be triggered by NPLs reported from these restructured loans. This represents a big threat from the point of view of recapitalization of the banking system.

RECAPITALIZATION EXPERIENCE

With the crisis, the equity capital of Russian banks stopped increasing in the second half of 2008. While official equity capital under Russian accounting standards went up by USD 30 billion from September 2008 to September 2009, this was a reflection of the USD 28 billion injection in the form of subordinated loans, mainly to state-owned banks, and of the direct equity injection into the second largest state-owned bank, VTB.

The Russian government came up with several initiatives to recapitalize banks. First, the large 50 per cent market share of state-owned banks meant that direct injections by the state into their equity capital have a material effect on the sector. The government has already delivered a RUB 180 billion state injection into tier-one capital of VTB through the purchase of new ordinary shares. Sberbank, the largest state bank, recently approved the issue of new ordinary shares, which could provide the bank with RUB 525 billion in tier-one equity.

Second, Russian banks are also receiving subordinated loans, considered to be tier-two equity capital, from Vnesheconombank (VEB) and the Central Bank. This was a two-step process. Initially, a total of RUB 257 billion were provided, including RUB 200 billion for VTB, RUB 25 billion for RosAgrobank and RUB 32 billion distributed among Alfa Bank, Nomos Bank, Khanty-Mansiysk Bank and Gazprombank. The CBR, as a shareholder of Sberbank, has provided it with RUB 500 billion. VEB is also about to distribute another RUB 70 billion to banks. In total, RUB 827 billion, or USD 25 billion, are to be injected through 10-year subordinated loans. The request for shareholders to contribute to the banks' support efforts has been the key obstacle to a more comprehensive use of subordinated loans by VEB. This limits the list of possible candidates that have access to this instrument.

Third, with the goal of helping private banks, the Russian government has prepared a law allowing banks to issue preferred shares in exchange for government OFZ bonds (rouble-denominated government bonds). The idea is that the Finance Ministry will acquire preferred shares of banks, but instead of injecting money it will put OFZ on the asset side of banks' balance sheets. Banks will later be able to pledge these bonds with the CBR to receive refinancing support or to sell them on the market. The Finance Ministry is expected to provide banks with RUB 450 billion through this instrument.

The trouble with this proposal lies in the fact that the CBR is providing only short-term liquidity to banks, that is with a maturity of less than a year. Even if de jure banks are showing an increase in their equity capital, in reality, they are receiving short-term financial support which has to be renewed annually. Thus, the proposal to exchange preferred shares for OFZ is unlikely to be accepted by the largest Russian banks, as they have access to refinancing support from the CBR. On the contrary, the real question is whether the Finance Ministry will be willing to acquire preferred shares of smaller banks with unclear business models. As a result, it is unlikely that Russian banks will make much use of this law.

The expected USD 21 billion increase of Sberbank's and VTB's equity capital, USD 25 billion in subordinated loans provided or approved, and the plan to inject USD 14 billion by swapping preferred shares for OFZ, still leaves Russian banks with hidden NPLs in their balance sheets. The current level of provisions does not provide the additional long-term resources necessary to cover the gap, so banks will have to restore the eroded capital themselves. This suggests that in 2010–11, the net profit of the Russian banking system may be close to zero; that is all operating profit will be used to replenish equity capital. For the real economy, this means that banks will be unable to increase lending, as their capital adequacy ratios will remain flat.

USING CRISIS AS OPPORTUNITY

The period of the economic and banking crisis should be used to enhance the mechanisms for oversight and management of systemic risks in order to prepare for a new phase of growth and to bolster stability within the financial system.

The obvious task is to use the current environment to strengthen banking supervision. Even though more than 900 banks are members of the Deposit Insurance System, the CBR is not comfortable offering a refinancing option to all these banks. During the fall of 2008, only around 120 banks had access to CBR's enlarged refinancing facilities. The need to create a special list of 'reliable' banks suggests that there is a potential opportunity to reduce the number of banking licenses and to improve regulation.

More rapid consolidation would be a very welcome trend made more urgent by the crisis. At present, 200 banks control about 90 per cent of the country's banking sector. This suggests that there are important opportunities for smaller banks to improve the efficiency of their business by consolidating and finding synergies through which to address the current crisis. Consolidation would also considerably simplify the Central Bank's bank monitoring responsibilities.

Traditionally, the Russian banking market has not been very rich in merger and aquisition deals in the banking sector. In part, this is a result of a number of smaller banks in the market that retain a 'one shareholder, one depositor, one borrower' model. In this environment, buying banks is not a guaranteed way to diversify business, since shareholder-clients will tend to leave the bank after the deal is closed.

This low level of diversification within the banking business explains why the move of foreign banks in the Russian market has been such a slow process. Apart from a couple of large deals, like Société Générale buying a stake in Rosbank, most deals were largely unimportant. For this reason, the share of foreign banks represents about 12 per cent of total banking assets, a figure which has remained stable in the past three to four years. The majority of major banks, like Citibank, preferred to grow organically. This is in part because of the low degree of transparency in the banking merger and aquisition environment.

The strong presence of state-owned banks in the Russian banking sector provides the other explanation for why the presence of foreign banks has remained so low. Sberbank continues to be the largest institution, responsible for 25 per cent of total corporate lending, 30 per cent of retail lending and 50 per cent of retail deposits. Altogether, five of the largest state-owned banks control 50–60 per cent of key banking markets. Their strong position is maintained by the fact that in Russia, enterprises still choose to open salary accounts at the banks that provide them with loans. Establishing these salary accounts at other banks is too expensive and usually impossible. Typically, if companies can receive relatively inexpensive loans from one of the larger banks, they will transfer all their accounts to that same banking institution. Last but not least, the size of the bank matters: with a 25 per cent credit risk exposure per borrower, Sberbank is able to provide a loan to an enterprise of up to USD 5 billion, while the largest privately-owned bank can offer only USD 500 million per company.

Finally, structural reforms provide a convenient way to reduce the number of monopolies of state-owned banks. The role of pension reform is crucial in this process. At present, a significant portion of pensions continue to be paid by state-owned banks, particularly Sberbank, which accounts for the bank's strong presence in the retail deposits market. Developing a system of defined-contribution pensions would gradually de-monopolize pension flows and affect market distribution in the retail banking area.

However, the low penetration of banking services suggests that Russian banks will sooner or later return to strong growth trend. First, the Russian economy as a whole is not highly leveraged by global standards. Russian companies' debt amounts to around USD 800 billion, or 60 per cent of 2009 GDP. By way of comparison, corporate debt in the East Asian economies, which were overwhelmed by the crisis of 1997, accounted for up to 150 per cent of GDP. This suggests that the ability to use credit leverage to boost growth is strong.

Second, compared to other countries, the household sector in Russia is not as leveraged. As opposed to a number of Eastern European countries, where households have accumulated significant debt in foreign currency, the Russian population was borrowing mainly in roubles. Additionally, the majority of retail loans were short-term and thus, the deleveraging process has occurred quickly. Obviously, concern remains about how fast households will be able to renew lending in case the economy does not recover. It is not surprising that during the previous years of double-digit real disposable income growth, the population was comfortable borrowing increasingly more. The big question is whether households will continue to do so under economic stagnation. One of the obvious explanations is that in Russia labour regulation is constructed very much in favour of the employer, bringing little social obligations to the corporate sector. This presents a structural constraint for a lending-driven recovery, but the low saturation of demand for banking loans will clearly allow some growth looking forward.

All in all, under the present economic circumstances, the focus should remain on continued economic reforms. The downside potential of the Russian economy appears to be limited. The question is whether it will be able to generate growth. After bad loans peaked in the second half of 2009, the Russian economy managed to restart growth. This crisis offers an excellent opportunity for much-needed consolidation in the banking sector, which is key to generating sustainable lending expansion.

16. Post-crisis business models of banks in CEE – the case of Raiffeisen[1]

Herbert Stepic

The aim of this chapter is to present the perspective of Raiffeisen International, the second-largest bank in Central and Eastern Europe (CEE).[2] Before I come to the point of what we will change as a result of the financial crisis, let me touch upon what we have done, what our old model looked like, how we have been affected by the crisis, how we reacted, what we expect for the near future, and how we see the mid- to long-term perspective.

We have been pioneers, Austrian banks specifically.

When I am being asked the question: 'Mr Stepic, are you unhappy about your investment in Central and Eastern Europe, wouldn't it have been better you had invested in China, or in Turkey or anywhere else?' The answer is always the same: 'No, I'm very happy with our business model because we are in a very specific situation in Central and Eastern Europe. This is a region with 360 million new customers, millions of new owners and new investors in a changing political system and economic transformation.'

If you want to earn money, you can earn a lot of money in a period of change and/or in a region of change.

When we had GDP growth in the western hemisphere before the crisis of 0.2 per cent and 0.3 per cent we were very happy: 'Ok, this is a growth year'. In CEE, in contrast, we were talking about 4.5, 5.5, 6 or 7 per cent of GDP growth. The average growth in CEE in the ten years up to 2008 has been 6.5 per cent per year. In the ten years up to 2008, the average growth of industrial production has been 6.8 per cent. We have doubled incomes in those last ten years in CEE, in euro terms. Real salary increases.

Many things happened in a very short period of time. People ask me 'Why does this go so slow?' This is nonsense. What happened in CEE in a very, very short period of time is a miracle. It is a real miracle! Here in Austria, we also had to learn democracy. We should never forget that we were killing each other in two world wars in the last century and we should remember that when we talk about CEE or any other emerging market.

CEE needs time to learn democracy. That is something very important. And many of the countries have learned democracy very fast. Most of the countries managed the process of transformation within a matter of five or six years. Look at our neighbouring country, Slovakia. It is a miracle, what they have achieved. So, at Raiffeisen we went into CEE because we believed, I believed, that this was a galactic window of opportunity.

Austria is overbanked; what should I therefore do in Austria? We are stepping on each other's toes. We had the whole 'new' Europe in front of our house. This is where we had to go, and where our services were in demand. So, we offered our banking services – namely universal banking for corporates, mid-market, micros, private individuals and some investment banking services to start with. This was our model, the 'old model'. When we started with loans, the conditions were horrible, and this is why I am convinced that what will come after the recent financial crisis, is nothing compared to what we have already brought behind us.

When Raiffeisen came to CEE, we came to an area that was the Wild, Wild East. We had no balance sheets, no reporting, no credit institutions. In 1993 we wanted to take our security in Slovakia out of a leasing transaction, but one afternoon a truck with gangsters armed with Kalashnikovs came and told us to better not take over this sawing mill which we had as a security. At this point we thought we should better go back to Austria. But we stayed, learned from this transaction and have since had very profitable and good business in Slovakia.

I think you will agree that those times are over and that the times we are looking forward to are difficult in economic terms but definitely not, and by no means, comparable to what we went through in the past.

How did we react when the crisis started?

Banks usually do not die of lack of capital, but they die of lack of liquidity. This is an iron rule. So, what did we do after the Lehman bankruptcy? The time in the future will apparently be divided between before Lehman and after Lehman; this will be the new denominator in banking, in risk assessment, in wrong policies by state officials and many more.

Our biggest fear was a banking run, a deposit run – this is the nightmare of any banker. We are working with borrowed funds and we lend money to others. And if some of those people who give us their money, who deposit their money with us, come to us overnight, we can run into troubles. This happened with Northern Rock. At 3 o'clock in the morning people came with biscuits and tea, waiting until Northern Rock opened at 9 o'clock in the morning and then asked, 'Where is my money?'

And this has also happened to us. It also happened to us due to false allegations through the Internet in a neighbouring country. People started to run on their deposits at Raiffeisen following almost three million messages sent through the Internet that Raiffeisen was about to go bankrupt.

So, what was the thing to do? We had to ship tons of money to this neighbouring country. Truckloads of cash in euro, in dollars. We had our banks open until midnight, Saturday, Sunday, and we announced in the newspaper, whoever wants to have money from Raiffeisen, please come now. After three days, the whole thing was over and we had business as usual.

The biggest risk for any bank is a banking run on deposits. So this is what I had to prepare for. That means we built up enormous amounts of cash in all our banks. In Russia, we built up about USD 2 billion in cash to be prepared for the big run. In Ukraine, we built almost EUR 1 billion in cash to be prepared for the big run; and that is what we did in all the other countries. Of course, that meant costs in the profit and loss statement because that is an auxiliary measure that you take in order to survive. We never knew whether the worst-case scenario would materialize or not. We just did not know. In February and March 2009, the system was on the edge. And, therefore, we said 'We better make sure to build up as much cash as we can, wherever possible, in order to be among the surviving parties'.

Now the situation is totally different. What is it like now?

The situation changed radically from one quarter to the other, from underliquidity to overliquidity. We now have an overliquid market.

After Lehman, the market dried out completely. Then, supranational institutions, mainly the European Central Bank (ECB), pumped EUR 300 to 400 billion into the market every month. I want to take this opportunity to thank them and I want to thank the International Monetary Fund (IMF) for what they have done. Without that we would not have survived. They were very instrumental, specifically the IMF has been extremely fast and very instrumental; and the Russian Central Bank (RCB) of course. The RCB acted faster than any other central bank in the world, frankly speaking, with huge amounts; they have been very alert.

We have overliquidity now; from a time of underliquidity we moved, after four months, to a time of overliquidity. At the moment there is very little demand for loans and credits. If any politician tells you in newspapers or in broadcasting 'Banks should lend', I can only say 'Yes, my friend, come. We will lend to you'. But there is currently not enough demand. The reason is that we are still in a crisis. We are going from minus 6.5 per cent GDP growth in 2009 in CEE – as mentioned before – to a slow 2 per cent growth in the region in 2010.

So, what will change in the future?

Will something change, and what will change? I would say, change of what we do as universal banks? No. Change of how we do our banking exercise? Yes.

Of course, we had bitter lessons to learn. That means we had a risk tsunami that we never expected. I would say, after the crisis, those banks which used the time to also change their internal organization – they will come out as much better banks than they entered the crisis. Because that is the time to strengthen your internal procedures and this is what we have also done as Raiffeisen International.

What will change? Money will become more expensive. It will get scarce again when the ECB and others are going to withdraw the liquidity from the markets, and I am quite sure that will happen at some point in 2010, and then we will see how the markets will work without the liquidity from supranationals. That will be a very touchy time and has to be very carefully watched, also by ECB officials and other central bankers.

Capital will be much more expensive. We need more capital. Banks are requested to hold more capital. Raiffeisen International is holding 10.5 per cent of core tier 1 capital. So, a lot of capital. And that is expensive. That means we need more capital for every single loan, for every single euro we are lending out. Therefore we are facing a situation with additional costs, as also liquidity will become more expensive. Specifically, long-term liquidity.

Also the risk people will not forget the crisis, which will result in additional credit and country risk charges. All these parameters, the risk and cost parameters are burdening the product lending in the future. Therefore, we have to look for other complementary activities to balance these additional costs. We nevertheless still believe that we will make very good business in CEE.

And why is that the case? Because I am talking about a very privileged region. The transformation process has been interrupted but not ended. The transformation process of the last twenty years has gone one-third of the total way. We still have two-thirds ahead of us. That means at least another two generations of growth, and that means two generations of successful banking business; indeed with higher capital costs and with higher liquidity costs than before, but still, a very juicy banking business.

NOTES

1. Transcript of statement made by Herbert Stepic at the OeNB Conference on European Economic Integration on 17 November 2009.
2. Jack Ewing (2009), 'The financial fix that saved Eastern Europe', *Business Week*, 6 November 2009.

17. Post-crisis business models of banks in CEE – the case of Intesa Sanpaolo

György Surányi

It is well known that the Central and Eastern European (CEE) countries used to outperform the industrial economies when it came to growth rates and potential growth rates (see Figures 17.1 and 17.3). Their growth models, especially those of small open economies, were pretty simple. We were convinced that if growth was dependent on exports and investments (see Figure 17.2) on the one hand, and on the fast inflow of foreign capital on the other hand, the results would be a given. This growth model has been seriously hurt throughout the crisis and is now being questioned severely. Even if the critics are right, I believe that it would be wrong to simply drop the model – much rather, we should revise it.

If we take the investment and exports figures in the pre-crisis period, they are impressive, just like the catching-up process has been impressive in terms of real convergence. However, it is obvious that the distance is still sizeable, and this should inform our interpretation of the data. If we take, for instance, the current account, it must be said that the current account deficits were in line with the growth model (see Figure 17.4).

There was an ever growing external imbalance, which finally turned out to be unsustainable. And much to many observers' and analysts' surprise, the current account imbalances were not primarily driven by fiscal profligacy, or by vague fiscal policies (see Figure 17.5). On the contrary, especially the Commonwealth of Independent States (CIS) countries, but even the CEE countries demonstrated quite a bit of fiscal discipline in general. The GDP ratio of the CEE countries and the new European Union (EU) member states are significantly below that of the major market economies.

To be able to better characterize the countries in the region, it is best to divide them into two groups, at the cost of necessary simplifications. On the one hand there is Poland, the Czech Republic, Slovakia and Slovenia. On the other hand there is Romania, Bulgaria, the Baltic States and

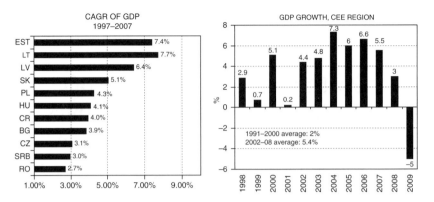

Abbreviation key: EST: Estonia, LT: Lithuania, LV: Latvia, SK: Slovakia, PL: Poland, HU: Hungary, CR: Croatia, BG: Bulgaria, CZ: Czech Republic, SRB: Serbia, RO: Romania.

Note: Before the crisis the consensus view was that in case of small, open, converging economies the sustainable growth strategies are export and investment-driven growth strategies – actively supported by capital inflows (both debt- and non-debt type financing) (C/A deficits!)

Source: Eurostat (n.d.a), IMF (2009a).

Figure 17.1 GDP growth rates well above the EMU average

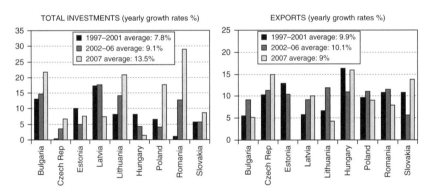

Source: Eurostat (n.d.b).

Figure 17.2 Export and investment-driven growth strategies

Ukraine. In the first category we might see low inflation, healthy fiscal balances, acceptable external imbalances and no asset price bubble. On the contrary, in the latter group of countries, we have high inflation, accelerating inflation, huge external imbalances (meaning high double-digit

GDP/CAPITA (PPP, EU-27 average = 100)

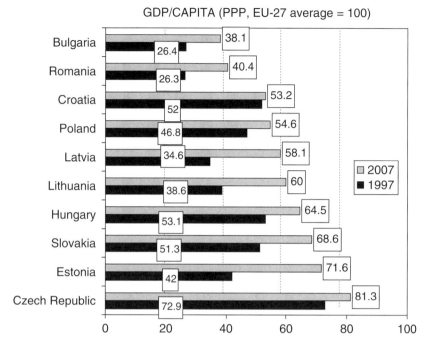

Source: Eurostat (n.d.c).

Figure 17.3 Strong growth rates pushed ahead real convergence

current account deficits), asset price bubbles, which is a clear indication of the unsustainable, overheated position of the economies. Hungary, Serbia and Croatia fall in between those two groups.

The dynamics of household consumption also serve to characterize these developments. After the crisis, growth rates collapsed, both in CEE and the CIS countries; imports went down dramatically by roughly one-third, while exports also declined by a quarter in CEE and by more than a third in the CIS countries (see Figure 17.6). Net capital inflows not only decelerated, but declined, which has got a dramatic impact on the growth model (see Figure 17.7).

If we take fiscal policies and the fiscal response, there are striking differences in the region vis-à-vis the major market economies (see Figure 17.8). In the region, we can, at best, talk about the invitation and application of the automatic stabilizers, whereas the Western countries opted for counter-cyclical policies in order to mitigate the crisis. Finally, household consumption has contracted, and the unemployment rate has obviously

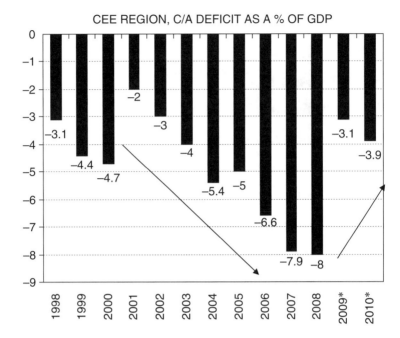

CEE REGION, C/A DEFICIT AS A % OF GDP

Note: * = forecast in 2009Q4. In the CEE region almost all countries ran external deficits or to put it another way: net domestic savings were negative. Before the current crisis it was considered a sustainable natural 'side effect' of the catching-up process.

Source: IMF (2009d).

Figure 17.4   Current account deficit a regional phenomenon

been increasing fast. All this has led to a serious change in real per capita income (see Figure 17.9).

Turning to the banking sector, we can see that credit growth had been unsustainable. Real annual average credit growth was pretty high in almost every country, especially in Serbia and in other countries where credit growth rates were in excess of 20% (see Figure 17.10). It is also interesting that the correlation with the degree of financial deepening may have increased with the crisis. Before the crisis, there was a general understanding that the greater the degree of financial deepening, the better for the given country. During the crisis the opposite turned out to be true. It is the ratio of foreign borrowing. I will come back to that.

If we analyse the loan-to-deposit ratios, they are not particularly high as compared to the euro average or the euro region on average (see Figure 17.11). However, they are obviously high. What is important is that in

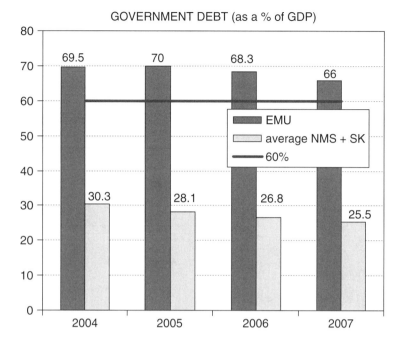

Source: Eurostat (n.d.d).

Figure 17.5 Low debt levels

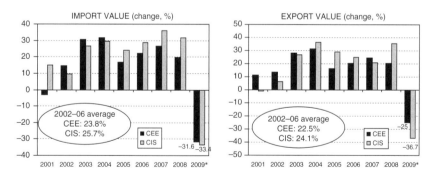

Note: * = forecast in 2009Q4. Exports are down approximately 25–35 per cent year-on-year.

Source: IMF (2009a).

Figure 17.6 Export markets collapsed

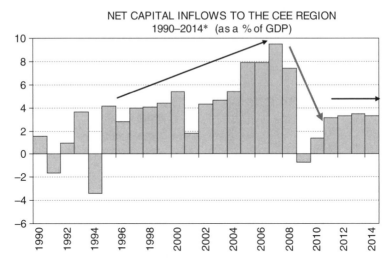

Note: * forecast.

Source: IMF (2009b), IMF staff estimates.

Figure 17.7   Sudden stop of capital inflows

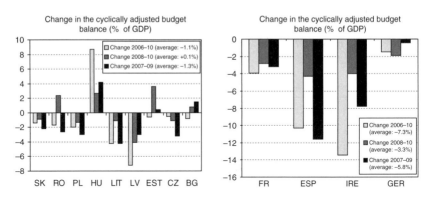

Abbreviation key: SK: Slovakia, RO: Romania, PL: Poland, HU: Hungary, LIT: Lithuania, LV: Latvia, EST: Estonia, CZ: Czech Republic, BG: Bulgaria, FR: France, ESP: Spain, IRE: Ireland, GER: Germany.

Note: Sustainability fears (even in case of low debt countries), the appearance of roll-over risks. Fiscal policies are not in a position to give a counter-cyclical boost to the economy.

Source: Eurostat (n.d.e), Brussel Commission.

Figure 17.8   Fiscal policies are not able to provide a shelter

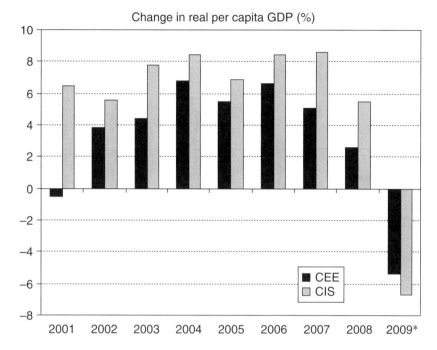

Change in real per capita GDP (%)

Note: * = forecast in 2009Q4

Source: IMF (2009c).

Figure 17.9 Real convergence came to a halt

the small and open, export-driven economies, which possess a liberalized FOREX regime, the monetary policies are losing their independence and their stabilizing roles.

On the point of the famous unhedged FOREX positions, I would like to emphasize that it should not have come as a surprise that those positions were building up in the first place. The emergence of those positions is a necessary consequence of the long-lasting external imbalances. If countries run a high current account deficit for many years, if not decades, it should not come as a surprise if they have unhedged domestic foreign currency positions. The policy option is how to allocate the unhedged position, whether to the public sector or to the corporate sector, or to the household sectors. If net domestic savings are insufficient as in the case of the CEE countries, an unhedged position will be created. So unhedged positions are not really an issue of the banking sector. What actually matters is whether the external position of the given countries, or group

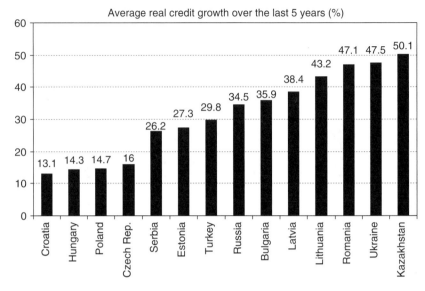

Source: IMF (2004–08).

Figure 17.10   Before the crisis: strong credit growth across the region

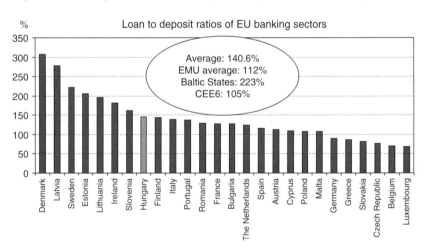

Note: The growth strategies built on cheap external financing are not sustainable any more. Domestic savings will not be sufficient to substitute external funding.

Source: ECB, NBH (2009), data as of end-2008.

Figure 17.11   The crisis: sudden stop of credit

of countries, is sustainable enough. If it was not sustainable, there would obviously be problems, regardless of which sector the FOREX position was allocated to.

The development of the so far unhedged FOREX positions has been driven by several factors: as explained, they have been the result of external imbalances. Second, they have been driven by the interest rate differentials, by the really tight monetary policy, which reflects the total inefficiency of the monetary authorities in the face of real open external accounts. Borrowers benefited not only from the interest rate differential, but also from the trend appreciation of the currencies, provided these countries were about to catch up with the major market economies. So borrowers were not gaining by chance, but rather by necessity. Third, there is the lack of medium- to long-term domestic currency funding, so even if price differentials had not made foreign currency borrowing so attractive, it would have been necessary because of the lack of well-functioning capital markets in these countries.

Now, how dangerous is the FOREX position? I would say I am a bit schizophrenic on this point. I was absolutely against liberalizing foreign currency transactions among residents. But since the International Monetary Fund, the Organization for Economic Cooperation and Development, the European Union and the European Central Bank were unilaterally pushing each and every country to abolish even the last foreign currency restrictions, it is a bit cynical for them to say to the region 'Why did you allow the banks and the borrowers to borrow in foreign currency?' If this was a prevailing phenomenon, it was a prevailing wind, that is, there was no way to lean against this prevailing wind. Also, were the unhedged foreign currency positions indeed so dangerous that they were the real reason for the crisis? I challenge this approach. In case of the closed and big economies, unhedged foreign currency positions are really deeply dangerous, since in such economies the nominal variables have no correlation with the exchange rate movements. Yet in the case of small and open economies, the foreign currency, the exchange rate level is in fact the only efficient nominal anchor for stabilizing inflation. So, if there is a monetary policy committed to price stability, the exchange rate has to be stabilized. If this is the case, central banks provide a kind of implicit hedging to the borrowers. Otherwise the inflation is going to be uncontrolled.

Second, there is another wave of defence, namely the trend appreciation of the real effective exchange rate. If it is true that on a longer term (15- to 20-year) horizon the exchange rate appreciates, borrowers have to win. Obviously, as a banker, I am absolutely well aware of the fact that the exchange rate is volatile, therefore there are ups and downs and there is a risk in the mean time, which has to be managed by the banks and their risk management functions. But I also have to say: if we are pointing out the huge risk related to foreign exchange positions, we must at the same time talk about the interest rate risk denominated in domestic currency. If the central banks stick to their price stability policies, they immediately have to tighten their belts and increase interest rates once the exchange rate falls. And the borrowers, even if they have borrowed in domestic currency, will find themselves saddled with an unhedged position – in this case not with a foreign exchange-related, but with an interest rate-related unhedged position.

Third, and this is also very important, these countries lack adequately deep long-term fixed income markets. The fixed income instruments are absorbed and crowded out by the fiscal authorities. Hence banks cannot offer medium-term or long-term funds at reasonably fixed interest rate levels. So, finally, I would like to say that the foreign currency risk is a very real risk. However, risk is our profession, so we have to be able to manage it. And I would say that the real issue in these countries is actually the sustainability of credit growth. The growth of credit, be it credit denominated in foreign currency or domestic currency, proved to be far too fast before the financial crisis struck. The authorities were unable to control credit growth. And partly they were unable to control it because the central banks had lost their autonomy, their independence. They were no longer in a position to control the dynamics of domestic demand.

To conclude, it is my opinion that the growth model is indeed going to be changed, but I would like to draw your attention to the fact that a simultaneous move by the authorities, governments and banks in the same direction might not deliver an optimum result. Why? Imagine that governments were to tighten their fiscal policies at the same time as central banks and supervisors were to tighten lending conditions and equity requirements, at the same time as banks were to tighten loan-to-deposit ratios, and at the same time as banks and authorities were to take action to reduce foreign currency lending. Taken by themselves, all these measures make real sense. However, if we simultaneously introduce these changes in the field of regulation, in monetary policymaking, in the everyday operations of the banks, on the macro level, this is going to be incredibly detrimental for the take-off of the economies.

REFERENCES

ECB, NBH (2009) Report on Financial Stability, April, available at: http://www.mnb.hu/Engine.aspx?page=mnbhu_stabil&ContentID=12306.

Eurostat (n.d.a), available at: http://epp.eurostat.ec.europa.eu/tgm/table.do?tab=t able&plugin=1&language=en&pcode=tsieb020.
Eurostat (n.d.b), available at: http://ec.europa.eu/economy_finance/publications/ publication16055_en.pdf.
Eurostat (n.d.c), available at: http://epp.eurostat.ec.europa.eu/tgm/table.do?tab=t able&init=1&plugin=1&language=en&pcode=tsieb010.
Eurostat (n.d.d), available at: http://epp.eurostat.ec.europa.eu/portal/page/portal/ government_finance_statistics/data/main_tables.
Eurostat (n.d.e), available at: http://ec.europa.eu/economy_finance/publications/ publication16055_en.pdf.
IMF (2004–08), Global Financial Stability Report, Table 1.1, available at: http:// www.imf.org/External/Pubs/FT/GFSR/2009/01/pdf/chap1.pdf.
IMF (2009a), World Economic Outlook, April, available at: http://www.imf.org/ external/pubs/ft/weo/2009/01/pdf/tblpartb.pdf.
IMF (2009b), World Economic Outlook, April, available at: http://www.imf.org/ external/pubs/ft/weo/2009/01/pdf/c1.pdf.
IMF (2009c), World Economic Outlook, October, available at: http://www.imf. org/external/pubs/ft/weo/2009/02/pdf/tblpartb.pdf.
IMF (2009d), World Economic Outlook database, available at: http://www.imf. org/external/pubs/ft/weo/2009/01/pdf/tables.pdf.

Index

adoption of euro *see* euro adoption
  and rapid euro adoption
Ahearne, Alan 157, 158, 160, 163, 164
Albania 110, 112, 115, 116, 122
Anderson, S.A. xv
Andrle, M. 53
animal spirits xvi–xviii
  Keynesian xxi
Australia 145, 149
  and Board of Statistics 150–52
Austria 120, 121–2, 153, 156, 180 *see
  also* Raiffeisen International

Babanin, O. 188
balance of payments (BoP) assistance
  8–9
Balassa–Samuelson effect 15, 85, 153
Baldwin, Richard 13, 51
Baliño, Tomás 90
Baltic States 8, 215
banks/banking systems 119–23, *see
  also* European Central Bank
  (ECB)
  Bank of Slovenia 50
  Central Bank of Russia (CBR) 203,
    204–5, 207–8
  in Central and Eastern Europe
    (CEE) 211–14
  Citibank 209
  Czech National Bank 53, 56, 68
  and Deposit Insurance System 208
  Eesti Pank (Estonia) 77
  foreign ownership of 176–7
  Intesa Sanpaolo *see main entry*
  KIT-Finance Bank 203
  National Bank of Serbia (NBS)
    23–33
    and consumer protection issues 25
  National Bank of Slovakia (NBS)
    50, 84–5
  Nordic 77

Oesterreichische Nationalbank 14,
  110
  and ownership of SEE banks 119
  ownership structure of 25
  Raiffeisen *see main entry*
  Russian 201–9
  trust in 116, 119
    deterioration of 120–23
  and trust in local currencies 123
  UniCredit 211
Basel II prudential requirements 181
Bayoumi, T. 50
Beddies, Christian H. 90
behavioural macroeconomic model
  xiv–xvi
Belgium 155–9
  house prices in 152
  manufacturing ULC in 162
Bénassy-Quéré, A. 141, 142
Berthou, A. 132, 133, 134
Blanchard, Olivier 162
Bosnia and Herzegovina 23, 110,
  113–17, 121–4, 179
  and IMF programme 10
bottom-up systems/rules xii–xv,
  xvii–xviii
Branch, W. xv
Brock, W. xv
bubbles 184–8, 190, 192–5 *see also*
  overconfidence *and* Ukraine
  bursting of 194, 195
  commodity price 184, 190, 195
  definition of 194
  housing 5
  speculative 184–5
Bufman, Gil 90, 93, 98
Buiter, W. 38
Bulgaria 23, 110, 111, 116, 120, 122,
  215
business cycle theories xviii–xix
  behavioural model xviii